CLAUDE
LANZMANN'S
SHOAH KEY ESSAYS

EDITED BY STUART LIEBMAN

CLAUDE LANZMANN'S SHOAH

KEY ESSAYS

OXFORD
UNIVERSITY PRESS

2007

OXFORD
UNIVERSITY PRESS

Oxford University Press, Inc., publishes works that further
Oxford University's objective of excellence
in research, scholarship, and education.

Oxford   New York
Auckland   Cape Town   Dar es Salaam   Hong Kong   Karachi
Kuala Lumpur   Madrid   Melbourne   Mexico City   Nairobi
New Delhi   Shanghai   Taipei   Toronto

With offices in
Argentina   Austria   Brazil   Chile   Czech Republic   France   Greece
Guatemala   Hungary   Italy   Japan   Poland   Portugal   Singapore
South Korea   Switzerland   Thailand   Turkey   Ukraine   Vietnam

Published by Oxford University Press, Inc.
198 Madison Avenue, New York, New York 10016

www.oup.com

Oxford is a registered trademark of Oxford University Press

Library of Congress Cataloging-in-Publication Data
Claude Lanzmann's Shoah : key essays / edited by Stuart Liebman.
     p. cm.
Includes bibliographical references.
ISBN 978-0-19-518863-9; 978-0-19-518864-6 (pbk.)
1. Shoah (Motion picture).   2. Holocaust, Jewish (1939–1945), in motion
pictures.   3. Lanzmann, Claude.   I. Liebman, Stuart.
D804.3.C55 2006
940.53'18—dc22   2006019704

9 8 7 6 5 4 3 2 1

Printed in the United States of America
on acid-free paper

Acknowledgments

Many people have helped me in various ways to prepare this volume. First and foremost, I thank the contributors to this book and/or their publishers for agreeing to allow their texts to be reprinted. I also want, however, to single out several for special thanks. Professor Antony Polonsky of Brandeis University generously offered me his extensive clippings file about the original public screening of *Shoah* in Oxford, England, in 1984 and about the debates it engendered. Raye Farr and Regina Longo of the United States Holocaust Memorial Museum in Washington, D.C., provided several key documents and important information about their efforts to preserve the nearly 350 hours of footage originally shot for the film. Elissa Schein of the Museum of Jewish Heritage in New York City invited me to serve as Claude Lanzmann's moderator at a series of screenings of and discussions about *Shoah* in September 2005. Claude Lanzmann graciously supported the project by granting the translation and publication rights to several of his articles, by translating his text "Hier ist kein Warum" into English, and by providing many stills to illustrate the volume. Dan Talbot, the president of New Yorker Films, was immediately supportive of my idea for an anthology about *Shoah* even as he had been the first in the United States to recognize the film's importance and to arrange for its public distribution. In addition to contributing his memoir about distributing the film, he and the New Yorker Films' staff gave me access to their extensive files on the reception of *Shoah* in the United States and also agreed to allow Oxford to publish stills from the film in this anthology. My wife, the photographer Lois Greenfield, painstakingly shepherded me through the inscrutable processes of contemporary photographic reproduction and then organized the production of most of the images that were finally selected as illustrations. I thank Elissa Morris, my first editor at Oxford, for agreeing to take on the project as part of Oxford's Casebooks in Criticism series, as well as Shannon McLachlan, who succeeded her as film books editor and who has so ably and cheerfully husbanded the book through to the final copyediting and production process. Christine Dahlin expertly and patiently responded to my questions concerning the final preparation of the manuscript for publication. Finally, I want to thank my research assistant, Thomas Meacham, at the CUNY Graduate Center for stalking down some of the more difficult to find texts on *Shoah*. Students in my seminar on Holocaust cinema at CUNY Graduate Center during the fall of 2005—Guillermo Calderon, Sharron Eisenthal, Rebecca Finkel, Tim Hughes, Mariko Ogawa, and Chong Wojtkowski—were kind enough to listen to my thoughts and responded with comments that challenged and expanded my thinking, as did participants in my seminar organized by Professor Peter Hayes and sponsored by the Holocaust Education Foundation at Northwestern University in June 2006.

My family and friends of many years sustained my efforts in many different ways, most often through their good-humored responses to my years-long preoccupation with films about the Holocaust. Thanks, first of all, to those nearest, dearest, and most constantly confronted with my intellectual interests: Alex, Jesse, and Lois. Colleagues often questioned my assumptions and challenged my interpretations by sharing their intellectual perspectives or providing key documents. I have learned much from them, so much, in fact, that I cannot summarize their contributions in any tidy way. I will therefore simply list their names here, knowing full well that such a cursory mention is too small thanks for all they have meant to me or done for me over the years: Monika Adamczyk-Garbowska, Joyce Block, Jonathan Buchsbaum, Christian Delage, Peter Hayes, Sylvie Lindeperg, Hanno Loewy, Ronny Loewy, Tony Pipolo, Krystyna Prendowska, Leonard Quart, and, especially Henry Weinfield.

I dedicate this volume to two extraordinary individuals. I must first single out my teacher and friend Annette Michelson, who more than three decades ago transformed my notion of what the discipline of film studies could be and whose intellectual passions still inspire me to work in the expanded field she did so much to open. Second, I dedicate my efforts to understand the role of the Holocaust in contemporary life to the memory of Amos Gunsberg, the remarkable man without whom I would not be who I am.

Credits

Timothy Garton Ash, "The Life of Death." *New York Review of Books* 32 (December 19, 1985): 26–39. Reprinted in abridged form by permission of the *New York Review of Books* and the author.

Fred Camper, "*Shoah*'s Absence." *Motion Picture* 1 (Winter/Spring 1987): 5–6. Reprinted in revised form by permission of the author.

Marc Chevrie and Hervé Le Roux, "Site and Speech: An Interview with Claude Lanzmann about *Shoah*." *Cahiers du Cinéma*, no. 374 (July–August 1985): 18–23. Reprinted in English translation by permission of *Cahiers du Cinéma*.

Simone de Beauvoir, "Preface." *Shoah: An Oral History of the Holocaust* (New York: Pantheon Books, 1985), pp. iii–vi. Reprinted by permission of Georges Borchardt, Inc.

David Denby, "Out of Darkness." *New York Magazine* (October 28, 1985): 130–133. Reprinted by permission of the author.

Georges Didi-Huberman, "Le Lieu Malgré Tout." *Vingtième Siecle*, no. 46 (April–June 1995): 36–44. Reprinted in English translation by permission of the author.

Marianne Hirsch and Leo Spitzer, "Gendered Translations: Claude Lanzmann's *Shoah*." In Miriam Cooke and Angela Woolacott, eds., *Gendering War Talk* (Princeton, N.J.: Princeton University Press, 1993), pp. 3–19. Reprinted by permission of Princeton University Press and the authors.

Jan Karski, "*Shoah*." *Together* 1 (July 2, 1986): 14–15.

Gertrud Koch, "The Aesthetic Transformation of the Image of the Unimaginable: Notes on Claude Lanzmann's *Shoah*." *October*, no. 48 (Spring 1989): 15–24. Reprinted by permission of the author.

Dominick LaCapra, "Lanzmann's *Shoah*: 'Here There Is No Why.'" *Critical Inquiry* 23 (Winter 1997): 231–269. Reprinted by permission of University of Chicago Press and the author.

Claude Lanzmann, "From the Holocaust to 'Holocaust.'" *Dissent* (Spring 1981): 188–194. Reprinted by permission of *Dissent* magazine and the author.

Claude Lanzmann, "Hier ist kein Warum." *Nouvelle Revue de Psychanalyse*, "Le Mal," no. 38 (Fall 1988). Reprinted in English translation by permission of the author.

Marcel Ophüls, "Closely Watched Trains." *American Film* (November 1985): 16–22, 79. Reprinted by permission of the American Film Institute.

Anne-Lise Stern, "*Ei Warum, Ei Darum*. Pourquoi." In her *Le Savoir deporté: Camps, histoire, psychanalyse*, edited by Nadine Fresco and Martine Lebovici (Paris: Éditions du Seuil, 2004), pp. 202–208. Reprinted in English translation by permission of Éditions du Seuil and the author.

Jean-Charles Szurek, "From the Jewish Question to the Polish Question." From *Au sujet de "Shoah"* (Paris: Éditions Belin, 1990). Reprinted in English translation by permission of the author. An epilogue has been added for this volume.

Daniel Talbot, "Distributing *Shoah*." This chapter was written for this volume and is printed by permission of the author.

Elie Wiesel, "A Survivor Remembers Other Survivors of 'Shoah.'" *The New York Times* (November 3, 1985). Reprinted by permission of the *New York Times*.

Leon Wieseltier, "*Shoah*." *Dissent* (Winter 1986): 27–30. Reprinted by permission of *Dissent* magazine and the author.

Contents

CLAUDE LANZMANN'S *SHOAH* KEY ESSAYS

Introduction

STUART LIEBMAN

No filmmaker has ever begun a project about a more immense and devastating historical topic and with less tangible prospect of success than the French intellectual, editor, and film director Claude Lanzmann. "I began precisely with the impossibility of telling this story," he noted in a 1985 interview with *Cahiers du Cinéma* about the massive work he had just released to extraordinary critical acclaim:

> I placed this impossibility at the very beginning of my work. When I started the film, I had to deal with, on the one hand, the disappearance of the traces: there was nothing at all, sheer nothingness, and I had to make a film on the basis of this nothingness. And on the other hand, with the impossibility of telling this story even by the survivors themselves; the impossibility of speaking, the difficulty—which can be seen throughout the film—of giving birth to and the impossibility of naming it: its unnameable character.[1]

The impossible story Lanzmann referred to is, of course, what we in the United States and England generally refer to as the Holocaust, but what the

French, following the title Lanzmann chose for his film, now tend to call the "Shoah." After Lanzmann's first film, a ranging, three-hour portrait of Israel in the years following the Six Day War, received warm reviews both in Israel and abroad,[2] he embarked on his research for what would become his second film in 1974. Although a modest pledge of financial support quickly proved inadequate for this continually expanding undertaking, it did start Lanzmann on an eleven-year journey around the world to make a film about the Nazis' mass murder of European Jewry.

Eventually, he would locate several dozen key Jewish survivors, German perpetrators, and Polish peasants who were eyewitnesses to the mass gassings of Jewish victims at Chelmno, Treblinka, Auschwitz-Birkenau, and other death camps. He would record some 350 hours of wrenching testimony, much of it providing details about this painful history that had never before been revealed.[3] He then faced the arduous task of condensing and shaping his vast array of material into a form that might somehow communicate to an audience something of the degradation and horror experienced by millions of innocents. What emerged from this long process was one of the longest and most demanding films ever released, the nine and one-half hour *Shoah*. Commentators usually refer to it as a documentary on the Holocaust; Lanzmann insists that it is a work of art, an "originary event" constructed with "traces of traces." Critics as well as increasingly large audiences around the world rightly regard it as one of the most powerful films ever made. More than that: it was—and remains—a cultural achievement of the greatest magnitude.

Shoah's Paris premiere in April 1985 was heralded in the pages of France's leading newspaper, *Le Monde*, by no less a French cultural icon than Simone de Beauvoir. "I would never have imagined such a combination of beauty and horror," she wrote:

> True, the one does not help to conceal the other . . . it highlights the horror with such inventiveness and austerity that we know we are watching a great oeuvre. A sheer masterpiece.[4]

Few French intellectuals disagreed with her assessment. With only a handful of exceptions, critics in the United States were no less lavish in their praise. "Certain sequences, hallucinatory and obsessive, are haunting," Elie Wiesel wrote in the *New York Times* shortly after *Shoah* was released in New York on October 23, 1985. "This is a film that must be seen." "The rhythm of *Shoah* envelops and mesmerizes. Reading about this movie isn't enough: You must see it," David Denby concluded his review for *New York Magazine*. The discerning New York Film Critics Circle acknowledged *Shoah*'s stature by naming it the Best Documentary of the year. Perhaps the highest praise came from the eminent documentarian Marcel Ophüls, a director celebrated for his groundbreaking cinematic account of Vichy France, *The Sorrow and the Pity*: "I consider *Shoah* to be the greatest documentary about contemporary history ever made, bar none, and by far the greatest film I've ever seen about the Holocaust."

The substance and tenor of such encomia would soon be echoed in dozens of reviews and articles in newspapers and intellectual journals across the United States.[5] Even critics who disliked the film—and there were not many— acknowledged the incredible intellectual daring that animated the project.[6]

A resounding success with the critics, *Shoah* attracted larger than antici- pated audiences in France and a truly astounding response in the United States.[7] Certainly within American Jewish communities, which since the 1970s had increasingly made the memory of the German destruction of European Jewry into a cornerstone of their group identity, word of mouth played a large role.[8] This interest was primed, however, by a carefully crafted plan of distri- bution in cities with large Jewish populations, including special benefit screen- ings, often with Lanzmann in attendance. These presentations were conceived by Dan Talbot, the head of New Yorker Films, a distinguished distributor and exhibitor of foreign features by Godard and Bertolucci, among other leading figures in the European New Waves. He had been the first American to recog- nize the importance of Lanzmann's project and, as his memoir written for this volume makes clear, he made an extraordinary effort to secure distribution rights to *Shoah* and then to build a momentum sufficient to carry it over into successful theatrical runs.

For such an unprecedentedly lengthy and detailed—indeed, demanding and exhausting—work, the box office receipts far exceeded those imagined by anyone, including Lanzmann and Talbot.[9] For years, in fact, *Shoah* remained the most profitable documentary film ever released in the United States. The film, it seemed, had tapped into a long suppressed need to hear, directly from those Jewish survivors, Polish bystanders, and German perpetrators closest to the killing process, precisely what had befallen the European Jews. Although for decades survivors had come forward to share their stories, these stories had almost always been disseminated in books and newspapers.[10] Few reached wide audiences. Even as increasing numbers agreed to record their terrible experiences for posterity on film or videotape, their accounts were almost al- ways simply deposited in archives such as Yad Vashem in Israel or in the vaults of the nascent Fortunoff Archive at Yale University. They were rarely, if ever, distributed and seen by the general public. That is perhaps one reason why the powerful testimonies in Lanzmann's film had such an overwhelm- ing impact on Jewish as well as non-Jewish audiences. Today Holocaust scholars and the Jewish community generally have come to regard *Shoah* as Ophüls did upon its release: as the most important film about the Holocaust ever made.

Indeed, an admittedly crude historiography of Holocaust cinema might divide the sixty years of filmmaking since World War II into a period before and after *Shoah*. Twenty years after its premiere, we can say with confidence that this work of surpassing ambition, which almost single-handedly changed the very name by which we refer to the slaughter of European Jews in World War II, marked a caesura in the representation of a vastly complicated histor- ical episode, the horrors of which are paradoxically ever more present in

Western imaginations even as they continue to resist any totalizing portrayal. Many filmmakers before Lanzmann, of course, had attempted to convey the unprecedented human catastrophe on film. Alain Resnais's short *Night and Fog* (1956), long a mainstay of Holocaust education in France and the United States, comes immediately to mind. So too do a number of serious, if now too little known, feature-length movies from the late 1940s through the 1970s that tried to portray something of the disaster that had engulfed millions.[11] But none of these important and generally well-intentioned films had faced the awful facts of the *Jewish* genocide head on, without political distortion or mystification. Some communist directors (including several of Jewish origin) in the new, East European "People's Republics," and even such a gifted and humane artist as Resnais, had instrumentalized Jewish suffering to serve political causes that occluded the particularity of the Jews' fate as the Germans' principal victims. Most had resorted, moreover, to dramaturgical formulae or documentary conventions that, intentionally or inadvertently, transformed the slaughter of Europe's Jews into something less momentous and more comprehensible than it was. Such films mitigated—and thereby evaded—the terrible truths Lanzmann wished to place at the very center of his work.[12] Perhaps even more significant is the fact that no filmmaker before Lanzmann had devoted so much time to reflecting not only on *what* to represent in a film about the Holocaust, but also on *how* to do so. Finally, no director had ever demanded so much dedication and forbearance from his audience in order to confront what many Jews and non-Jews alike, though for different reasons, did not wish to think about. In short, *Shoah* set imposing standards of seriousness and rigor for anyone who wished—or still wishes—to make a Holocaust film. Its significant historical contributions and demanding modernist form continue to throw into relief the evasions, banalities and trivializing efforts of directors who exploit the Holocaust merely as a background for sentimental stories of rescue and deliverance.[13] *Shoah* was, and remains, as the French say, "*un film clef.*"

In a 1979 essay ostensibly about the recent American blockbuster television miniseries *Holocaust*, Lanzmann observed that the extermination of the Jews was "a nameless crime, which the Nazi assassins themselves dared not name, as if by doing so they would have made it impossible to enact. It was literally an unnameable crime."[14] What to call his film about this unnameable crime, in fact, bedeviled Lanzmann for the decade and more he worked on it. What was at stake in this act of naming was the way he conceived the construction, both thematic and formal, of his immense subject. His important essay "From the Holocaust to 'Holocaust,'" reprinted in this volume, provided ample grounds for rejecting the word "holocaust," which had become the dominant way of naming the Judeocide in the English-speaking world. He refused to consider it as a possible title for his evolving work for several reasons. First, it was already the name of a bad film that, Lanzmann believed, betrayed the reality of Jewish suffering by its use of banal, "idealized" movie conventions.

"The Holocaust," wrote Lanzmann, "is unique because it created a circle of flames around itself, a boundary not to be crossed since horror in the absolute degree cannot be communicated. Pretending to cross that line is a grave transgression." According to Lanzmann, *Holocaust* had repeatedly crossed the line by misrepresenting the character and fate of the Jews who were murdered. Gerald Green, the screenwriter, and director Marvin Chomsky had not dared to present the unendurably brutal end of the majority of those killed, who, by West European standards, seemed alien in their dress and manner, who were famished, humiliated, and terrified to the point of derangement, and who were finally whipped, clubbed, and bayoneted with unspeakable brutality until they entered the gas chambers. Rather, "as good form prescribes," the authors of *Holocaust* chose a familiar-looking, middle-class German family who went stoically to their deaths. By presenting a fantasy of a death with dignity in the gas chambers, *Holocaust* had fashioned a myth of the Holocaust; it perpetrated, according to Lanzmann, "a lie, a moral crime; it assassinates memory."[15]

Lanzmann also could not accept the theological implications of "holocaust"—a word meaning "burnt offering" and derived from the Septuagint, the Greek version of the Hebrew Bible—because it implied that the Jews were sacrificial offerings.[16] It is not clear whether Lanzmann ever considered the less familiar *hurban*, another biblical word with strong Jewish historical and Yiddish connotations. It referred to the destruction of Solomon's Temple and was one of the first choices by Jews in Palestine who learned of the mass murders as they were taking place.[17] It was, in fact, only at the last moment, just before the first screenings in Paris, that Lanzmann spontaneously opted for the word *shoah*, by then a term firmly ensconced in Israeli discourse but not widely used in France or any other Western country. As he wrote two decades later, "The word *shoah* imposed itself on me at the end since, not knowing Hebrew, I did not understand its meaning, which was another way of not naming it [the events and the film]." This choice would later prove controversial, as some scholars would contest the extensions of the word's original biblical meaning.[18] Despite these objections, and in large measure as a result of the film's resounding worldwide success, "shoah" has since become a "borrow word" in several languages to refer to the German Judeocide.[19]

"Shoah" conveys something of the essence of Lanzmann's project as it crystallized. The word appears thirteen times in the Hebrew Bible, where it consistently refers to the ravages of a natural disaster such as an earthquake or a flood. By the mid-1940s, however, the word had increasingly become central to pre-state, and later Israeli, public discourse about the catastrophe that had engulfed the European Jewish diaspora; its original referents had already begun to expand to include the "catastrophe," "destruction," or "annihilation" wrought by the Nazis. Lanzmann, however, did not simply adopt the biblical term, nor did he embrace ordinary Israeli usage. Rather, as he later wrote, for him " 'Shoah' was a signifier without a signified, a brief, opaque utterance, an impenetrable word, as unsmashable as an atomic nucleus."[20] For Lanzmann, the word's opacity for all nonspeakers of Hebrew poses a challenge to discern the scope and meaning of its referent(s). Its foreignness casts a kind of numinous remoteness on the events, making them impervious to ready comprehension. That is not to say that Lanzmann intended to mystify the slaughter of the Jews during World War II. Far from it. For Lanzmann, the catastrophe that befell the Jews was rooted in historical events and social and religious values that had been part of European traditions and practices for nearly two millennia. *Shoah*'s conceptual architecture is, in any case, deeply informed by historical knowledge, and Lanzmann has often acknowledged that the film could not have come into existence but for the work of scholars who had established the principal time lines, procedures, and consequences of the extermination process. Yet Lanzmann has also somewhat paradoxically insisted that the Judeocide cannot be explicated strictly in historical terms. Some have incorrectly taken this apparent paradox for inconsistency on Lanzmann's part, and that perception has led them to misunderstand his aims and cinematic strategies.

Indeed, almost no other topic of recent history has attracted more in-depth historical research than the Holocaust. For nearly three generations historians have sought to establish the root causes that made it possible. Every possible factor and combination of factors have been weighed: the centuries of Christian anti-Judaism; the emergence of *Völkisch* and pseudoscientific, racist, anti-Semitic ideologies in the nineteenth century; German national humiliation at the end of World War I; the incompetence of Weimar democracy and the rise of extremist, right-wing political parties; the social and economic dislocations of the 1920s, culminating in the Depression and unprecedented German unemployment; the treachery of German military and business elites; Hitler's psychopathology; the moral failures of Christian churches; simmering ethnic animosities in the East—the list is long and could be extended. Lanzmann knew this material extremely well. After embarking on his project, he first studied as much of the relevant historical literature—in several languages—as he could for an entire year, and he kept abreast of new Holocaust studies as his work progressed. Yet, in one of his first and most important published reflections on these issues, he rejected the idea that social and political circumstances, either singly or together, were sufficient to generate, let alone to explain, what the Germans and their allies did. "The destruction of Europe's Jews," Lanzmann wrote,

> cannot be logically deduced from any such system of presuppositions. Between the conditions that permitted extermination and the extermination itself—the *fact* of the extermination—there is a break in continuity, a hiatus, an abyss. The extermination was not "generated" and to wish to account for it thus is, in a way, to deny its reality, to shut one's eyes to the outbreak of violence; it is to wish to clothe the implacable nakedness of the violence, to disguise it and thereby refuse to

confront it in all its bleak singularity. In a word, to weaken it. All discourse that speaks about the "engendering" of violence is an absurd dream of the nonviolent.[21]

In *Shoah*, therefore, Lanzmann did not want to offer a grand causal narrative explicating how the atrocities came to be perpetrated, for this terrible fact could not be explained. Nor did he want merely to invoke a *memory* of the past, which would have yielded only a pale recollection of the systematic destruction of countless Jewish lives. He formulated his rejection of "memory" in characteristically trenchant terms:

> A film on the Holocaust has to set out from the principle of the rejection of memory, the refusal to commemorate. The worst moral and artistic crime that can be committed in producing a work dedicated to the Holocaust is to consider the Holocaust as past. Either the Holocaust is a legend or it is present; in no case is it a memory.[22]

Instead, Lanzmann wished to expose "the implacable nakedness of the violence" as it erupted into the historical continuum. He sought to make new for viewers a perception of the Germans' unprecedentedly cold-blooded fury, and thereby to restore a sense of the palpable *presence* of the crimes for contemporary audiences. Underlying this project was an ethical perspective that insisted on the moral proximity of the Shoah to those who watched the film. He wanted to wound his audience by a new, more vivid awareness of what had taken place and thereby impel an intensely personal engagement with the innocent men, women, and children who were slaughtered.[23] The film's narration, therefore, had to be anchored in precise facts, however brutal, that had either eluded the grasp of historians or whose extreme violence had been weakened by the narratives they constructed.[24] Only by restoring this sense of the immediacy of the Holocaust for contemporary viewers could the past become present without adulteration, and with its ironies and horrors intact in all their grisly complexity. With this purpose in mind, he began to seek out those who, in various roles, had been at the very center of the Hells at the extermination centers of Auschwitz-Birkenau, Treblinka, Sobibor, and other sites.

The sheer immensity of the historical events Lanzmann wished to evoke and the paucity of witnesses to assist him in developing what he regarded as his crucial focus on the actual killing process made work on the film consistently challenging and often tedious. With the aid of several archives, he formulated a reconnaissance plan, first locating key survivors and then persuading them to speak on camera. The case of Abraham Bomba, a barber from Częstochowa, Poland, who had been forced to shear the hair of women in the very gas chambers at Treblinka, is instructive. Lanzmann heard of this man at Yad Vashem, the Holocaust museum, memorial, and research center in Jerusalem. Bomba was said to be living in New York City. To find him, Lanzmann walked the streets, asking at barber shops if anyone knew Bomba. Eventually his efforts brought him to the door of Bomba's home in the Bronx. They spent a weekend together, during which Lanzmann learned about the barber's activities during the war and Bomba promised to cooperate in the filming of his testimony when the funding for filming was secured. About a year later Lanzmann returned to New York to shoot the interview, only to find that Bomba had retired and moved to Israel. Returning to Israel once again, Lanzmann located a fellowship group of survivors from Częstochowa who put him back in touch with Bomba, and filming finally began.[25]

Making contact with former German perpetrators was even more difficult, although for different reasons. German officers and SS guards were obviously wary of possible prosecution or simply wished to have their sordid activities forgotten. They were hardly eager to speak with a Jew about what they had done. In order to get them to tell their stories, therefore, Lanzmann was usually forced to work under a pseudonym and with a hidden camera and offer them false assurances that he would not disclose their identities. He thereby routinely risked exposure and physical harm. His luck ran out at least once. After his clandestine filming had been discovered by irate family members of a German war criminal, they destroyed his equipment and Lanzmann ended up in a hospital for eight days.

His first recorded interview—with Benjamin Murmelstein, the last *Judenälteste* of the Theresienstadt Ghetto—appears to have taken place in December 1977; the filming of other subjects continued until 1981 and editing began in earnest in 1983/1984.[26] In some cases those Lanzmann sought out had already publicly commented on their experiences. Some had testified at or been the subject of criminal trials; several had even published books and articles about what they had been through. Their earlier remarks often inform what they say on camera.[27] Nevertheless, Lanzmann was able to coax vivid, uniquely detailed, and revealing statements from nearly all who spoke to him; their facial expressions and gestures, moreover, add a dimension unavailable in print. For example, the moment when Filip Müller's strangely calm demeanor breaks down is, in my opinion, one of the most heartbreaking in the history of cinema. This Czechoslovak Jew, who miraculously survived several shifts as a member of the *Sonderkommando* that cleared bodies from the gas chambers and then stuffed them into the roaring crematoria at Birkenau, bursts into tears as he remembers the women of the Czech "Family Camp." Even when facing their imminent death, they urged him not to despair and die with them but to live to tell their story. Recalling this is more than Müller can bear, and the version he recounts through his tears in the film has an even greater intensity than the one he reports in his memoir.[28] Many others—for example, the Polish peasants who had stood by as trainloads of Jews were forced into the camps or were mute witnesses to the packing of gas vans from the steps of their village church—were speaking for the first time on camera, and their spontaneous gestures and facial reactions are often as telling as what they say. Even today, after tens of thousands of survivors have recorded their testimonies under the auspices of the Fortunoff Foundation at Yale or Spielberg's "Righteous Persons" project, the interviews Lanzmann recorded a quarter century ago remain intensely moving, permanent additions to the historical record.

One common misunderstanding of Lanzmann's purpose in making *Shoah* is that he wanted to provide a comprehensive history of the Holocaust in all its dimensions. This is simply not the case. For all the stunning details he elicits, and despite the solidity of the historical framework underlying the film's complex narrative weave, Lanzmann does *not* attempt to provide a complete history of the Holocaust. About the so-called German *Einsatzgruppen*'s brutal murders at close quarters of nearly a million Jews under the cover of the *Wehrmacht*'s "Operation Barbarossa" during the summer of 1941 in Eastern Poland, Ukraine, Belorussia, and other western Soviet states, *Shoah* says next to nothing.[29] Nor does Lanzmann take note of the uncounted thousands of Jews shot in the street or tortured to death by German sadists and their Ukrainian, Latvian, Lithuanian, Hungarian, Croatian, or Rumanian collaborators (although he does occasionally adopt their physical points of view when he places his camera on the tops of the train cars over which Latvians or Ukrainians once stood guard).[30] Despite a revealingly evasive interview late in the film with Dr. Franz Grassler, a former adjutant to the German commander of the Warsaw Ghetto and one of those most responsible for the misery of the hundreds of thousands of Jews trapped inside, there are few allusions in the film to the countless number who perished from starvation and disease in the East European ghettos.[31] Even more surprising, perhaps, is that he includes surprisingly little about the Jews' heroic efforts to maintain communal life under impossible conditions or about the superhuman efforts by a few to resist the Germans by either passive resistance, sabotage, or armed struggle. With the exception of Rudolf Vrba, who escaped from Auschwitz in order to warn the world of the imminent destruction of Hungarian Jewry, Lanzmann does not include any information about how his interviewees managed to cheat the death the Germans planned for them nor is he interested in the lives they fashioned for themselves after the war. Finally, Lanzmann never highlights the shameful collaboration in the deportations of their Jewish citizens by West European governments such as those in Norway and the Netherlands. Even more astoundingly, he never mentions the vile Vichy regime in France, against which he himself fought as a teenage member of the Resistance, while it shipped more than 76,000 resident Jews to points east. (Only some 2,500 returned.)

To argue that *Shoah* is inadequate because of these omissions is to forget that Lanzmann's focus is elsewhere: on what he takes to be the Holocaust's most distinctive horror. All the witnesses in the final film testify to the systematic manner in which the Germans, from relatively improvised beginnings in December 1941 at Chelmno, organized the transport and increasingly more efficient gassing of millions of Jews from early 1942 onward in the specially designed "Operation Reinhard" death camps at Bełżec, Sobibor, and

Treblinka as well as at Auschwitz-Birkenau.[32] We hear, for example, from the only two Jewish prisoners who survived Chelmno out of the approximately 400,000 murdered there. Simon Srebnik, a thirteen-year-old during the "second period" of executions, describes how he burned the bodies of those who had been asphyxiated, including some who were cast into the ovens while still alive. Michael Podchlebnik, who survived the first "castle" period at Chelmno, recounts how he unloaded bodies—including those of his wife and children—from the gas vans and put them into mass graves.[33] The Polish locomotive driver Henrik Gawkowski tells how he pushed, *not* pulled, the cattle cars loaded with Jewish victims into Treblinka; then, after reenacting the journey to the Treblinka depot at Lanzmann's request, he spontaneously draws his hand across his throat, a gesture he says he used to warn the doomed Jews. Richard Glazar, a member of the *Sonderkommando* at Treblinka, also recalls seeing a peasant boy making this gesture when he was riding in a boxcar to the camp, but he notes that he and the other Jews failed to understand its meaning. A Polish peasant whom Lanzmann interviews says that he too had tried to warn the Jews in this way, but we quickly perceive from his demeanor that, rather than fellow feeling for the victims, the gesture expressed the sadistic pleasure he took—and still seems to take!—in their fate. By contrast, another Pole, a railway worker at the Sobibor train station during the war, speaks, still apparently stunned by the experience, of the eerie, "ideal" silence that descended when, within hours of the arrival of the first large Jewish transport, the human beings it contained seemed simply to vanish within the confines of the camp located only a few steps away from the station. At the beginning of the film's "Second Era," one's stomach turns as the film returns to an interview with Franz Suchomel, who had been an SS *Untersturmführer* and a guard at Treblinka. While filming clandestinely by means of primitive mobile television technology, Lanzmann induces him to chant the words of the jaunty ditty that those few Jews, the so-called *Arbeitsjuden*, who had temporarily been spared, were obliged to sing as they marched to work. This is a song, Suchomel confides to Lanzmann with oily bonhomie, that "no Jew today knows." Throughout the film, Lanzmann seeks out unsuspected, concrete, telling details that, while scrupulously adhering to historical accuracy, take on a level of immediacy that statistical abstractions cannot achieve, by provoking a striking, unfamiliar encounter with the awful events described.

Each face and voice offer something unique and personal that contributes not only to an understanding of the larger event we call the Holocaust,[34] but also to our growing awareness of its vast scope and the diverse multiple perspectives on it. Each individual is asked for and reports only on what he or she directly experienced, or, as in the case of Simon Srebnik, what he cannot believe he witnessed, but did.[35] No one who Lanzmann interviews is in a position to speak about "the Holocaust," the global abstraction historians use to refer to the sum of all these events. All are witnesses to only an aspect—but often an extraordinarily revealing one—of the terrifying whole.[36] Their impact is all the greater because, through the agency of the unsuspected detail or the often surprisingly cool tone in which they report their experience, they pierce viewers' defenses against the full force of the horror, defenses variously informed by ignorance, abstractions, or presumptions of knowledge. The details—the beauty of summer days during which thousands of bodies were burned every day, the unbelievable stench saturating the killing fields for miles around, the fountains of blood spurting from mass graves, the military green color of the gas vans, the jocular tone in which SS men told reassuring lies to those about to die—revivify and powerfully alter our sense of the texture and flow of the events. It should not be forgotten, too, that the testimonies are not presented chronologically and are embedded in a larger mosaic of nonnarrative material. It is only in and through this complex structure that they constitute what Lanzmann calls "an incarnation, a resurrection," and that they make, as he puts it, "the whole process of the film . . . a philosophical one."[37] I will return to this point.

Perhaps surprisingly, historical documents do not figure very prominently in this mosaic. Lanzmann's research was, of course, profoundly informed by both published and unpublished documents, and he does occasionally quote from primary texts, often to powerful effect. For example, we hear the Rabbi of Grabów's agonizing last letter announcing the imminent end of his community when Lanzmann reads it on camera in front of a furniture warehouse that was once the Grabów synagogue. At the end of the film's "First Era," Lanzmann in voice-over reads a letter to the Saurer company from "Just," an experienced SS manager of the exterminations. While the camera is placed in a car following a modern Saurer truck on a highway in the Ruhr industrial district, we hear Lanzmann flatly read Just's breathtakingly precise and proper bureaucratic language as he asks for structural modifications to the gas vans that the Saurer company had expertly engineered so that the Jews could be destroyed even more effectively. At a *Bierstube* in Munich, Lanzmann displays a photograph of Christian Wirth, a major architect of the extermination process at Bełżec and Treblinka, while trying to provoke a response from the man working the bar: he is Joseph Oberhauser, one of Wirth's principal assistants and a war criminal whom German justice had set free before the end of his prison term. In each of these cases, the documents open unexpected depths of horror within, or lend a poignant perspective to, the misleadingly banal subjects we see in the image.

One type of document—archival film clips of the camps, survivors, and victims—is conspicuously lacking, however. The absence of such "documentary" images, in fact, makes *Shoah* virtually unique among Holocaust documentaries. Theodor Adorno had been perhaps the first to question the use of such images.[38] Indeed, Lanzmann has on occasion indicated that Adorno's proscriptions had an impact on his thinking, and from the outset he seems to have followed Adorno's lead in rejecting them as well.[39] Depicting the atrocities in graphic detail, he believed, were not necessary for remembering or memorializing the horrors. On the contrary, there were many reasons for avoiding such depictions. By the end of the 1940s, moving pictures describing the

Nazis' rise to power taken from such propaganda films as Leni Riefenstahl's *Triumph of the Will* and German *Wochenschau* newsreels, or the awful pictures of the camps taken by Allied cinematographers at the war's end, had already been endlessly recycled in a host of "documentary" shorts as well as several fictional features.[40] These images served various purposes: they were used in newsreels, in propaganda and training films, in films shown at trials of war criminals, and so on, and they have appeared and—sad to say—sometimes to misleading effect in countless films since then. Their use was often highly problematic, and Lanzmann recognized this fact before many others did.[41]

First and foremost, Lanzmann regarded the truth value of these pictures as deeply suspect. Nazi newsreels and the rushes the *Propaganda Kompanien* of the *Wehrmacht* recorded but never made into finished films, for example, do not fairly represent the Jewish victims. Nazi ghetto footage was clearly made with an eye toward attributing the bestial conditions to their victims' mores and certainly avoided taking any responsibility for what German authorities were deliberately causing to happen in the starving, filthy slums into which they forced the Jews.[42] Footage of this kind thus presents a biased, and at best a partial picture of what happened.[43] The Nazis, furthermore, strictly prohibited any cinematic documentation of their death squads and camps. Today we know of only a single, 90-second clip recording a mass execution (at Liepaja, Latvia), filmed by a German soldier and amateur cinematographer named Wiener, which now figures prominently in exhibits at the U.S. Holocaust Memorial Museum as well as in several films.[44] Finally, the often gruesome footage shot by Russian and Polish camera teams in the summer of 1944 and January 1945, and by American and British army photographers during the spring of 1945, did not show the death camps in action but primarily recorded some of the gassing installations, the pathetic medical victims, the bodies "stacked like cordwood," and the survivors in the aftermath of the death marches. Certainly these films portray *some* of the results of Nazi bestiality but, horrible as they are, they are woefully inadequate to portray the process, scale, and brutality the Jews faced *in the extermination camps*, all of which constitutes *Shoah*'s central focus.[45] Lanzmann, in any case, dismissed documents of this kind as "images without imagination," inexact visual renderings that allow viewers to indulge in an unsavory and misleading spectacle at the expense of a past that could be tapped only by a strenuous effort of listening, learning, and imaginative engagement. Even if the Germans *had* recorded their foul deeds for posterity, he added, their actions would make a spectacle too shameful to reproduce. Indeed, years after Lanzmann had completed *Shoah,* he observed that if he were to come across any authentic images of the extermination process, he would destroy them.[46] A firm principle thus anchors Lanzmann's film: mimesis, the pictorial reproduction of the awful circumstances in which the Jews met death, is not essential for—indeed, is a hindrance to—anamnesis, the calling to mind of the process of their destruction.

In *Shoah*, the voices and bodies of those who had seen or themselves been through the worst, and yet were still capable of making their experiences come alive in the present, bear the principal burden of conveying the truth of what happened. However, Georges Didi-Huberman, in his chapter translated in this volume, insists on the importance of Lanzmann's own comment in "Site and Speech" and other interviews that *Shoah* must also be regarded as a "topographical" film. If *Shoah* is memorable principally for the unforgettable close-ups of those who speak about the mass murders, it is equally a work that returns, again and again, to the scenes where the crimes they describe took place. Lanzmann refers to these places as "non-sites of memory."[47] As is well known, the Germans took great pains to erase all trace of their crimes, ex-huming and burning their victims' bodies and destroying the facilities with which they had accomplished the genocide. At Treblinka and Bełżec they even planted trees and various crops on the blood-soaked fields. When Lanzmann came to these extermination sites, all that was left were rapidly disappearing traces of structures like the one Srebnik walks past in the forest clearing out-side Chelmno. At others locales, perhaps most movingly at Treblinka, the Pol-ish authorities had established commemorative monuments of shattered stones to symbolize the destroyed Jewish communities. Whether the traces of the killing process have been submerged in innocent-looking fields and ver-dant forests or supplanted by symbolic sculptures, Lanzmann directs our at-tention to the sites in two ways. In some locations his "characters"—Srebnik at Chelmno, or Piwonski and Lanzmann himself at Sobibor—walk through or skirt the perimeters of the camp sites. Even more imposing, however, are the many camera movements that relentlessly and repeatedly traverse these spaces. Sometimes these "obsessive," seemingly unmotivated movements are accompanied by the voices of those who suffered there; sometimes they un-fold in an eerie silence. The long gliding tracks down the symbolic rail bed into Treblinka or the more agitated pans around the Treblinka stone monu-ments seem desperate attempts to measure the scale of the camp, to mark its boundaries, to insist upon the very slope of the ground on which it formerly stood. Surveyed in this way, the spaces themselves are made to testify to cen-tral truths of the exterminations in a way, Lanzmann believes, that simulacra of the murder sites, as reconstructed in so many fictional movies, never can.[48]

In order to stimulate their testimony, Lanzmann brought some of his witnesses—Srebnik is the best example—back to the very sites where they had suffered. While a child prisoner at Chelmno, Srebnik had been forced to row down the river Ner, singing popular Polish songs or German military ditties while his SS guards cast the ashes of cremated Jews into the current.[49] More than thirty years later Lanzmann asked him to recreate this painful scene for his camera. The result is haunting: the simple images are imbued with an as-tonishing, almost mythic density as Srebnik, a modern incarnation of Or-pheus crossing the river Styx, appears to call the dead back to life. Similarly, Lanzmann asked Bomba, although he was already retired, not simply to tell his story, but to give a haircut while describing how, standing at the threshold of Treblinka's gas chambers, he was forced to cut the hair off naked women who had only minutes to live. Lanzmann carefully coordinates the setting, its framing and composition, and the movement of those he refers to as "characters" through the spaces he constructs. In this Tel Aviv barber shop, so far removed from wartime Poland, the people reflected and refracted in the complicated, unstable spaces of the facing mirrors invoke invisible spectral presences that haunt Bomba's—and our—present. Indeed, the image of a woman with short-cropped hair in an advertisement just visible in the illusory depths of the frame makes the presence of the women who died uncannily palpable.

Lanzmann points to subtle compositional and mise-en-scène techniques such as these to insist that *Shoah*—*pace* Marcel Ophüls and countless others—is not a documentary on the Holocaust but an original work of art. This notion may confound viewers who observe *Shoah*'s resemblance to other "talking heads" films on historical topics. Yet those who diminish the complexity of Lanzmann's film by likening it to these all too familiar models ignore those aspects of *Shoah* that explode crucial features of the talking heads genre, transforming it from a mere history lesson into something much greater: a meditation, emphatically modernist in form, on the genocide of the European Jews.

Shoah clearly resists certain organizational principles typical of the historical documentary genre and also adds materials that are utterly foreign to it. As has already been noted, Lanzmann abandons chronological narration of the genocide because he believes that it is grounded in an ultimately misleading conception of historical causality that he rejects. To conceive of the Holocaust merely as a tragic story that could be narrated as a linear process and then digested in a straightforward manner, moreover, would be to impose closure on the Germans' unspeakable crimes and thereby to circumvent the kind of personal engagement that is a crucial dimension of Lanzmann's project. Rather, Lanzmann circles around key reference points (the first time something happened, the harrowing journeys in the cattle cars) and around some of the themes that obsess him (the bitter cold, the Poles' lack of remorse), moving freely—for the uninitiated, perhaps a bit too freely—back and forth in time. Toward the end of the film, for example, Jan Karski, a former courier for the Polish government in exile, offers an account of his clandestine visit to the Warsaw Ghetto in the fall of 1942. This is hours after we have heard the odious Suchomel speak about testing the primitive gas chambers and burial techniques in Bełżec and the "improved" operations at Treblinka where most of the Warsaw Jews were killed during the late summer of 1942.

That is not to say that no narrational structures undergird the historical facts in the film. Lanzmann organizes *Shoah* into large thematic sections that move broadly from the initial implementation of the extermination process, through the time when the "industrial production line of death" (Suchomel's phrase) was working at maximum efficiency and speed, to the disingenuous or sincere struggles which some reported on and others denied all responsibility for, to how the Germans' "Final Solution" was implemented; the film concludes with the bitter despair of some survivors who, though they resisted, know the futility of their efforts. After the Warsaw Ghetto Uprising was defeated, Simha Rottem, one of its former leaders, recounts how he returned through the sewers to the shattered remnants of the former Ghetto. The words he strains to utter are the last we will hear in the film: "I remember a moment feeling a kind of tranquility, of serenity. I said to myself: 'I am the last Jew. I'll wait for morning, and for the Germans.' "

Instead of using chronology as a conceptual armature, Lanzmann stitches together a number of smaller, local narratives[50] whose overlapping accounts and echoing resonances constitute a temporality that is unique to the film. It refuses to subsume the stories of those who testify before his camera into a more encompassing narrative, for to do this would be to impose a false coherence on the radically disjunctive experiences that are the crucial basis of both the survivors' testimonies and of his own project. Leon Wieseltier's chapter in this volume elegantly conjectures what Lanzmann's motive may have been: to spare his witnesses "from the perfections of narrative," to prevent its sweep and drive from supplanting the voicing of the particulars of their experience. This unusual strategy imposes an uncommon burden on the spectators of *Shoah*, one that requires commitment, sharpened attention, and reflection. Only by negotiating the shifting chronologies of these scraps of time, by listening to painful words uttered through forced smiles or squeezed out through tears solely by means of a survivor's grim determination, by gathering and putting together the fragments of vanishing traces, can one *re-member* the actions that today cannot otherwise be made accessible.[51] Only by doing so can viewers restore and make present in almost carnal, physically tangible terms the experiences beyond any human limits evoked by these witnesses.

Not all spectators prove up to the challenge. Some viewers are put off by the delays in translating comments from Polish, Hebrew, or Yiddish into French, because these extend the film's length.[52] Further obstacles to some viewers are the lengthy takes of boxcars in motion or extended tracking shots down rail beds leading to former sites of destruction where piled memorial stones constitute mute signs of the agonies experienced by the victims. Lanzmann's use of extended takes that are not necessarily thematically motivated—long shots of empty forests and fields—can be frustrating to those who prefer to get on with the story. But this method of interpolating blocks of imagery that resist any simple, legible rationale is purposeful in several ways. It has the effect of punctuating and affording visual relief from the medium and close shots of the witnesses Lanzmann cajoled—indeed, at times prodded—to push their recollections ever farther. When accompanied by voice-overs, the landscapes gradually disclose an unsuspected past and compel the viewer to strain to reconcile the deceptively tranquil present with the horror of former days. When silent, these images of a peaceful countryside allow time for reflection on the enormity of the losses. They mysteriously bolster in distinctly nonverbal ways the sense of portentous menace that will forever haunt these lands where thousands upon thousands of human beings went up in smoke.

Both on and off screen, Claude Lanzmann presides over *Shoah*. As his French compatriot Marcel Ophüls does in his own films, Lanzmann plays several key roles in this one: the audience's testy surrogate; the mediator of the conversations he conducts; a questing, questioning hero seeking truth, always persistent, sometimes exasperating, often ironic or condescending, or all of these simultaneously. The process of integrating *Shoah*'s fabric of voices and spaces, of time past and time present, would not have been possible without him. Off screen, he is, of course, responsible for the timing of the sequences, their shuffled order, the folds and fissures of the narration he constructs. Lanzmann is, as all great editors are, a kind of conductor, and thus it makes sense that he has likened the structure of *Shoah* to that of a symphony grounded in several complicated logics. Perhaps it does not matter that these patterns will not be apparent to all viewers. Some will find the potency of the testimonies sufficient to sustain their attention and admiration. And just as many people are moved to meditation by a great piece of music while understanding little of the complex harmonic, instrumental, or rhythmic relationships that make it stirring, so too will *Shoah*, even without a sophisticated comprehension of its stylistic dynamics, induce reflection and empathy as viewers are brought face to face with one of the defining events of the twentieth century.

For audiences, today and in the future, few films will engage a more important moral subject; even fewer will dare to redefine the nature of cinematic achievement itself with greater rigor and ambition than Claude Lanzmann's *Shoah*.

Notes

Special thanks are due to Richard Maxwell, and above all to Henry Weinfield, who read an earlier version of this chapter and made many helpful suggestions.

1. See the complete translation of this text in this volume.
2. *Pourquoi Israel* was released in France in 1973 and had its premiere at the New York Film Festival on the very day the Yom Kippur War began in October 1973. Note that the title conspicuously lacks a question mark, though the grammar would seem to call for it, and many early reviewers incorrectly added it. Lanzmann was making an affirmative statement about Israel, its diversity and social and political tensions; he was not raising any question about the existence of the Jewish state.
3. All the footage (as well as transcripts of the interviews) is now deposited in the archives of the U.S. Holocaust Memorial Museum in Washington, D.C., where it is being meticulously catalogued and preserved.
4. This text forms the introduction to the published English-language script of the film included in this volume. As is well known, Lanzmann and de Beauvoir were involved both professionally in the publication of the famous intellectual journal *Les Temps Modernes*, as well as personally. Their relationship has recently been portrayed—not very insightfully—in an unfortunately salacious book, *Tête à Tête: Simone de Beauvoir and Jean-Paul Sartre* by Hazel Rowley (New York: HarperCollins, 2005).

5. See the complete reviews by Wiesel, Denby, Ophüls, and Wieseltier in this volume for a representative sampling of the praise that greeted the film in major newspapers and intellectual weeklies.

The most notable negative review in the American press was by Pauline Kael. It was buried in a late December 1985 issue of the *New Yorker*, more than two months after the New York premiere. (It appears that the editors deliberately delayed publication.) Her attention span being overtaxed by the film's uncommon length and what she called its "ritualistically" repeated camera movements, she was annoyed by the delays caused by the translations into French of witnesses testifying in Polish, Yiddish, or Hebrew. She also objected to the relentless intensity of the "tyrannically close" close-ups, which she likened to the "invasions of a face." As was her wont, Kael substituted words of dismissal for anything resembling a thoughtful analysis. She accused Lanzmann of "slackness" and his film of "diffuseness"; she charged Lanzmann's approach with a "lack of moral complexity," and she built to a nasty put-down: " 'Shoah' is a long moan." Reading this diatribe by someone who was the most influential American film critic of the day is dismaying. Fortunately, she does not seem to have had much impact on the film's success with American audiences. She was far closer to the truth when, in passing, she called *Shoah* "oral history treated on a grand scale as an elegy or meditation."

6. Upon its release, critics tended to focus on three objections: (1) Lanzmann's methods, which often involved subterfuge (as in the false promises he made to keep Franz Suchomel's identity secret); (2) his sometimes aggressive interview techniques that pressed survivors to remember what they at times seemed desperately to want to forget; and (3) his alleged affronts to Polish national pride. The first objection, perhaps correct in principle, is utterly wrong when matters concern former murderers who had to be approached with the greatest circumspection in order to obtain their crucially informative comments. The second objection results from ignorance of the trust Lanzmann had established with survivors beforehand and overlooks the gentleness with which he elicits their stories. The case of Bomba, who had already told his story to Lanzmann and agreed to be filmed, is instructive in this regard. The last issue is bound up with the ways the Polish communist martial law regime attempted to drum up opposition to Lanzmann to shore up its waning fortunes. Full accounts are provided in the chapters by Timothy Garton Ash and Jean-Charles Szurek in this volume.

7. In fact, similar acclaim has greeted the film wherever it has been shown, from Europe through Latin America to China.

8. See Peter Novick, *The Holocaust in American Life* (Boston: Houghton Mifflin, 1999). For a slightly different perspective mapping the presence of the Holocaust in the public sphere on American television and the social discourses surrounding it, see Jeffrey Shandler, *While America Watches* (New York: Oxford University Press, 1999).

9. Twenty years after its completion Lanzmann wrote: "As for myself, I thought that my film would be seen by 3,000 people and that was enough for me." "Ce Mot de 'Shoah,' " *Le Monde* (February 26, 2005). As of 2006, countless millions in China, Europe, and the Americas have seen the film, mostly on television but also in theaters as well as on videotape and DVD.

10. A major exception to this trend was Sidney Lumet's *The Pawnbroker* (1965). It focused on an embittered, unlikable, un-Christian survivor whose personal humiliations and losses in German camps were clear but formed only the background to the

contemporary problems he faced. The most famous and widely seen film about a Holocaust subject was, of course, *The Diary of Anne Frank* (George Stevens, 1959), but Anne had not survived and her diary focuses entirely on her family's life in hiding.

11. For a general overview of Holocaust cinema, see Annette Insdorf, *Indelible Shadows*, 3rd ed. (New York: Cambridge University Press, 2003).

12. In a sense, Lanzmann's project continued the thrust initiated by Ben Gurion's efforts to make the Jewish genocide a central topic in both Israel's and the world's awareness and discourse. See, among many others, Hannah Arendt, *Eichmann in Jerusalem* (1965; New York: Penguin, 1994); Annette Wieviorka, *Le Procès Eichmann, 1961* (Brussels: Editions Complexe, 1989); and Hannah Yablonka, *The State of Israel vs. Adolf Eichmann* (New York: Schocken Books, 2004).

13. I have in mind filmmakers such as Roberto Benigni or Robin Williams, or even (according to Lanzmann) Steven Spielberg. See Lanzmann's "Why Spielberg Has Distorted the Truth," *The Guardian Weekly* (April 3, 1994): 14.

14. "From the Holocaust to 'Holocaust,' " in this volume.

15. Ibid. This stinging last phrase was later taken up by leading Jewish scholars, among others Yosef Yerushalmi and Pierre Vidal-Naquet, who rebutted those who deny that the Holocaust occurred. See the latter's *Assassins of Memory*, trans. Jeffrey Mehlman (New York: Columbia University Press, 1992). See also Lanzmann's comments in "Site and Speech" in this volume: "The American series *Holocaust* was rubbish in every respect. Fictionalizing such a history is the most serious sort of transgression: it shows the Jews entering the gas chambers, arm in arm, stoically, as if they were Romans. It's Socrates drinking the hemlock. These are idealist images that permit all kinds of reassuring identifications. *Shoah*, however, is anything but reassuring."

16. Claude Lanzmann, "Ce Mot de 'Shoah.' "

17. Uriel Tal, "Excursus on the Term: *Shoah*," *Shoah* 1, no. 4 (1979): 10.

18. Henri Meschonnic fulminated against using the word "Shoah" in "Pour en finir avec le mot 'Shoah,' " *Le Monde* (February 20–21, 2005).

19. "Ce Mot de 'Shoah.' " Lanzmann's remarks emerged as a response to a debate concerning the naming of the Holocaust in the pages of *Le Monde*. Jacques Sebag began the debate in "Pour en finir avec le mot Holocauste," *Le Monde* (January 27, 2005); Meschonnic, "Pour en finir avec le mot 'Shoah.' " See also Michel Henochsberg, "*Shoah*, nom propre," in *Les Temps Modernes* (March–June 2005): 27–35; and Didier Epelbaum, *Pas un mot, pas une ligne* (Paris: Éditions Stock, 2005), p. 15.

20. "Ce Mot de 'Shoah.' "

21. "From the Holocaust to 'Holocaust,' " in this volume.

22. Ibid.

23. Dominick LaCapra provides a searching analysis and critique of these strategies in his chapter in this volume.

24. It seems that the other crucial dimension of Lanzmann's film—its circular shape and structural links based on corroborating testimonies, for example—emerged later. Lanzmann has promised a written memoir of his experiences while making the film that will undoubtedly provide insights into the evolving process.

25. Lanzmann told this story on the stage of the Museum of Jewish Heritage in New York City on September 25, 2005.

26. Personal communication from Regina Longo, a former archivist at the U.S. Holocaust Memorial Museum, who has been studying the documentary and cinematic record (July 19, 2005).

27. Rudolf Vrba, who escaped Auschwitz with fellow prisoner Alfred Wetzler on April 10, 1944, published the first eyewitness report, *German Extermination Camps— Auschwitz and Birkenau*, later that year. See also Jan Karski, *Story of a Secret State* (Boston: Houghton Mifflin, 1944); and Filip Müller, *Eyewitness Auschwitz: Three Years in the Gas Chambers* (New York: Stein and Day, 1979). (Lanzmann wrote the introduction to the French translation of this book.) German SS man Pery Broad, whom Lanzmann also interviewed but did not include in the film, also wrote "Reminiscences," which has also been published in *KL Auschwitz Seen by the SS* (Oświęcim: The Auschwitz-Birkenau State Museum, 2002), pp. 103–147.

28. See his *Eyewitness Auschwitz: Three Years in the Gas Chambers*. Jacques Derrida makes a similar point when he writes that "*Shoah* would have been much less powerful and credible as a purely audible document. The presentation of the traces is neither a simple presentation nor a representation, nor is it an image. It is incarnated in the body, harmonizes gestures with speech, as it recounts [a story] within a landscape in which it is inscribed." "Le Cinéma et ses fantômes," *Cahiers du Cinéma* (April 2001): 81. Marianne Hirsch and Leo Spitzer incisively highlight the way in which the memory of women serves as triggers for male emotions in *Shoah* in their chapter included in this volume.

29. In large measure, *Shoah*'s silence about the SS killing squads in the USSR results from Lanzmann's frustrated efforts to obtain testimony from German participants. As is noted above, Lanzmann was beaten so badly by the family of one of the former *Einsatzgruppen* officers that he ended up for an extended stay in the hospital. Personal communication with the author.

30. Such was the fate of the now celebrated Polish-Jewish writer Bruno Schulz, who was murdered in his home town of Drohobycz (formerly in Poland, now part of Ukraine) by a German officer as retaliation against another officer who was, for a time, Schulz's protector.

31. Lanzmann's inventory of the rushes of interviews he filmed during the development of the film include fourteen hours of discussion with Murmelstein, but none of the footage was included in *Shoah*. The rushes and transcripts of this interview are in the Steven Spielberg Archive at the U.S. Holocaust Memorial Museum in Washington, D.C.

32. It is true that Lanzmann does not significantly treat the thousands of Poles, Russian POWs, and Gypsies who were also gassed at these sites.

33. The transcripts of all testimonies in the film are available in French in Claude Lanzmann, *Shoah* (Paris: Gallimard, 1985). An English version, which Lanzmann has repudiated, was published in 1985 by Pantheon Books in New York.

34. Lanzmann took seriously the remarks of his principal historical mentor, Raul Hilberg, who appears in *Shoah*. Hilberg notes that all the while he was writing his great history of the Holocaust, he was always afraid to ask large questions for fear of obtaining only small answers. He preferred to focus on details, as does Lanzmann when, for example, he asks Podchlebnik, what colors the gas vans at Chelmno were.

35. See Srebnik's comments in Lanzmann, *Shoah*, pp. 24–25.

36. *Pace* Shoshana Felman in her well-known, challenging, and deeply problematic essay, "In an Era of Testimony: Claude Lanzmann's *Shoah*," *Yale French Studies*, no. 79. Perhaps the longest text on the film yet produced, it was too long to include in this anthology. The essence of Lanzmann's subjects' testimonies is not impersonal, nor do any who are testifying (in a metaphorical sense; they are not appearing, after all, in a court of law) aim for an impersonal expression of what they experienced. Much to the contrary, as Felman does observe. Neither the gaps in their diverse accounts nor the inevitably radical differences in their viewpoints that she carefully articulates (and the different languages they speak—German, Yiddish, Hebrew, Polish) necessarily imply what she calls the "incommensurability" of their statements. Indeed, as she notes, Lanzmann deliberately sets up a "logic of corroboration" among the different witnesses. Those collected, structured testimonies, to be sure, do not constitute what Felman calls a "community of witnessing" based on shared visual perceptions of what took place, although why she restricts testimony to what was seen (as opposed to, say, experienced) is unclear.

37. "An Evening with Claude Lanzmann" (May 4, 1986). Cited in Felman, "In an Era," p. 48.

38. Michael Rothberg intelligently reviews the nuances of Adorno's thinking as it changed over time in *Traumatic Realism* (Minneapolis: University of Minnesota Press, 2000), pp. 25–58.

39. Clearly, Lanzmann did not follow Adorno's ambivalence about making artworks about the Holocaust, since he has always insisted that *Shoah* be considered a work of art. See previous note.

40. A partial list of documentaries would include Aleksander Ford's *Vernichtungslager Majdanek, Cmentarzysko Europy* (1944); *Les camps de la mort* (Anonymous, 1945); K. Czyński's *Swastyka i Szubienica* (1945); the U.S. Army Signal Corps' *Nazi Concentration Camps* (1945) and Roman Karmen's *The Crimes of the German Fascist Invaders* (1945), both presented at the first Nuremberg Trial; Don Siegel's *Hitler Lives* (1945); G. Kanin and C. Reed's *The True Glory* (1945); Hanuš Bürger's *Todesmühlen* (1946); R. Karmen's *Oświęcim* (1946); I. Setkina and R. Karmen's *Vernichtungslager Majdanek* (1946); G. Fowler, Jr.'s *Seeds of Destiny* (1946); Henri Cartier-Bresson's *Le Retour* (1946); Richard Brandt's *Todeslager Sachsenhausen* (1946); R. Karmen and E. Svilova's *Sud Narodov* (1947); Frank Capra's *Your Job in Germany* (1946); Ernst Lubitsch's *Here Is Germany* (1946); and Leo Hurwitz's *Strange Victory* (1948), as well as unfinished projects such as Sidney Bernstein and Alfred Hitchcock's *The Memory of the Camps*. Three feature films also make extensive use of such footage: Aleksander Ford's *Border Street* (Poland, 1948); Alfred Radok's *Distant Journey* (Czechoslovakia, 1949); and Saul Goskind and Nahan Gross's *Undzere Kinder* (Poland, unreleased, 1949).

41. The problems include inaccurate identification of sources, taking images out of context, and using specific images to make general points or vice versa without proper annotation. Adding to the problems are the fact that some fictional films modeled their images on specific documentary sources or developed authentic-looking images which were then incorporated as "documentary" shots in later work. See, for example, images Wanda Jakubowska made for her docudrama *Ostatni Etap* (1948) that were recycled in, among others, Alain Resnais's *Nuit et brouillard* (France, 1956), Leo Hurwitz's *The Museum and the Fury* (United States, 1956), and Allan Holzman's *Survivors of the Holocaust* (United States, 1996).

42. Propaganda footage exists of deportations in the Będzin region, and color as well as black and white images of the Warsaw Ghetto were also taken, though as far as we know they were never used. Later in the war the Nazis contrived to make several films to document their allegedly humane treatment of the Jews at both the Westerbork and Theresienstadt camps. Neither film was ever completed to serve their intended purpose.

43. Lucy Dawidowicz, "Visualizing the Warsaw Ghetto," *Shoah* 1, no. 1 (1978): 5–6, 17–18. A close examination of the Nazi footage of the Warsaw Ghetto reveals how events (such as the capture of a Jewish criminal by the Jewish police) were staged for a sophisticated network of German cameramen who filmed them.

44. Lanzmann interviewed Wiener but did not include any of the footage in *Shoah*.

45. See his comments in this volume in "Site and Speech" about "images without imagination."

46. Claude Lanzmann, "Why Spielberg Has Distorted the Truth." In recent years Lanzmann and Godard have engaged in a series of skirmishes about the existence and ethics of images of the exterminations. Libby Saxton follows the debate and provides useful bibliographic references in "Anamnesis and Bearing Witness: Godard/Lanzmann," published in Michael Temple, James S. Williams, and Michael Witt, eds., *Forever Godard* (London: Black Dog Publishing, 2004), pp. 364–379. These debates have also been joined by authors, such as Georges Didi-Huberman, who have written about photographs of the camps,. See his essay "Images malgré tout" in Clément Cheroux, ed., *Mémoire des camps* (Paris: Marval, 2001), pp. 219–241, as well as his responses to the criticisms of many in Lanzmann's circle in his book of the same title published by Les Éditions de Minuit in 2003.

47. See "Site and Speech." Lanzmann's description of the killing fields as "non-sites of memory" alludes to the work of French historian Pierre Nora, the principal author and organizer of the large historical project *Les Lieux de mémoire*. For a précis, see his "Between Memory and History: *Les Lieux de Mémoire*," *Representations* (Spring 1989): 7–24.

48. Constructing simulacra of the conditions in the camps and ghettos, of course, has grounded many cinematic fictions from *Morituri* and *The Last Stop* (both 1948), *Kapo* (1959), and *Jakob der Lügner* (1975) through *Schindler's List* (1993), *Life Is Beautiful* (1997), *Jakob the Liar* (1999), *The Grey Zone* (2001), and *Fateless* (2005). But for Lanzmann these reconstructions invoke fundamentally false memories, or as Derrida has noted, provoke at best a drastically weakened form of memory. "Le Cinéma et ses fantômes," p. 81.

49. In her chapter in this anthology, Anne-Lise Stern provides a subtle reading of the revealing mistakes Srebnik makes when singing the words of the German marching song.

50. Lanzmann uses the repetition of key details by differently positioned witnesses to corroborate the veracity of an event or characterization. The throat-cutting gesture already mentioned is one instance of this procedure, and the descriptions of riding in the cattle cars and the brutal unloading on the ramps repeated by several witnesses is another illustration.

51. The combining of broken fragments of tombstones is a prominent feature of many Holocaust memorial monuments in Poland and elsewhere. See James Young,

The Texture of Memory. Holocaust Memorials and Meaning (New Haven, Conn.: Yale University Press, 1993), pp. 185–208.

52. Such delays generate a kind of *temps morts* (literally "dead times") in which the flow of information momentarily comes to a halt, leaving viewers in limbo about the meaning of what has been said. They produce a suspenseful state of anticipation as viewers wait for the details of a process whose outcome all know all too well. These delays are thus a considered aspect of Lanzmann's narrational techniques. Some Polish speakers, by the way, have protested aspects of the translations into French. In general, however, the translator occasionally softened the nuances of some anti-Semitic utterances by the Poles who were interviewed.

PART I
Inception through Production and Distribution

From the Holocaust to "Holocaust"

CLAUDE LANZMANN

At the end of the war, the massive revelations of the genocide committed against the Jewish people—and of the way it was perpetrated—stunned the Western world. (The countries of Eastern Europe, long familiar with anti-Semitism, were not exempt from this reaction.) Infected to the marrow, as the European nations were, by the poison of anti-Semitism—and nearly all knowing themselves to be guilty in varying degrees—they recognized and understood at once, with instant, lightning certainty, the unique and unconscionable nature of the crime. Everything was now clear; no debate, no protest, no denial was possible. The Nazi crime was both unprecedented and unsurpassable—unsurpassable because, as we shall see, it was an absolute crime.

What gave rise to this horrified wordlessness was not the fact that, once again, the Jews had been the appointed victims: the European nations were not unaccustomed to such practices; and, indeed, the Holocaust could not have taken place had not 2,000 years of persecution and anti-Jewish hatred paved the way for it everywhere. No, stupefaction arose from the unbearable discovery that anti-Semitism, a patrimony and passion the nations shared, could reach such extremes and end in a slaughter unparalleled in the history of mankind. Things had gone too far: if anti-Semitism had led to Auschwitz, if anti-Jewish passion had resulted in Auschwitz, then anti-Semitism must be irrevocably banished. The feeling that prevailed at the time was that, this once, the Jewish people had paid the supreme price and for all time. Everything seemed to suggest that the Holocaust had established forever that theoretically anti-Semitism had become impossible.

The planned, methodical bureaucratic massacre of six million Jews was a long-term enterprise, carried out patiently and without passion in the name of ideological imperatives that were openly stated and explained. From the magnitude of the massacre, the human species took the staggering measure of its capacity to commit crimes against itself. For indeed it was mankind itself that was challenged by the monstrous crime perpetrated against the Jewish people. In order to judge the Holocaust, to grasp it fully, no ordinary existing laws are adequate; it has been necessary to resort to an entirely new juridical-metaphysical concept—namely, that of a "crime against humanity."

It was, factually, literally, a crime against the human essence, a metaphysical crime committed on the person of each murdered Jew against the being of Man. Once again—and one must hope, for the last time—the Jews performed their role of witness people. The cry that will rise into the skies of Auschwitz and Treblinka until the end of time testifies to the unsurpassable limits of inhumanity of which mankind is capable. There is and will be nothing with which Auschwitz and Treblinka can be compared. No one can mistake it, no one is so obscenely impudent as to deny the Holocaust its specific character, its uniqueness, by attenuating it, by burying it in a thesis of universal evil, by subsuming it under generalities such as "the horrors of war" or "the victims of fascism." Despite the millions of dead on both sides, despite the terror of Hiroshima or Dresden, we know that the six million murdered Jews were not victims like the others.

Their extermination is a crime of a different nature, of a different quality; it is a nameless crime, which the Nazi assassins themselves dared not name, as if by doing so they would have made it impossible to enact. It was, literally, an unnameable crime.

To say that the Holocaust is unique and can be compared with nothing else does not imply that it should be regarded as an aberrant phenomenon, which eludes intellectual or conceptual grasp, which occurred outside history or is to be denied the status of a historical event. On the contrary, I consider the Holocaust an unqualifiedly historical event, the monstrous, yes, but legitimate product of the history of the Western World. My film means to deal with this crucial aspect in the utmost detail and precision.

But the responsibility and guilt of most nations are too grave, their remorse and shame are too great, the crime is too burdensome: the Holocaust encumbers the conscience of the modern world like an indigestible patrimony. After the stunned acknowledgment of the brutal fact of the extermination in the years following the Second World War, after the recognition of the immeasurable nature of the crime, public response has steadily tended to reverse itself.

For the most part, the Holocaust has not been assimilated as a specific historical event, and one may doubt that it ever will be.

Indeed, only some thirty years after the catastrophe we are witnessing an extraordinary phenomenon of rejection. The "honeymoon" between the Jewish people and the world has definitely come to an end and we can take the measure of our illusion: like the indestructible phoenix, anti-Semitism is arising virtually everywhere from its own ashes, wearing its ancient disguises or the more modern, "democratic" mask of anti-Zionism. As for the Holocaust, the keynote seems to be "How do we get rid of it?" In the East as well as in the West, on the right as well as on the left, people are trying in every way to be quit of it, to forget it without ever having understood it, to falsify it, to deny it, the revival of anti-Semitism and the rejection of the Holocaust are dialectically interrelated. The true pursuit of anti-Semitism is the death of the Jew; therefore, the anti-Semite must deny that the extermination ever happened so as to regain the unhindered right to kill again.

The Holocaust is rejected by banalizing it, trivializing it, or excising it from history with the pretext that it was only an aberration.

After all, what happened to the Jews is common enough, nothing to make a great fuss about. History is one long series of massacres, and their names come tumbling to our lips—the massacre of Saint Bartholomew, the genocide of the Armenians in 1915, the Gulag, the tortures in Algeria, segregationist violence in the United States or Tell el Zatar. Thus Tell el Zatar has become the Warsaw Ghetto (an identification coldly made by some French papers a year ago). As for Sultan Abdul Hamid's Turkey, as everyone knows, it was the most developed and most modern nation in the Western world, the motherland of Goethe as well as of Kant and Schiller, the home of the Ruhr magnates, of Krupp and I. G. Farben. And the Sultan, too—in this a forerunner of Adolf Hitler—had established a coherent, universally applicable doctrine to justify the annihilation of the Armenians. One may make step-by-step comparisons among atrocities and point out the ideological flaws, absurdities, and perversities. But the goal has been attained; after a while, people no longer know what anything is about, everything is indistinguishable; the Holocaust has lost its unique particularity. It has been conjured away.

In this connection, it is by no means sure that the success of the American TV serial that was entitled *Holocaust* should be taken as a sign of an awakening of conscience. The sudden discovery of the martyrdom of the Jews, and the compassion it evoked among an immense TV audience, is perhaps the latest ruse of a kind of history that disposes of the Holocaust's singularity even as it claims to be portraying it. The treatment and the means used are highly suspect. The Jewish family with which millions of Americans and Germans are said to have identified was chosen precisely so that such an identification would be possible. In fact, and this is the essential point, the Jewish victims in the TV film are in no way distinguishable from the spectators or, for that matter, from their executioners. In order to make the "humanity" of these Jews obvious, to ensure that it would be recognized and felt, every trait that could have distinguished them was effaced, every trace of otherness was erased, and one was presented with an "assimilated" family; most of the actors were not Jewish. The contrary would have been far more appropriate: the humanity of the victims should have been made all the more evident and profound for us by virtue of their seeming different from the outset.

Could the world's television viewers have identified as readily with the Jewish men and women of Poland, of the Ukraine, or of Belorussia, with their different clothing, their traditions, their particular mannerisms, their strangeness?

The characters in the American documentary never lose their "humanity," even in the gas chambers. (Only a cast-iron disposition would dare represent what went on there; none of those who entered ever returned to tell us about it.) In *Holocaust*, people await death gravely and with dignity, as good form prescribes. In real life, things were different. After years of ghetto confinement, terror, humiliation, and hunger, the people who lined up in rows of five were driven by whips and bludgeons and knocked against each other as they entered the death chambers; they had neither the leisure nor the composure to die nobly. To show what really happened would have been unendurable. At the least, it would have precluded conscience-salving "identification." However, the film is a work of fiction. And in this instance, because the reality defies the resources of any fiction, *Holocaust* perpetrates a lie, a moral crime; it assassinates memory.

The Holocaust is unique because it created a circle of flame around itself, a boundary not to be crossed, since horror in the absolute degree cannot be communicated. To pretend that one has done so is to commit the gravest of transgressions. One must speak out and yet keep silent at the same time, knowing that in this case silence is the most authentic form of speech—maintaining, as in the eye of a hurricane, a protected, safe zone that is not to be entered. Here, to transgress or to trivialize are alike. The Hollywood serial transgresses because it trivializes, destroying the unique nature of the Holocaust, the thing that removes it from any comparison, that makes it the worst of all crimes to have been or ever to be committed.

Let me also say—and this is essential—that in my view anti-Semitism has an absolute specificity that can in no way be reduced to political or racial conflicts as they are generally understood. Anti-Semitism is much more than, and entirely different from, a particular instance of racism. Just as the destiny and the history of the Jewish people can be compared with no other, so also the cyclic character of anti-Jewish persecution and hatred (intense periods followed by remissions, wild hopes always shattered), the duration and the persistence of the persecution, the force and the extent of that hatred, with all the mythical and phantasmal spinoffs it constantly generates, make anti-Semitism a unique phenomenon and, sadly, make the periodic attempts to abate it ridiculous. The prodigious will-to-life of the Jewish people accounts for the persistence and the escalation of anti-Semitic hatred, which reached its peak in the Holocaust.

Raul Hilberg has summed this up in a splendid terse formula. "Christian missionaries had indeed said, 'You have no right to live among us as Jews'; the secular leaders who followed had proclaimed, 'You have no right to live among us.' The German Nazis finally decreed, 'You have no right to live.' "

To those today who regard the Holocaust as an anomaly, as an aberration so perfect that it eludes any appraisal, any historical interpretation, Hilberg's quotation would provide one response. Here are a few others:

First of all—if indeed it is a question of an aberration—the Jews have been its victims. The aberration lies at the very core of their history, it lays the foundation of that history, and they may be forgiven for wanting to find out its meaning. Twelve years of systematic persecution, of a slow process of destruction, carried out with the knowledge and in full view of the world and resulting in the annihilation of one-third of the Jewish people, allow them at least to ask themselves what made this anomaly possible.

However, essentially what the aberration theory aims to accomplish today is to get rid of the idea that any historical responsibility lies with Germany and the other nations. Yet the Holocaust was not the work of a handful of madmen. With regard to Germany, the process of destruction could have been carried through only on the basis of a general consensus of the German nation. The annihilation of six million Jews was an extremely difficult and complicated task, which posed numerous and vast problems for the murderers; in order to carry it out, the active, patient participation of the whole administrative machinery of a large modern state was required.

Furthermore, Germany relied on the existence of an aggressively anti-Semitic world: Poland, Hungary, Rumania, the USSR—not to mention others—were anti-Semitic. The famous Madagascar plan began as a Polish idea (the 1936 Lepecki Commission), and M. Georges Bonnet, the French minister of foreign affairs, coolly talked the matter over with von Ribbentrop. Mr. Ruthmund, the Swiss chief of police, was the first person responsible, as early as 1938, for the requirement that Jewish German refugees have their passports stamped with the letter "J." When Hitler condemned the Jews, he was not speaking an exotic foreign language; he was "communicating," he was understood and he knew he was understood. (See his comments after the Evian conference stalemate, or the Rublee-Schacht plan, or the entries in Goebbels's diary for 1942–43: "I am convinced that, deep down, the democracies are not dissatisfied that we should rid them of the 'Jewish trash' [*Jüdischen Riff-Raff*].")

If the democracies had been actively opposed to the persecution, or—what amounts to the same—had they opened their doors to the Jews and said, "You don't want them, so be it; we'll take them," the Holocaust would not have taken place or, at least, would never have reached such dimensions. The Holocaust was made possible in the first place because nations washed their hands of the Jewish persecution and left the Nazis alone with the "problem." Such are the historical responsibilities that one can follow, case by case, stage by stage, up to and including the shameful failure to rescue the Jews of Hungary: "What am

I to do with one million Jews?" Lord Moyne, then the British high commissioner in Egypt, asked.

We must hold fast to both ends of the chain: The Holocaust is unique but not aberrant. It is not the doing of a group of irresponsible atypical criminals, but, on the contrary, must be viewed as the expression of deep-seated tendencies in Western civilization. Basically, everyone agreed to the killing of those for whom there was no place.

Today the aberration theory of the Holocaust also allows for a new appraisal, a reevaluation of Nazism, and at last permits Germany to restore the missing link in its history. For thirty years Germany was unable to face up to the Holocaust and took the tack of pretending that Nazism had never existed. One simply did not mention Nazism. Germany was fat and affluent but it lacked a past, and her young men—those who are today between thirty and forty years old—were zombies presumably sprung up from nowhere. This discreet silence on the part of the great majority of Germans had one merit at least: implicitly it acknowledged that the Jewish question was absolutely central to Nazi ideology and practice; it admitted that the destruction of the Jews had been the very core of Nazism, that the Holocaust had been the only issue of Nazism.[1] Everything now has changed: time has done its work, new generations of Germans have come who have no reason not to wish to be linked to their history, a history that they have never been taught. And then, too, the Jewish people have survived; they are more alive than ever; and finally and above all, the State of Israel exists and, in its turn engages in violence. Through the instrument of their state, *the Jews have provided themselves with the means to resort to institutionalized violence.*[2]

The Jews also kill. This demonstrable fact is wonderful, liberating ("and what if the Jews were Nazis themselves!"). It delivers one from the old feeling of guilt and makes it possible to rewrite the history of Germany, integrating Nazism in it and while not completely denying the Holocaust, turning it into a secondary phenomenon of little consequence. Auschwitz is virtually obliterated. This is now the trend among even reputedly serious German historians, and this is the sense of the German films now being shown in Europe. The smashing success Joachim Fest's film *Hitler, a Career* has met with in Germany has no other explanation: in it are glorified—one is free at last to do this—the "positive aspects" of Hitler the man and his accomplishment. The Holocaust is pushed far into the background; that is the bad aspect of the man and of a period that in other respects had its excellent sides. And it is not at all certain that the bad outweighs the good; at the least, they may balance out evenly. In this way, anti-Jewish hatred becomes merely a personal aberration of Hitler's: "It's true, he didn't like Jews and he went too far." Does the aberration, then, lie in his own aversion or in the exaggeration of that aversion; does it lie in anti-Semitism or in an "excess" of anti-Semitism? In any case, one has come full circle: anti-Semitism, which had previously been banished and condemned to an underground existence, can now surface in broad daylight, based on and justified by reason of the very being of the Jew, with all the Jew's traditional characteristics. Thus the film of R. W. Fassbinder and Daniel Schmid, *The Shadow of Angels*, accepts with the most astounding innocence, as if it had reinvented them, all the stereotypes in the Nazi anti-Semitic lexicon.

This, then, is where we stand after thirty years. *The first question is not "How was the Holocaust possible?" but "How is it possible, thirty years after the Holocaust, that we should be where we are?"*

In point of fact, a tragic parallel can be drawn between the forgetting and the rejection of the Holocaust, on the one hand, and, on the other, the conditions that made it possible. Just as the Jews were murdered in the most heartrending solitude—derelict ears did not hear their calls for help, because, after all, the death of the Jews was only an insignificant happening in the context of universal history—so to remember this crime against humanity (which the Holocaust was) will not be the duty, the mission, the sacred trust of all mankind but something for Jews to harp on. Just as our people were left alone face to face with their exterminators, so will we remain alone to live with the gaping wound of a measureless crime.

As the philosopher Emil Fackenheim has admirably put it: "For us, the murdered Jews of Europe are not merely the past, they are the presence of an absence." This means that they have begot us, that they beget us daily, that we are born of them and will forever be born and reborn of them. Israelis and Diaspora Jews alike, we are anchored to (and in) the Holocaust, whose consequences and implications, far from disappearing with time, are continually and more deeply revealed to us. The destruction of six million of our people— an attempt to annihilate the entire people—has radically modified the Jewish universe, the Jews' perception of themselves, and their attitude toward others. The inflexibility of Israeli policy, so deplored and allegedly the root cause of its isolation, stems precisely from the fact that Israel knows it is the only— absolutely the only—guarantor of the sacred oath "Never Again," which we had believed all nations would subscribe to after Auschwitz.

Until now, all films dealing with the Holocaust have tried to generate it by using the expedients of history and chronological development. Generally, they begin in 1933, when the Nazis came to power—but sometimes earlier, presenting the various currents of German anti-Semitism in the nineteenth century (for instance, the *Volk* ideology, formation of the German national conscience) and seek to explain, year by year, step by step—one might say almost harmoniously—how these developments led to extermination. As if the extermination of six million men, women, and children, as if such a massacre could be "generated."

Obviously, there are reasons and explanations for the destruction of six million Jews: Adolf Hitler's character, his relationship to the Jew perceived as the "evil father," the German defeat in 1918, unemployment, inflation, the religious roots of anti-Semitism, the role of Jews in society, the image of the Jew, the indoctrination of German youth, the seduction of the whole German nation by the "charming rapist" Hitler, the Jewish spirit seen as the absolute opposite of the German spirit, and so forth. All these psychoanalytical, sociological, economic, religious, etc. explications, taken alone or together, are both true and false, which is to say, totally inadequate. If they were the necessary precondition for extermination, they were not a sufficient condition. The destruction of Europe's Jews cannot be logically deduced from any such system of presuppositions. Between the conditions that permitted extermination and the extermination itself—the *fact* of the extermination—there is a break in continuity, a hiatus, an abyss. The extermination was not "generated," and to wish to account for it thus is, in a way, to deny its reality, to shut one's eyes to the outbreak of violence; it is to wish to clothe the implacable nakedness of the violence, to disguise it and thereby refuse to confront it in all its bleak singularity. In a word, to weaken it. All discourse that speaks about the "engendering" of violence is an absurd dream of the nonviolent.

One must start with the naked violence and not, as is usually done, with the bonfires, the singing, and the blond heads of the Hitler Jugend; not even with the fanaticized German masses, the shouts of "Heil Hitler!"—the millions of raised arms; nor from the series of anti-Jewish laws that, beginning in 1933, gradually made life for German Jews impossible. Nor from the *Kristallnacht*. The chronological account that would begin with the boycott in April 1933 and culminate naturally in the gas chambers of Auschwitz or Treblinka would not be false, strictly speaking, but it would be miserably shallow and one-dimensional. No, in creating a work of art, one deals with another logic, another way of telling the story. For example, if one wants the spectator to be moved by the scandalous Evian conference, the conference must not appear in the film where chronologically it belongs in the twelve-year-long history of Nazism. One should begin with the ending, with the night of December 7, 1941, in the forest of Ruszow, when the 900 Jews of the little town of Koło, in the District of Konin (northwest of Lódź), had the privilege of being the first to be gassed in the Final Solution. In my film, the Final Solution could not be the culmination of the story, it would be its point of departure. The full impact of the Evian scandal will not be felt unless the gas trucks are already in action and the spectator has been gripped by the mind-boggling acceleration of history, between Evian and the first gassing of the Jews of Wartheland *only three years* passed.

The flowery rhetoric of Latin-American delegates at the conference, the customary hypocrisy of the British and American representatives, become murderous only when juxtaposed with the reality of extermination, extermination in the process of being carried out. For there to be tragedy, the end must be known. Death must be present at the very outset of the story, it must mark every episode, be the sole measure of the words, silences, actions, refusals to act, and the blindness that made that death possible. Because a chronological account is no more than a succession of befores and afters, it is essentially anti-tragic, and when death comes, it always does so in its own good time, which is to say that it is nonviolent and nonshocking. The six million massacred Jews did not die in their own good time, and that is why any work that today intends to do the Holocaust justice must, as a matter of principle, break with chronology. The suspense of the investigation itself—the difficulties and risks it entailed, which are an integral part of the film—will be intensified by yet another suspense that I have called "historic" and that will invariably arise from the juxtaposition of the exact moment of extermination with an incident, remote in time or space, in which a person desperately in need of help at that moment is denied it.

One does not kill legends by opposing them with memories but by confronting them, if possible, in the inconceivable "present" in which they originated. The only way to do this is to resuscitate the past and make it present, invest it with a timeless immediacy. The Holocaust today is legendary on several scores and has attained the dimensions of a mythical tale: knowledge of the unknowable, fuzzy, vague, stereotyped. As happens with all myths, increasing numbers of intelligent people who are not always necessarily ill-intentioned ask themselves whether, after all, these things really happened. If it is possible nowadays to write books on "the myth of the six million" or "the lie of Auschwitz," it is because the entire reality of the Holocaust is dissolving both in the reaches of time and in the stereotypical recoining of a myth where truth has never really been communicated. The essence of myth—the knowing of the unknowable, the unknowing of the knowable—is its capacity for infinite adaptation, its susceptibility to distortion, and, once distortion has occurred, its resistance to efforts to reestablish reality; myth is more stubborn than facts. How stale, how trivial the *memories* of survivors appear when compared with the nebulous inflexibility of myth!

This is the reason, then, why a film on the Holocaust has to set out from the principle of the rejection of memory, the refusal to commemorate. The worst moral and artistic crime that can be committed in producing a work dedicated to the Holocaust is to consider the Holocaust as past. Either the Holocaust is legend or it is present; in no case is it a memory. A film devoted to the Holocaust can be only a countermyth. It can only be an investigation into the present of the Holocaust or at least into a past whose scars are still so freshly and vividly inscribed in certain places and in the consciences of some people that it reveals itself in a hallucinating timelessness.

Notes

1. I entirely subscribe to the idea that the war waged by Hitler was, fundamentally, "a war against the Jews." The launching of the offensive in the East and the working up of the "Final Solution" were organically conjoined. The East was not only the great reservoir of Jewry; in the hallucinatory German *Weltanschauung* it was also the place of absolute indefiniteness, of the shapeless, the vague. *Everything is possible in the East*; people are exterminated in the East, people are deported from West to East (cf. the protocols of the Wannsee conference: *Von Westen nach Osten durchkämmen* (sweep from West to East). *The East is unsurpassed slaughter country.*

2. Violence and Nonviolence, the relation between Jews and violence, this is an-other chapter—an essential one. From the massacre of innocent people in Ponary, Sdolbunov, and Babi-Yar; from naked women running in rows of five to the gas chambers in Treblinka, terrified by the whips of the Ukrainian guards, to the heroism of the Jewish soldiers of modern Israel, not forgetting the desperate rebellion in the extermination camp of Sobibor or the Warsaw Ghetto, *the reappropriation of violence* by Jews is a central problem. No matter how brave certain groups and individuals were, the European Jews as a whole were condemned in advance because, being deprived of a *political status*, being turned into stateless persons by a bureaucratic definition, they had become "superfluous," "redundant," living-dead. In the world of nation-states, where the only protection one may enjoy is that of the state, they stood no chance.

Site and Speech

An Interview with Claude Lanzmann about *Shoah*

MARC CHEVRIE AND HERVÉ LE ROUX

Translated by Stuart Liebman

Claude Lanzmann: I have already said many things about *Shoah*, but I would very much like to talk about it as a film. Certain people have irritated me a lot: it is as if, having discovered things that took place yesterday, they are so overwhelmed by the horror that they develop a kind of sacred and religious attitude toward it and do not see the film itself. One has to understand why and how this horror is transmitted. In truth, I myself have difficulty in speaking about this because I can talk about it only in a circular fashion, as the film itself is constructed that way, and it remains in many respects opaque and mysterious. I will explain *Shoah*, using examples from *Shoah*, in a book I will write. Above all to tell the story of these ten years, in truth more than ten years, since I began to work on it in 1974.

1. To See and to Know

Cahiers: *How did the project come about? From what starting point?*

C. Lanzmann: I began by reading, for a year, every book of history that I could find on the subject, everything to be found by going through the archives—the written archives, not the photo archives. And I assessed the extent of my ignorance. Today Jews who do not want to go see the film say, "We know all about this." They make me laugh. They know nothing; they know only one thing: that six million Jews were killed, that's all. That is not interesting!

I did not know at all how I was going to proceed. I was obliged to make up budgets in order to get the money, and they always asked me, "What is your conception [of the film]?" That was the most absurd question: *I did not have any conception.* I knew that there would not be any archival materials in it. I had some personal obsessions, and I knew from the very moment I began that it would be difficult to make me let go of it. But the question about my conception was an abstract question, a historian's question, one that was meaningless. I therefore began by accumulating a great deal of bookish, theoretical knowledge. Afterward, armed with this knowledge that was not my own, this second-hand knowledge, and quaking a bit, I started to look for, to seek out witnesses. And I did not want just any witnesses. There are many deportees. There are swarms of them, as an anti-Semite would say. But I wanted very specific types—those who had been in the very charnel houses of the extermination, direct witnesses of the death of their people: the people of the "special squads."[1] I began to meet them.

I was like someone who has little talent for dancing but who takes lessons—as I did twenty years ago—and then tries and does not make it. There is an absolute gap between the bookish knowledge I had acquired and what these people told me. I understood nothing. First of all, it was difficult getting them to speak. Not that they refused to speak. Some were crazy and incapable of conveying anything. They had lived through experiences so extreme that they could not communicate anything. The first time I saw Srebnik, the survivor of Chelmno, who was thirteen during the period—these were very young people—he gave me an account that was so extraordinarily confused that I understood nothing at all. He had lived through so much horror that it had destroyed him. I therefore proceeded by trial and error. I went to the places, alone, and I perceived that one had to combine things. One must know and see, and one must see in order to know. These two aspects can't be separated. If you go to Auschwitz without knowing anything about Auschwitz and the history of the camp, you will see nothing, you will understand nothing. In the same way, if you know without having been there, you will also not understand anything. It therefore requires a combination of the two. That is why the issue of the site is so important. I did not make an idealist film; it is not a film with grand metaphysical or theological reflections about why all this happened to the Jews, why they killed them. This is a film from the ground up, a topographical film, a geographical film.

Cahiers: *Yes, there are very precise notions of place, for example what the Nazi says about the narrow passageway at Treblinka,[2] and at the same time an absence of traces.*

C. Lanzmann: That's where I made the film. The sites I saw were disfigured, effaced. They were "non-sites" of memory [*non-lieux de mémoire*].[3] The places no longer resembled what they had been. I had shots (for example, those of Treblinka). And I had models (for example, the plaster model of the people descending into the gas chamber). I therefore made a film with the landscapes of today, with the present-day shots and models. A film in which one moves from a shot of a contemporary landscape, from a speech sounding over a contemporary landscape, to the model of a gas chamber, which often imbues it with an extraordinary power, and which is derived from the extreme internal sense of urgency I felt to understand and to imagine it all. These extremely detailed questions make the film powerful and vital.

Cahiers: *The film was made from a will to know and to communicate, all the while knowing that there will always be a part that . . .*

C. Lanzmann: . . . cannot be conveyed. Absolutely! That is why the American series *Holocaust* was rubbish in every respect.[4] Fictionalizing such a history is the most serious sort of transgression: it shows the Jews entering the gas chambers, arm in arm, stoically, as if they were Romans. It's Socrates drinking the hemlock. These are idealist images that permit all kinds of reassuring identifications. *Shoah*, however, is anything but reassuring.

Cahiers: *What's very powerful about the film is how it was made in the face of its own impossibility.*

C. Lanzmann: That's a very accurate observation about the film, because I started precisely with the impossibility of recounting this history. I placed this impossibility at the very beginning of my work. When I started the film, I had to deal with, on the one hand, the disappearance of the traces: there was nothing at all, sheer nothingness, and I had to make a film on the basis of this nothingness. And on the other hand, with the impossibility of telling this story even by the survivors themselves; the impossibility of speaking, the difficulty—which can be seen throughout the film—of giving birth to and the impossibility of naming it: its unnameable character. That is why I had so much trouble finding a title. Over the years, I thought of different titles. I had one that I liked a lot but it was a bit abstract: *Site and Speech*. There was a provisional title that I did not come upon myself because the film did not have one, but I was obliged to name it for the CNC:[5] *Death in the Fields*. I remember when I first said that I was going to tackle this project, a very dear friend who is now dead, Gershom Scholem in Jerusalem—a great Kabbalist—said, "It is impossible to make this film." He even believed to a certain extent that it should not be made. And in truth, yes, it was impossible and highly improbable to produce it and to succeed in doing so.

2. The Absence of Archives

Cahiers: *Was the absence of archival images foreseen from the beginning?*

C. *Lanzmann*: What do we have as archival material? There are two periods. The period between 1933 and 1939, during which the Jews in Germany were persecuted, not killed, but persecuted. There are photographs: of Nazis burning books, of the Storm Troopers, of *Kristallnacht* in 1938. And suddenly the war. One no longer knew anything about the people under German control; they were cut off from the world. For this period there are two or three little propaganda films shot by the Nazis themselves, the PK—the Propaganda Companies of the German army and the [Nazi] party–in the Warsaw Ghetto, where they had opened phony cabarets and forced the women to wear makeup, where they staged scenes in order to show that life was all right and that the Jews were hedonists. Other than this and some photographs of the Warsaw cemetery with handcarts transporting the cadavers, there is nothing. About the extermination strictly speaking there is *nothing*. For a very simple reason: it was categorically forbidden. The Nazis kept the extermination secret, so much so that Himmler formed a special squad, Commando 1005, composed of young Jews selected because they were sturdier than the others from among the death convoys that arrived. They made them open the trenches and erect gigantic pyres that burned for days, as the film says, in order to make the traces disappear. The problem of getting rid of the traces was therefore crucial in every respect.

The only thing I found—and I really saw everything—was a little film lasting a minute and a half by a German soldier named Wiener (whom I located and spoke to). It is the execution of Jews at Liepaja in Latvia. In it one sees—it is silent—a truck arrive, a group of Jews get out and run to an anti-tank ditch, where they are shot by a machine gun. It is nothing at all. Like such a film, Nazi images of the ghetto (that have since been combined with all kinds of sauces; one always sees the same ones without any indication that they are propaganda images) are not intended to say anything; in a certain sense, one sees such things every day. I call these "images without imagination." They are just images that have no power.

There were therefore no archival images. And even if there had been some, I don't much like montages of archival images. I don't like the voice-over commenting on the images or photographs as if it were the voice of institutionalized knowledge. One can say whatever one wants, the voice-over imposes a knowledge that does not surge directly from what one sees; and one does not have the right to explain to the spectator what he must understand. The structure of a film must itself determine its own intelligibility. That is why I knew and decided very early on that there would be no archival documents in the film. I have them: I have a mass of photos that come from the Institute for the Second World War in Warsaw. They do not mean anything. One had to make a film from life, exclusively in the present tense.

Cahiers: *Exactly, the film is made entirely of words and gestures around a kind of blind spot that is the absence of the images it speaks about.*

C. *Lanzmann*: Absolutely. But as a result, it is more thoroughly evocative and powerful than everything else. It so happens that I have met people who are convinced they saw images in the film, ones they hallucinated. The film forces the imagination to work. Someone wrote to me and, moreover, did so magnificently: "It was the first time I heard the cry of an infant in a gas chamber." That is how powerfully the sensation was evoked by the words.

Cahiers: *How were the interviews one sees in the film produced? Over what length of time?*

C. *Lanzmann*: There are three kinds of characters in the film: the Jews, the Nazis, and the witnesses (the Poles). Insofar as the Nazis are concerned, that is a story in itself. The presence of each Nazi in the film is a miracle. For the others, the primary difficulty—which meant that the interviews had to be very long, much longer than those in the film—was that the people had trouble speaking. One can see this in the scene with the barber who cut the hair of women arriving at the gas chamber. At the start, his discourse is sort of neutral and flat. He communicates things, but he does so poorly—first of all because it was very painful for him and he only conveyed things intellectually. He evaded my questions. When I said to him, "What was your first impression when you saw all these naked women and children coming for the first time?" he turned away and did not respond. It became interesting the moment when, in the second part of the interview, he repeated the same thing but in a different way, when I placed him in the situation and said to him, "How did you do it? Imitate the gestures that you made." He grabbed his customer's hair (whose hair would have been cut long before if the barber had really been cutting his hair, since the scene lasts twenty minutes!). And from this moment on, truth became incarnate, and as he relived the scene, his knowledge became carnal. It is a film about the incarnation of truth. That's a cinematic scene. Because in reality he wasn't a barber any longer: he was retired. I rented a hairdressing salon and told him, "We're going to shoot there." I found him in New York and I filmed him in Israel because he had left New York and now lived there. I knew that it would be difficult and I wanted to place him once again in a situation where his *gestures* would be identical. Every expression of feeling demonstrates something, and conversely, every proof of this sort is itself a form of emotion.

3. To Frame Is to Excavate

Cahiers: *Mise-en-scène therefore plays a role. That means that truth cannot emerge from archival images, but from restaging.*

C. Lanzmann: There are a lot of staged scenes in the film. It is not a documentary. The locomotive at Treblinka is *my* locomotive. I rented it at Polish Railways, which was not so easy to do, just as it was not a simple matter to insert it into the traffic schedule.

Cahiers: *Exactly. In the structure of the film there are pivotal elements: images of trains, of freight trains. There is the idea of retracing not only the gestures but also the routes, the journeys.*

C. Lanzmann: I wanted to do so at all cost. Treblinka is a triage station: there are trains, the boxcars—the *same* ones—are there, and it's shocking to see them. I filmed them from top to bottom; I got up into the trains and we filmed, filmed without exactly knowing what I was going to do with the material.

Cahiers: *You even filmed from the interior of the boxcars, from the point of view of the Jews arriving in Treblinka. You crossed the line with a very violent cinematic act.*

C. Lanzmann: It's one of the things that I have trouble understanding today. It was the middle of winter. I said, "Let's get into the boxcar and film the sign for Treblinka." The distance between past and present was abolished, and everything became real for me. The real is opaque; it is the true configuration of the impossible. What does it mean to film reality? Making images from reality is to dig holes in reality. Framing a scene involves excavating it. The problem of the image is to create a hollow space within a full image. I had another terrible time at Birkenau: the cameraman trembled as he executed a handheld tracking shot while descending the steps into the crematorium, and he fell and smashed his face. I reshot what he had done. I was petrified by the truth and the pain. The first time I went to Treblinka, I did not yet have in my head a conception of the film and I said to myself, "What's the point of filming all this?" Then, since I am not very imaginative and have little gift for fictionalizing, I could not shoot anything but the reality before me. I went back there and filmed the stones like a madman.

Cahiers: *About the train: there was also the idea of having the driver play his former role and to make the terrifying gesture of cutting his throat. I had the impression that he did so on his own.*

C. Lanzmann: Exactly. I found him by chance. It was in winter, in Treblinka. Night had already fallen, and I was going around the farms looking for witnesses. It was the first time that I had come to Poland. At the beginning, I did not want to come. I thought much like one of the women in the film who, when I asked her, "Haven't you ever returned to Poland?" responded, "What would I see there? Nothing is left." I thought that the destruction of Judaism in Eastern Europe was like the destruction of a forest. Once a forest is destroyed, the climatic conditions are altered for kilometers around. I said to myself that Poland is a non-site of memory and that this history had been "diasporized," that one could recount it anywhere—in Paris, New York, or Corfu. Poland had become a sort of eye of the hurricane where I could not go.

Then I arrived at Treblinka, and I saw the camp and these symbolic commemorative stones. I discovered that there was a train station and a village called Treblinka. The sign for "Treblinka" on the road, the very act of naming it, was an incredible shock for me. Suddenly, it all became true. These places have become so charged with horror that they have become "legendary." Right then and there I went beyond my theoretical knowledge of the legends that could exist only in my own imagination, and into a confrontation with the real. In going to the farms, I noticed that when given the opportunity, the Poles began to speak about this history as a kind of legendary experience. I perceived that it was very alive in their consciousness, that scars had not yet formed. They spoke to me about the conductor of a locomotive. I arrived at his house at ten o'clock at night, at a farm 10 kilometers from Treblinka, where he lived with his wife. There were crucifixes all around. He received me with an extreme gentleness, he hid nothing from me, and I set about speaking with him without giving everything away in advance.

Cahiers: *Have you always adopted such an approach: so as not to give away in advance what is to go on in front of the camera?*

C. Lanzmann: Absolutely. When I had the locomotive and came back to film him, I said to him, "You are to get up into the locomotive and we are going to film the arrival at Treblinka." I said nothing else. We arrived at the station; he was there, leaning out, and on his own, he made this unbelievable gesture at his throat while looking at the imaginary boxcars (behind the locomotive, of course, there were no boxcars). Compared to this image, archival photographs become unbearable. This image has become what is true. Subsequently, when I filmed the peasants, they all made this gesture, which they said was a warning, but it was really a sadistic gesture.

Cahiers: *Did you ask that they do so?*

C. Lanzmann: It was a collective gesture. I induced them to make it and they did so voluntarily. We learn about it via a detour, by returning to the survivor, Glazar, who witnessed it—they had made it to him—and to other Polish witnesses who made the gesture. At this moment everything becomes clear: the film is based on corroboration, hence its length: the truth is constantly attested to at different levels; one must dig for it. At the same time, correspondences emerge because I always posed the same questions. The circularity of the film is derived from the obsessional character of my questions, my personal obsessions: the cold, the fear of the East (the West for me is human; the East scares the hell out of me). I became aware that I asked everyone these questions: about the cold, always the cold, the idea that these people waited for death in this passageway, that they drove them on with lashes of the whip.

But to return to this idea of drilling [for truth], of archaeology, and of its importance for the editing: there is a tracking shot in a car through the little village of Wlodawa where the guy, very gently and quietly, explains that there was a Jewish home here, and over there a Jewish shop. I had to be satisfied with this. And one day, during my second "Polish campaign," while going to Chelmno I saw a sign: Grabów. I had read in Poliakov's book[6] the letter of the rabbi of Grabów that I read in the film. I stopped and I decided to return to film there. This scene seemed to come from a real Western: the wooden houses, the types of people sitting on their front doorsteps, the women looking out from behind the curtains. The fact that I arrived there with a camera and a team must have made me look something like a lawman coming to demand justice. They experienced it that way. In comparison with Wlodawa, where the guy took me around and showed me the Jewish houses, it was the same story, except that here I questioned those who lived in the houses: I got into greater depth. And the old medieval Christian anti-Semitism of the Polish peasants became blatant. If I had placed this scene at the beginning, the film would have been polemical, violent, aggressive, but such things needed to be discovered gradually.

Cahiers: *That is also what differentiates the staging from the "reassuring" mise-en-scène of* Holocaust.

C. Lanzmann: Yes. Shoah *is a fiction rooted in reality [*fiction du réel*], which is something entirely different.

4. The Paradox of Character

Cahiers: *The first sentence—it is written—in the film is: "The action begins . . ."
and further on, a subtitle describes one of the people interviewed as the "next
character," that is, in fictional terms.*

C. Lanzmann: Fictional, yes, or theatrical. It is as if saying, "by order of appearance on stage."

Cahiers: *Yes, even while refusing a fiction of the* Holocaust *variety, you describe
a person who is there, in front of us, who has experienced certain events, as if he
were a character.*

C. Lanzmann: They are the protagonists of the film.

Cahiers: *The characters of History?*

C. Lanzmann: Yes, not the characters in a reconstruction [of the past], because the film is not one, but in a certain way these people had to be transformed into actors. They recount their own history. But just retelling it is not enough. They had to act it out, that is, they had to give themselves over [*irréalisent*] to it.

That's what defines imagination: it de-realizes. That's what the entire paradox of the actor is about. They have to be put into a certain state of mind but also into a certain physical disposition. Not in order to make them speak, but so that their speech can suddenly communicate, become charged with an extra dimension.

The film is not made out of memories, I knew that right away. Memory horrifies me: recollections are weak. The film is the abolition of all distance between past and present; I relive this history in the present. One sees memories every day on television: the guys with ties behind their desks who talk about things. Nothing is more annoying. It is through staging that they become characters. I found a guy from the *Sonderkommando* at Auschwitz, a Hungarian Jew who arrived there in 1944 and who was immediately led to the crematorium at a moment when there was a glut of traffic since they had to kill 450,000 Jews in two and a half months, and instead of burning the Jews in the ovens, they burned them in immense pits. This guy arrived there from a ghetto. You can imagine the shock. Terrifying. When I found him, he was a butcher in a little town in Israel. He was the most taciturn, the most silent man I have ever known. I came to see him many times and we spoke about present-day matters. I finally dragged out of him that the only thing he really liked to do was to go to the seashore and fish. I also like to fish, and I said to myself, "When I come back to film him, I will take a fishing pole and we'll go fishing together and try to talk." I could not do so because he was dead before I could return. But it was precisely through such a maneuver, by fishing together today, above all because it no longer involved remembering, that he would have become a character.

The barber also became a character because he was no longer a barber. The simple fact of filming in the present allows these people to pass from the status of witnesses to History to that of actors. When I conducted the interview with Filip Müller, who tells the story of the massacre of the Czech family camp in the second part of the film, it was very difficult. At first he did not want to speak. I filmed with him over the course of three days, and presenting the discussion as it occurred was out of the question. But I edited his words, his voice, setting them over the contemporary landscapes, constantly moving back and forth from synch-sound to voice-over. When I used voice-over, the difficulty was to preserve the interior rhythm of the voice even as I refined it. The transition from on- to off-screen sound is fundamental to the film: the voice exists over the landscape and they reinforce each other. The landscape lends the words an entirely different dimension, and the words reanimate the landscape. With Filip Müller I did not stage anything; it was impossible: I placed him on his sofa and began to film. But the staging is created by the editing.

5. Montage: The Method and Its Object

Cahiers: *Did you know very quickly that the film would be so long?*

C. *Lanzmann*: I did not know how much time I would need to do it, but very quickly it seemed to me that it would be no less than six hours long. There were content requirements—there were some fundamental things that I had to say—and formal requirements, architectural considerations that made it so long. It could have been longer: I shot 350 hours of footage. Of these 350 hours, roughly speaking, about 100 had to be jettisoned: silent shots, the beginnings of the interviews, things that were ruined. But there were also magnificent things. It broke my heart not to use them in the editing, yet at the same time, not so much. The film took shape as I made it, and an underlying form shaped all that followed. Even if it was something very important, abandoning some things did not make me suffer too much, since the general architecture compelled me to do so. I was absolutely driven crazy during the editing by problems of length. I said to myself, "If it's too long, who will go to see it?" I was reluctant to make three films, each three hours long, since I said to myself, "No, the film is round, a circular film, and it must end as it began." The end of the first film is a gas van traveling, a contemporary Saurer[7] van. And the second film ends the same way, except that it is no longer a van but a train.

Cahiers: *How did the architecture of the film emerge from the enormous quantity of material you had?*

C. *Lanzmann*: That was terrifying. It took five and a half years to edit. It was like being on the north face of a peak and having to invent a way up, to devise a route to the top. I had to invent both the method and the object. I had first of all to internalize this immense amount of material. I started by deciphering and typing all the speeches, everything that was said: 5,000 or 6,000 pages of text. And I had to learn the images. I began by shutting myself up for a month in a house with one of the women who worked with me, and then with the principal editor in order to develop a tentative structure. I constructed a film of four and a half hours exclusively about Chelmno. Now, the film had to be a structure encompassing everything. At the same time, all these attempts and mistakes were a way to learn the material: I had to go through this process. After I constructed the first half hour, the form emerged and hinted at the rest that was virtually present. But I had to make progress, to go forward. The construction is a symphonic construction with themes that are initiated and then shift at pivotal moments that I will tell about in the book. These led me to make a lot of progress. For example, the history of the Jewish cemetery at Auschwitz: two million Jews were killed there, and the only thing that remains is the cemetery of the Jews who formerly lived there. All the attempts at theoretical constructions were absurd and failed. I did not immediately come upon the idea to end the first film by returning to the beginning, with the first survivor of Chelmno, or to put the ghetto at the end. I was obliged to make the film with what I had: there were wonderful scenes that constituted pivot points around which I had to construct the film—for example, the massacre of the family camp when Filip Müller breaks down and cries. It is a major story because it incarnates what for me are a lot of fundamental issues: knowledge and ignorance, deceit, violence, resistance. The same for the ghetto: I had this Pole[8] who visited it and I had to integrate this part. When I say that I constructed the film with what I had, this means that the film is not a product or derivative of the Holocaust; it is not a historical film: it is a sort of original event, since I filmed it in the present and I myself had to construct it with traces of traces, with what was powerful in what I had shot. The structure is rooted in several complicated logics. The difficulty was that there is no concessive proposition in cinema: you cannot say "although." You can say that in a book, via a detour in a sentence, but if you want to say it in a film, what you want to *insert* immediately becomes a kind of absolute, killing what precedes it and determining what will follow.

Cahiers: *That becomes a major proposition.*

C. Lanzmann: Yes, and I confronted this difficulty during the entire time it took to edit. I had to preserve the general architecture of the film and, once the sequence was edited, I had to reproject everything that preceded it to see how it connected. At times I discovered that the sequence was too linear, that it became boring or intolerable, and that I had to interrupt it by inserting something else. For example, when I questioned the peasants at Treblinka, I asked the fat guy—this guy was a pig—if he remembered the first convoy of Jews coming form Warsaw on the 22nd of July 1942. He said that he remembered it very well and then forgot that we were speaking about the first convoy and placed it in the routine course of the extermination, among the convoys that he saw arrive every day. And, moreover, there is the guy from the station at Sobibor who speaks of the silence ("the ideal silence") after the arrival of the first convoy. Logically, I should have placed it at the end. I tried to do so but the difference between the manner of the two men's accounts was too large: they did not come together at all. The fat guy put himself into the logic of routine while the other, by his comment about the silence, suddenly became conscious of having been a witness to an unprecedented event. He takes on this almost legendary tone I was speaking about a moment ago. I was keen that he be in the film, but I did not know where to put him. It was only further on that I placed him, after listening to the Nazis who explained the urgency of beginning the extermination, the fact that there were too many bodies they did not know what to do with and too many living people who had not yet been killed. It is a parenthesis in the logic of the film, but it is very important that it does not come immediately after the fat guy's statements. It was also important to place the ghetto at the end, after one knows how radical and total death was, in order to show that the logic of the ghettos, where one starved to death, was part of the extermination process.

There was another reason: in order for there to be a tragedy, and also in order for there to be suspense, you have to know the end at the beginning. You have to know what will happen, all the while having the feeling that this should not happen. That's what Sartre called "the defeatist tone" in American crime films like *Double Indemnity*[9] after the war. The structure was also dictated by questions of morality. I did not have the right to bring about a meeting between characters. It was out of the question that the Nazis would meet with the Jews—not that I would have gotten them to meet physically, which would have been more than obscene, but even that I would make them meet through the editing. These are not former combatants who meet forty years later on television for a virile handshake. That is why the first Nazi enters only after two hours have gone by. No one encounters anyone else in the film. Neither do Jews and Poles, except the survivor of Chelmno.[10] At the church he is there, silent; he understands everything and he is terrorized by them, as he was as a child. And then he is alone in the forest clearing. He is split: he does not even meet himself.

Cahiers: *How did you think about the audience and the extent of its knowledge when you were constructing the film?*

C. Lanzmann: That's a real question, and one that increasingly imposed itself since I refused all commentary. The film is absolutely historically rigorous. You can say to me, "You have not dealt with this or that." I know. But one cannot take me to task. There are a thousand things that I dealt with and filmed but did not edit into the film. And there are some things that I did not deal with for the simple reason that, in certain cases, the destruction succeeded and there are entire episodes where there is no one, not a single witness, nothing. But it is an important question: What does the audience know? What does it not know? Up to what point may one preserve the mystery? Finally I said to myself that I did not have to say everything, that people ought to ask questions. The film is made so that the people continue to work at it—during the screening, but also afterward. The massacre of the family camp (why did they keep them for six months before killing them?), even if one roughly knows the reasons, remains mysterious. One must preserve the mystery and make the imagination work: one does not have to explain everything.

Notes

1. Lanzmann is referring to the so-called *Sonderkommandos*, composed of Jewish prisoners who were forced to operate the crematoria, instruct the victims about "the showers," then clear and incinerate the bodies, etc.–Tr.

2. This passageway was also known as the *Schlauch* or *Himmelfahrtsweg* and is discussed in *Shoah* by Suchomel, a German guard at Treblinka, as well as by former prisoners Abraham Bomba and Richard Glazar.–Tr.

3. Lanzmann is referring to the famous collective historical project on national memorial sites in France, *Les Lieux de mémoire*, edited by the French historian Pierre Nora (Paris: Éditions Gallimard, 1984).–Tr.

4. The television series *Holocaust*, written by Gerald Greene and directed by Marvin Chomsky, aired in 1978 in the United States and provoked an enormous response in West Germany and other European countries.–Tr.

5. Le Centre National de la Cinématographie.–Tr.

6. French historian Léon Poliakov wrote *Bréviaire de la haine: le IIIe Reich et les Juifs*, preface by François Mauriac (Paris: Calmann-Lévy, 1951), among many other books.–Tr.

7. The German firm Saurer made the gas vans used in Chelmno and elsewhere.–Tr.

8. Lanzmann is referring to Jan Karski, a courier of the Polish Underground Army who was charged by Jewish leaders in the Warsaw Ghetto to report his eyewitness accounts of ghetto conditions and the facts of the extermination camps when, in late 1942, Karski managed to travel clandestinely to the West. His discussions with Churchill, Eden, Roosevelt, and Frankfurter, among others, proved fruitless. These are recounted in his classic *Story of a Secret State* (Boston: Houghton Mifflin, 1944), pp. 320ff.–Tr.

9. Directed by the German Jewish refugee Billy Wilder and released in the United States in 1944, *Double Indemnity* starred Fred MacMurray, Barbara Stanwyck, and Edward G. Robinson.–Tr.

10. Lanzmann is referring to Simon Srebnik, the boy singer of Chelmno, the first survivor we meet in *Shoah*.–Tr.

Hier ist kein Warum

CLAUDE LANZMANN
Translated by Claude Lanzmann

Perhaps the question needs only to be asked in its simplest form: "Why did they kill the Jews?" Its obscenity is instantly glaring.

There is indeed an absolute obscenity in the project of understanding. Not to understand was my ironclad rule during all the years *Shoah* was in the making: I braced myself on this refusal as on the only possible attitude, at once ethical and operative. Keeping my guard high up, wearing these blinkers, and this blindness itself, were the vital condition of creation.

Blindness should be understood here as seeing in its purest form, the only way not to avert the gaze from a reality that is literally blinding: blindness as clear-sightedness itself. To face the horror head-on, one must renounce all distractions and evasions, and above all, first and foremost, the most falsely central question, that of why, along with the endless academic frivolities and low tricks it constantly entails. *Hier ist kein warum* ("Here there is no why"): Primo Levi recounts that an SS guard taught him the rule of Auschwitz the very moment of his arrival. "There is no why": this law also holds for whoever assumes the responsibility of such a transmission. For only the act of transmission matters, and no intelligibility, that is, no true knowledge, exists prior to the transmission. Transmission is the knowledge in itself.

You cannot split what is radical. No why, but also no answer to why the refusal of the why—for fear of falling again into the obscenity that has just been named.

Distributing *Shoah*

DANIEL TALBOT

Presenting *Shoah*, as both an exhibitor and a distributor, was the most thrilling event of my life's work in film. It was also a profound emotional experience. While knowing the general outline of the Holocaust, I knew little—indeed, almost nothing—about the specifics. The film put me on a track which I have never left. I began reading extensively about this historical episode. I am still reading. It has become an obsession. I was seriously thinking of abandoning film distribution about six months after opening *Shoah*. I thought that there was no point in continuing, for everything after this film would be anticlimactic, trivial, depressingly boring.

I found *Shoah* through the *New York Times*. I had heard about it a year before from my friend Lia Van Leer, the director of the Jerusalem Cinematheque. Lanzmann was still working on it at the time, so I simply forgot about it, hoping it would surface soon. Then on May 2, 1985, the *New York Times* man in Paris, Richard Bernstein, wrote a long, vivid article in the paper about the film and its maker, Claude Lanzmann. After my wife, Toby, and I read it, I turned to her and said, "We have to fly to Paris immediately to see this film." She agreed. Although I had never met Lanzmann, I knew about his relationship with Jean-Paul Sartre and especially Simone de Beauvoir, with whom he had lived for seven years.

I had seen his first film, *Pourquoi Israel*, at the New York Film Festival. I admired it but was unable to spring for it since my company, New Yorker Films, was in one of its periodic cash crunches at that time. A dozen years later our prospects had improved, and I called Lanzmann to ask if we could see the film right away and then meet with him. Since he knew about our work as a significant distributor of foreign language films in the United States, he was pleased to hear from us. I told him I would call him upon arriving in Paris the next day.

It was early morning when we arrived in Paris. We were tired and wanted to nap, but our room was not ready. So we left our bags in the lobby and went to a nearby café for a coffee. I called Lanzmann and he met us at the café within thirty minutes. I recognized him from the photo in the *Times*. At sixty years old, he looked quite youthful, a rugged fellow, a cross between a boxer, a movie star, and an anxious intellectual. He strode into the café with a shopping bag full of reviews, as if he were a Left Bank version of Willy Loman. He began reading some of the reviews; they were raves. He seemed eager for us to like and want to distribute the film. We returned to the hotel to secure our room and then, tired, on the edge of jet lag, afraid that our judgment might be impaired, we took some benzedrine pills before driving with Lanzmann in his snappy red Rover to the Monte Carlo Theatre on the Champs-Elysées, one of the three theaters playing the film in Paris.

At the theater, detectives frisked every patron at the door. A bomb had been set off several weeks before at an Israeli film festival, and people feared further violence wherever *Shoah* was playing. Inside the theater were two plainclothes policemen monitoring the crowd, walkie-talkies pinned to their ears. The print had no English subtitles and our command of spoken French is poor, so Lanzmann sat behind us and whispered the English equivalents in our ears. In no time at all we fell into the powerful rhythms of its testimonies, its searching pans and tracks over the landscapes of the killing grounds of Poland. There were interviews with Michael Podchlebnik, one of two survivors out of 400,000 who were murdered at Chelmno; with Abraham Bomba and Filip Müller, formerly members of *Sonderkommando* teams who had been forced to observe the last moments of thousands of their fellow Jews at Treblinka and Auschwitz, respectively; with Franz Suchomel, the deputy commander of Treblinka ("No, Herr Lanzmann, you are mistaken, we only processed twelve thousand people in a day, not fifteen!"); with Polish peasants admonishing Simon Srebnik, the other survivor of Chelmno ("The Jews were paying for having sinned against Christ"); with Jan Karski, the aristocratic former courier of the Polish underground who is brought to tears as he recounts his visit to the Warsaw Ghetto shortly before the Germans destroyed it; and with Itzhak Zuckerman, a former leader of the Zionist Fighting Organization in Warsaw, who survived the destruction of the Ghetto, had become an alcoholic, and died of a damaged heart shortly after his interviews with Lanzmann. These and other interviews in the film overwhelmed us. At the end of the first part we found it difficult to discuss the film with Lanzmann. We arranged to meet him later in the evening.

We left him and strolled around Paris for a few hours, agitated by what we had seen. At the Luxembourg Gardens, one of our favorite Paris haunts, we sat and discussed the film. We were astonished at our staggering ignorance about the Holocaust. Over the years we had seen repeated stock or fictionalized footage on television and on theater screens—the smokestacks emitting fumes, the piles of corpses, the starved prisoners in striped clothing, the yellow stars—and having seen this, thought we knew something. But I realized that we knew nothing.

After we watched the entire film the next day, Lanzmann told us how he had come to make it. After seeing *Pourquoi Israel*, some Israeli friends suggested that he make a film on the Holocaust. At that time Lanzmann, fed up with his leftist anti-Israeli friends, was persuaded that the time was ripe for a big Holocaust film. The starting point was an arranged meeting between him and the Prime Minister, Menachem Begin, who approved of the project.

It took Lanzmann twelve exhausting years to make it. He told us about the stops and starts in the production after he had depleted the insufficient amount of money he received from Israel; of his round-the-globe travels tracking down Holocaust survivors for interviews; of the hundreds of hours of footage left on the cutting-room floor, incredible material that would not fit honorably into the narrative; of the dangers he encountered (he was beaten to a pulp outside of Munich by a gang of neo-Nazi toughs, requiring a month in the hospital); of his attempts to find completion money in America at a private screening in the home of a well-known billionaire (the latter tuned out after twenty minutes and slept through four hours of film, and, of course, didn't give a dime, knowing well in advance that the screening was a one-on-one fund-raiser), and so on.

The day after the screening of Part Two I met with Lanzmann and his lawyer. In short order we worked out the terms of a distribution deal. There was no haggling. They mentioned that two other American distributors were interested in the film. One of them was Roger Corman of New World Pictures. Corman produced and distributed mainly action films—horror movies, westerns, crime stories. First-time directors such as Peter Bogdanovich, Martin Scorsese, and Monte Hellman were in his stable. In the 1980s Corman had ventured into foreign films, which were not as profitable as his low-budget actioneers. Given Corman's history, his pursuit of *Shoah* seemed odd to me. I could never figure out why he wanted the film. Corman was a down-home, nuts and bolts, thrifty, practical man. For someone like Corman, whose low-budget films were all safe bets, *Shoah* represented a huge gamble. And, as far as I know, Corman is not Jewish, so the ethnic motivation was not there. The other person interested in the film shall go nameless, since he was known in our business as a certified crook. Yet he had a nose for off-beat artistic films. For many years he earned a living as a bagman for some famous producers, depositing their illegal gains in Swiss banks. Enough said.

After signing the agreement, we returned to New York. I began work on the film immediately, ordering one brand-new 35 mm print. The first person for whom I screened the film was Lucjan Dobroszycki, an important historian and archivist who worked at the YIVO Institute for Jewish Research in New York. His groundbreaking book, *The Chronicle of the Lodz Ghetto, 1941–1944*, was published here in 1984, a year before *Shoah* opened. I had met him years before through Elie Wiesel. Lucjan was my neighbor on the Upper West Side of Manhattan. He and his wife loved movies and often came to my theaters. His response to Lanzmann's film was important to me. I had to start word-of-mouth going, and Lucjan was a good mouth. He was overwhelmed by the film and called it a masterpiece. I then held many screenings during the summer of 1985, all of them at a professional screening room in the Gulf and Western Building at Columbus Circle, where Trump International Hotel and Tower now stands. I invited friends for whom I knew the film would resonate: Irving Howe, Philip Roth, Cynthia Ozick, Alfred Kazin, Elie Wiesel, Robert Brustein, Albert Goldman, Morris Dickstein, and many others. I consulted frequently over the summer with Lanzmann. He fed me articles and advice, and we became close.

Distributing a nine-and-one-half-hour film in America, which is notorious for its short attention span and hostility toward foreign films with English subtitles, was a big challenge. I had not the foggiest notion as to whether the film would succeed. But I was consumed by the film; I thought about it and little else day and night; I slept little. I was energized, however, to make it work as no other film I had ever handled. I tried to get Lincoln Center to do a pre-opening "event" screening and failed—the cost of renting a hall there was prohibitive. No matter. By the time I was ready to open the film at The Cinema Studio in the fall of 1985, I had already held many screenings. I sensed a buzz on the film.

In 1976 I had taken over the theater then known as The Studio, on the east side of Broadway and 66th Street. It had had only one large auditorium of 600 seats and catered to a Hispanic audience. I changed its name to the Cinema Studio and split the space into two theaters, one with 300 seats and the other with 185, because the economics of our business dictated such a move. In the late 1970s I had trouble getting the films I wanted from distributors, since the theater had no track record for foreign and independent films. Having the good fortune of being a distributor at the time, I put my own films into the theater. R. W. Fassbinder's *The Marriage of Maria Braun* ran one full year. *Tree of Wooden Clogs* was very successful. Distributors took notice and I had a steady flow of "product." By the time I opened *Shoah* there, the theater had a considerable following.

After *Shoah* opened on October 23, 1985, I brought Lanzmann to New York for interviews. With the notable exception of Pauline Kael, an old friend who was then the foremost film critic in the United States, the press was virtually unanimous in its praise. There were lines around the block on opening day. Lanzmann was visibly moved by what he saw. He draped his arms around me and wept.

The film ran twenty-six weeks at the Cinema Studio. The audience was mostly an older crowd, conservatively dressed, unlike the hip, modish-looking group who regularly frequented the theater. They were, in effect, coming to a secular *shul* to watch a film about the most devastating event in Jewish history. It grossed $729,290 during the run, an unprecedented figure for a film of this size. Phones rang off the hook at New Yorker Films. I began organizing openings around the country and devoted one full year to the theatrical distribution of *Shoah*. I did all the selling, launching, and publicity by myself, wearing several hats that had been on a rack for a few years. The cost of distributing this film was staggering; each of the six subtitled prints I had cost $15,000.

The usual pattern of distributing a foreign film in America is to open in New York City, sometimes in Los Angeles on the same day, and then a few weeks later to fan out to all the major cities. With *Shoah*, I hit upon another strategy. Since I was working with only six prints, I decided to target cities with large Jewish populations—Chicago, Los Angeles, Cleveland, San Francisco, and so on. I couldn't afford lengthy runs because of the wear and tear on prints, so I selected an exhibitor in each city on the basis of his ability to do strong marketing with the Jewish audience. I restricted each exhibitor to two weeks. Instead of the usual percentage arrangement, I sold the film for a very high flat rental—a minimum of $20,000, and often more, depending upon the size of the city and its Jewish population. Since the picture could be shown only a limited number of times in a two-week period, I allowed the exhibitor to use the film as a fundraiser for a Jewish nonprofit organization in his city. Also I made the exhibitor pay for 100 percent of all advertising and publicity. In this way, New Yorker Films had an assured film rental and no expenses beyond the print and shipping costs.

Jewish groups in every city wanted the film desperately, and they put their money and their shoulders behind it. A competition surfaced among these groups, not unlike those mammoth fundraisers for the State of Israel that usually took place at the Waldorf Astoria Hotel. Once I attended such an event at the Waldorf. When Menachem Begin came on stage, there was an explosion of applause. After his rousing speech, ending dramatically with his Job-like intonation, "Never again, never again," people in the audience pledged huge sums of money, none less than a half million dollars, each pledge topping the previous one. In the same manner there were groups in many cities who bid against each other in a frenzy for the privilege of playing *Shoah*. The film had a talismanic depth to it. For an exhibitor not to get it would amount to a *shanda*.

The largest theatrical event after New York City took place in Chicago. I gave the film to an organization that held frequent cultural events. My point man was Rabbi Joel Pupko, a cultural swinger who drove around Chicago in a convertible. Over the years he had staged many events for this outfit. Over the phone he sounded thin, bearded, wired. He spoke show-biz lingo—"heads" (audience), "hires" (critics), "toilet" (an inferior theater). He read *Variety* and was schooled in theatrical grosses around the country. He talked rapidly, his thoughts tripping over his tongue. I never met him, but I felt that I knew him well, since I had run into whirling types like him in my business. We hit upon the idea of playing the film in a 2,000-seat auditorium in Skokie, a suburb of Chicago that had more Holocaust survivors than any other city in America. We *hondled* gently with each other over the deal—percentages, number of shows, fees, and the like. I didn't have to travel to Skokie for this important exhibition. Rabbi Pupko, my alter ego, choreographed everything. He was juiced up by all the excitement. We spoke to each other five, six, seven times a day. When I sent Lanzmann to Skokie to attend the showing, Rabbi Pupko took him in hand. Claude spoke to me often about the audience reception. A predominantly survivor audience was struck strongly by this leviathan film. Claude couldn't get over the effect the film had on such a large body of survivors. I later sent Claude to other cities to defend, as the Europeans say, the film. A strong personality who doesn't suffer fools gladly, Claude behaved well. The showings in America were larger and grander and wider than in any other country in the world, and I sensed his gratitude.

The film played in over a hundred cities and towns. It was one of the most successful films in the history of my company.

While the film was playing in theaters around the country, we embarked on a plan to get it shown on the PBS network. In order to do so, we had to raise money. I enlisted Sue Weill, a high-level executive at WNET, to help us. Sometime before she got on board, Claude and I had met with a well-known financier. He had read that I had taken the film on, and he had been so interested in our project that he phoned to ask if he could buy a 35 mm print. I turned him down but remembered his call when the financing of the PBS broadcast came up.

That he granted Claude and me a meeting was no small matter. At the time, wealthy people flocked to him, begging him to take their money to invest. (The minimum investment he would accept was rumored to be $10 million. I had heard that even Henry Kissinger, ever alert to a smart investment, had visited him with several lawyers to check him out, though I never learned the outcome.) But he was also known to be generous, and this proved to be true. Claude and I had our rendezvous with the financier and his wife at the bar in the Algonquin Hotel. They were excited both by Lanzmann and his film and they offered to help in any way possible. We told them about our need to raise $1.5 million to cover the costs of the PBS broadcast. They promptly offered to hold a fundraiser in their mansion in Mt. Kisco, New York.

A week later my wife and I accompanied Claude to their home, along with Henry Orenstein, a warm and colorful Holocaust survivor and self-made man in America who, shortly after *Shoah* opened, had handed Claude a check for $25,000 in gratitude for his having made such an important film and to help Claude pay some of his debts accumulated over the eleven long years of research and production. As we entered the mansion's large living room, we noted the usual suspects on the walls—Renoir, Matisse, Cezanne. Billionaire investor Carl Icahn and his young attractive Czech wife were there as well as a member of the Bronfman family and a prominent Hollywood director whose name I have forgotten, along with others of wealth in the room whose names

I didn't catch. Henry Orenstein spoke passionately about the film. Our host pledged $200,000; others joined in. We were still short of our goal, but with Sue Weill's help and the generous contributions of many individuals, we managed to put the necessary money together within a few months.

When I embarked on distributing *Shoah*, I did not think much about the commercial possibilities of the film. I was prepared to guarantee personally all losses. I did not want to mix money and Holocaust work. For me it was an emotional undertaking. To my surprise, the film was a considerable commercial success. Lanzmann was gratified by this success, though much of his earnings went toward reducing the debts he incurred while making the film. He hoped to live on the balance so that he would not, as he put it, "die in misery." The profits from the film that New Yorker Films made did not go into fur coats or champagne parties at *Le Bernadin*. I plowed the monies I got back into a slate of new films, all of which went down the tube, so that two years after the success of *Shoah*, I was back to square one. But for me, the biggest reward was the national PBS airing of the film. Over ten million people saw it.

A week after the film aired on television, Toby handed me a note written by one of her students at The New School, where she teaches a course on documentaries: "The prisoners are to be transported to Germany, secretly . . . these measures will have a deterrent effect because (a) The prisoners will vanish without leaving a trace; (b) No information may be given as to the whereabouts of their fate." This was an excerpt from Hitler's "Night and Fog" decree, which affected primarily political prisoners. Any information about the fate of the Jews was to be effaced without a trace. Claude's film ensured that Hitler's final plan to erase the memory of those he exterminated would not succeed.

Twenty years later the film remains etched in my brain. I know of no other film like *Shoah*. It is a highly artistic work, unlike any other "documentary" I have ever seen. Lanzmann's powerful camera zooms in on the geography of faces and places with a high sense of drama. These are not ordinary interviews. They are more like confrontations between an inquisitive, angry artist and damaged souls. His relentless traveling shots by car and railroad train are like search engines into hitherto unknown landscapes. He is not at all interested in morality or "history." There are no discussions of Jewish history prior to the devastation, no attempt to make links or explanations. He could just as well be filming life on the moon. He made no restrictions upon himself as to the length of the film. Despite its length, there is not one boring moment in the film.

I can think of few films in the past few decades that have haunted me as much as *Shoah*. I have had the good fortune to be involved as a distributor and an exhibitor with a score of films that live permanently in my memory: Krzysztof Kieślowski's magisterial *Decalogue*, R. W. Fassbinder's *Ali: Fear Eats the Soul* and *Berlin Alexanderplatz*, Andrei Tarkovsky's *The Sacrifice*, Satyajit Ray's *Apu Trilogy*, the Dardenne Brothers' *La Promesse* and *Le Fils*, Hirokazo Kore-Eda's *After Life*, Werner Herzog's *The Land of Silence and Darkness* and

Kaspar Hauser, Theo Angelopolous's *The Traveling Players*, Ousmane Sembene's *Borom Sarret* and *Moolaade,* and of course Yasujiro Ozu's *Tokyo Story*, Kenji Mizoguchi's *Sansho the Bailiff,* and Orson Welles's *The Magnificent Ambersons.* These works inform and nurture the soul and have made my work meaningful. But then along came *Shoah* and . . .

Sometime in November 1985 a rabbi and his wife came to the Cinema Studio to see Part One of *Shoah*. They drove fifty-five miles from Livingston, New Jersey, to see the film. I seriously doubt that either had ever seen a movie before. When the film ended, the rabbi lingered in the lower lobby, just outside the auditorium. Ushers were guiding people out and, once everybody left, they went to clean the hall in preparation for the next showing. An usher politely asked the rabbi to leave. When I saw the rabbi still lingering, I interceded and told the usher to leave him alone. The rabbi then went back into the auditorium and, facing a wall, his body rocking back and forth, he prayed. He was blessing the theater.

PART II
Appreciations, Close Readings, and Celebrations

Shoah

SIMONE DE BEAUVOIR

Shoah is not an easy film to talk about. There is a magic in this film that defies explanation. After the war we read masses of accounts of the ghettos and the extermination camps, and we were devastated. But when, today, we see Claude Lanzmann's extraordinary film, we realize we have understood nothing. In spite of everything we knew, the ghastly experience remained remote from us. Now, for the first time, we live it in our minds, hearts, and flesh. It becomes our experience.

Neither fiction nor documentary, *Shoah* succeeds in recreating the past with an amazing economy of means—places, voices, faces. The greatness of Claude Lanzmann's art is in making places speak, in reviving them through voices and, over and above words, conveying the unspeakable through people's expressions.

Places. The Nazis' great concern was to obliterate all traces. But they could not wipe out all the memories, and Lanzmann has succeeded in ferreting out the horrible realities hidden beneath camouflage, like young forests and fresh grass. In ditches on that green field, trucks dumped bodies of Jews who had died of asphyxiation during the journey. Into that pretty little stream were thrown the ashes of incinerated corpses. Here are peaceful farms where Polish farmers could hear and even see what was happening in the camps. Here are villages with fine old houses from which the entire Jewish population has been deported.

Claude Lanzmann shows us the Treblinka, Auschwitz, and Sobibor railway stations. He walks up the now grass-covered ramps, down which thousands of victims were herded into the gas chamber. I found one of the most heartrending sequences a heap of suitcases, some unpretentious, others more expensive, but all carrying name and address tags. Mothers had carefully packed into them milk powder, talc, baby food. Others had packed clothes, food, medicines. But no one ever had any need of them.

Voices. During most of the film all the voices tell of the same things: the trains that arrived, the wagons being opened and corpses tumbling out, the thirst, the unawareness riddled with fear, the stripping and "disinfection" procedures, the gas chambers being opened. But never does it seem repetitive.

First, because of the different voices. There is the cold, objective—with a few emotional tremors at the beginning—voice of Franz Suchomel, the SS *Unterstürmführer* at Treblinka. It is he who gives the most precise and detailed account of the extermination of each consignment. There are the slightly flustered voices of some Poles—the driver of the locomotive, whom the Germans sustained with shots of vodka but who could not stand the cries of thirsty children; the Sobibor stationmaster, worried by the sudden silence that had fallen over the nearby camp.

But often the peasants' voices are indifferent or even a little mocking. And then there are the voices of the very rare Jewish survivors of the camps. Two or three have managed to master a seeming serenity. But many can hardly speak—their voices break down and they burst into tears. The fact that many times they speak about the same events does not tire you. To the contrary. You think of the intentional repetition of a musical phrase or leitmotiv. For, with its moments of intense horror, peaceful landscapes, laments, and resting places, what *Shoah*'s subtle construction calls to mind is a musical composition. And the whole work is punctuated by the almost intolerable din of trains rushing toward the camps.

Faces. They often say much more than words. The Polish peasants express compassion. But most of them seem indifferent, ironic, and even satisfied. The faces of the Jews match what they say. The oddest are the German faces. Franz Suchomel's remains impassive, except when he sings a song glorifying Treblinka and then his eyes light up. But the embarrassed, foxy expressions of the others give the lie to their protestations that they did not know and are innocent.

One of Claude Lanzmann's great skills has in fact been to tell us the story of the Holocaust from its victims' viewpoint, as well as from that of the "technicians" who made it possible but reject all responsibility for it. One of the most typical is the bureaucrat who organized the transport. He explains that special trains were made available to holiday or excursion groups at half-fare. He does not deny that the trains sent to the camps were also special trains but claims he did not know that the camps meant extermination. He says he assumed they were work camps where the weakest died. His embarrassed, evasive expression belies his claim that he did not know. A little later the historian Raul Hilberg tells us that the Jews who were "resettled" were regarded as vacationers by the travel agency and that the Jews, unwittingly, themselves financed their own deportation, since the Gestapo paid for it with the goods it had confiscated.

Another striking example of how an expression gives the lie to words is given by a German "administrator" of the Warsaw Ghetto. He wanted to help the ghetto survive, he declares, to protect it from typhus. But when Claude Lanzmann questions him, he mumbles an answer, his expression becomes distorted, his eyes turn shifty, and he is totally confused.

Claude Lanzmann's construction does not follow a chronological order. I should say it is a poetical construction, if I may use the word in connection with such a subject. The Warsaw Ghetto, for instance, is described only right at the end of the film, when we already know the remorseless fate of its walled-in inhabitants.

Here again the narrative is not univocal: it is a funeral cantata for several skillfully interwoven voices. Karski, at the time the courier of the Polish government in exile, yielding to the entreaties of two highly placed Jewish leaders, visits the ghetto to report back to the world on what he has seen (to no purpose, moreover). He sees only the ghastly inhumanity of the dying ghetto. The rare survivors of the uprising, crushed by German bombs, speak, on the other hand, of the efforts made to preserve the humanity of the doomed community. The great historian Hilberg has a long discussion with Lanzmann about the suicide of Czerniakow, who thought he could help the Jews in the ghetto but lost all hope the day of the first deportations.

In my view the end of the film is wonderful. One of the very few survivors of the ghetto uprising stands alone among its ruins. He says he experienced a kind of tranquility as he thought, "I'm the last of the Jews and I'm waiting for the Germans." And the film immediately cuts to a train hurrying another consignment to the camps.

Like all who have seen the film, I mingle past and present. I have said that the miraculous side of *Shoah* lies in this mingling. I should add that I would never have imagined such a combination of beauty and horror. True, the one does not help to conceal the other. It is not a question of estheticism: rather, it highlights the horror with such inventiveness and austerity that we know we are watching a great oeuvre. A sheer masterpiece.

A Survivor Remembers Other Survivors of *Shoah*

ELIE WIESEL

Shoah, the Hebrew title of Claude Lanzmann's monumental documentary at the Cinema Studio, translates into "Holocaust" in English. Both terms seem to me pale and inadequate to describe the systematic and inexorable annihilation of countless Jewish communities during the Nazi era. There are really neither words nor means to capture the totality of the event. Even if one were to add *Night and Fog, The 81st Blow, The Final Solution*, and all the other documentaries to *Shoah*, one could not encompass this tragedy comparable to no other. Certainly, in one sense, it is the most documented tragedy in history; but in spite of the testimonies, memoirs, and superhuman efforts of survivors, we will never know how Auschwitz and Treblinka were possible—for the killers as well as for the victims.

Claude Lanzmann, like so many others, has tried to understand and illuminate, devoting ten years of his life to *Shoah*. A scrupulous, pitiless, and indefatigable investigator, he pursues truth like a detective tracking down a criminal: he follows it step by step, relentlessly pushing it toward the place if not the time of the murder, uses one clue to get others. From his voyage to the end of the night, so close and so distant, he brought back 350 hours of footage condensed into 9½ hours of film. Certain sequences, hallucinatory and obsessive, are haunting. This is a film that must be seen.

And yet it is difficult for me to speak about *Shoah*. It touches me too closely.

These trains which ride, day and night, across occupied Europe, I remember them.

The barbed wire of Auschwitz, the watch towers, the lead ceiling pushing down on a merciless earth, I knew them.

The march at midnight, toward the platform and the selections; separation, last words, mute cries, suppressed sobs, the fear of hunger which is as keen as hunger: all this is in the film and in my memory.

These men who evoke, with a genuine simplicity, the past and its ghosts, Birkenau and Treblinka with their corteges of the condemned in a daze: I saw them, insofar as I could and dared to look then. And I remember them.

"At that time, had you been able to lick my heart, you would have been poisoned." This sentence is, for me, the most shattering, the most penetrating of *Shoah*. I knew the man who, almost inadvertently, says it.

Antek: legendary fighter, friend and deputy of the young commander of the Warsaw Ghetto uprising. In *Shoah* he recalls the horrors of that desperate struggle. After the war Antek moved to Israel, where he founded a kibbutz museum in memory of the ghettos and their heroes. We had been in contact for years; we were supposed to meet each time I visited Israel. There was always an unforeseen obstacle; we had stopped counting our missed reunions.

It was only in 1981 that we finally found each other. Seated behind his desk, Antek welcomed me without getting up. His legs were a source of pain. He seemed to me tired, sad. We spoke of Israel's wars, of anti-Semitic hatred which refuses to be appeased, the victory of time over memory. How does one combat both oblivion and the trivialization of a past so heavy with terror and mystery? We stayed together a few hours.

Then a leader of the kibbutz came to ask me to participate in an open-air meeting. Antek had to be carried out and was seated in the last row. A thousand people—from the kibbutz and elsewhere—listened to a number of speakers. When it was my turn to speak, I addressed myself directly to Antek. "Dear Antek," I began. Antek the visionary, Antek the man of action, discreet and humble hero. I told him what he represented for my generation and how we, in the little Jewish villages of the Carpathians, had heard of and relived the revolt of his ghetto.

I blended my memories with his, his hopes with mine. I did not want to cry, nor to make him cry, yet nevertheless he cried silently. For whom was he crying? For his massacred friends and mine? For a world that had remained indifferent? We embraced each other. The moment seemed endless. Antek shook his head, I did likewise. We said something or other. Perhaps it was our way of welcoming the sun setting over the Galilee.

Antek died a few hours later.

Shoah contains no historical scenes of the death camps, no old newsreels. Instead, the film begins with a middle-aged Polish Jew returning to Chelmno, the scene of his childhood, where he is welcomed by Polish villagers as though the Holocaust had never occurred. Then we meet the prisoner escaped from Birkenau who tried to warn Hungarian Jews. We see Polish anti-Semitism then and now—the peasants who worked their fields while, a few feet away, a Jewish convoy was being massacred, the train conductor who returned each evening from Treblinka to resume his family life, fortified by the vodka provided by the Nazis. We see the SS officer who explains Treblinka in detail to Lanzmann. We hear the masterly comments of the historian Raul Hilberg, and the terrifying and sober words of the survivors of the *Sonderkommando*—the squads of Jews in charge of burning Jewish corpses.

The mechanism of destruction is what Lanzmann takes apart—how the Nazi experts deceived the Jews at every stage so that things would run smoothly. Perhaps this is the secret of the tragedy: the executioner had more imagination than his victims. He always knew more than they did. And the system worked. In this death industry, all the wheels seemed well oiled, all the participants were in their places. The killers killed, the spectators observed, the victims fell, the children were hurled into flaming pits. It was as if, since the beginning of Creation, things had been meant to happen this way.

The Nazis made victims, but the term "Shoah" applies only to Jews. Watching this succession of images, words, faces, and landscapes, one understands better the uniqueness of the Jewish tragedy. What the Germans did to the Jews, they did to no other race, to no other people. The proof that *Shoah* provides is unquestionable. Nevertheless, the film does not try to diminish the suffering of other prisoners; it simply urges us to avoid facile comparisons.

However, ideology or explanation is not the point of the film. Its depth comes from its characters, wisely anchored by Lanzmann in a present-day landscape, as if to juxtapose the memory of trees and clouds and rocks with that of people.

I'd like to meet Rudolph Vrba, but I'm afraid.

Vrba, who is one of the survivors filmed by Lanzmann, is an authentic hero. He escaped from Auschwitz at the beginning of 1944 and tried to tell the world what was happening there. In his book, *I Cannot Forgive*, he tells how he succeeded in eluding the guards. Compared to his adventure, *The Great Escape* is a fairy tale.

But why am I afraid to meet him? Permit me to evoke a personal memory. I arrived at Auschwitz six weeks after Vrba had escaped. It was night. Plunged into this unknown universe of horror, I thought I was dreaming. Shouts, barking of dogs, beatings: the last convoy of Jews from my city advances, in the shadows, toward the flames which devour the sky. Suddenly, strange beings stop us, crying, "Idiots, why did you come here?!" Their anger surprises us. Someone answers, "You think we came here voluntarily?" "You should have resisted, run away, died at home rather than coming to Auschwitz." "But we didn't know!" "You should have known!" yell the prisoners. They run among our rows and tell us what will happen to us at any moment, in the shadows of the chimneys.

For a long time I could not understand their rage. Reading Vrba's memoir, I understood. Vrba and his friend Wetzler had escaped to save us, the Hungarian Jews. They knew that we had no inkling of what awaited us at Auschwitz, where the executioners were already preparing the installations to "treat" the one million Hungarian Jews. They decided to accomplish the impossible: to tear themselves from the kingdom of death, to alert the victims, to urge them to cheat death by hiding in forests, by organizing themselves to resist. And the two fugitives succeeded in their escape. They met with Jewish leaders and with representatives of the Vatican, drafted a detailed report on the death factory named Auschwitz . . . all in vain. The Hungarian Jews kept coming. The escape, risk, danger, and sacrifice of Vrba and his comrades had not helped the others.

That's why the prisoners greeted us with anger: they were part of the first squad that had to deal with us, the squad to which Vrba had belonged; they were aware of the escape plan. Why, then, if we had been warned, why did we come?

That's why I'm afraid to meet Vrba; I'm afraid of his questions.

Jan Karski: I discovered him in 1980. To be more precise, it was in 1980 that I learned he was alive and living in the United States. I was familiar with his clandestine activities during World War II. I had read his book, *The Secret State,* and felt toward the author boundless admiration and affection. In it, he tells more than he says in *Shoah.* He describes his conversations with the Jewish leaders of Warsaw, as well as his meeting with poor Shmuel Zygelbaum, a Jewish member of the Polish Parliament in exile, who committed suicide in London in an attempt to arouse mankind's conscience. He also recalls his visit to the Warsaw Ghetto and tells of having witnessed, from a close vantage point, the liquidation of a Jewish convoy. Karski reports his meetings with Roosevelt, Felix Frankfurter, Rabbi Stephen Wise, and other Jewish intellectuals and leaders. Hero of the Polish Resistance, he seemed to have disappeared after the war.

Then in 1980, while preparing an international conference of Liberators of Concentration Camps in Washington, I learned by accident that a certain Jan Karski taught at Georgetown University. A shiver went through me. Could this be the same man? It was.

We invited him to speak at the conference. No speaker affected the audience as much as Karski. There was laughter when he imitated Roosevelt, and there were tears when he described the Warsaw Ghetto and its misery. He received an ovation when he spoke of his vow never to forget what he had been allowed to observe "over there."

It was the first time that Jan Karski had agreed to speak of his past in public. He felt, no doubt, that he had tried hard to accomplish his mission to those in power and to the leaders of the Jewish world. It was not his fault that his voice had encountered walls of incomprehension, if not indifference to what was being done to the Jews of Europe.

His interlocutors refused to accept his testimony. "I don't believe you," responded Felix Frankfurter when Karski told him of the death camps. And seeing Karski's bewilderment, the judge added, "I didn't say you weren't telling the truth. I only said I'm not capable of believing you."

Jan Karski: a brave man? Better: a just man.

Filip Müller of the *Sonderkommando*. Watching *Shoah*. I listen to him and I think of his doomed comrades, forced by the killers to burn the victims' corpses. How did they manage to not yield to resignation, despair, madness? For them, the very sky had turned into ashes.

At Auschwitz, we knew of their existence. Bizarre rumors circulated about them: they lived in a separate prison, more isolated than ours; their faces and bodies covered with soot, they had only a vaguely human appearance.

Much later I had occasion to read the journals that a few of them had kept even in Auschwitz: Zalman Gradowski, Zalman Lewental, Leib Langfus. . . .

"Seeker," says Gradowski in his devastating memoir entitled *In the Heart of Hell*, "seeker, look everywhere, search every piece of land. Writings, mine and others, are buried here. . . ." Langfus, a pious believer and former rabbinical judge, recounts the last minutes of a newly arrived convoy. The condemned group learns from one of the *Sonderkommando* where they are. The scene is unreal, as the victims insist that the man from the *Sonderkommando* drink "*Lehayim*," to life. . . .

It's been years since I read the first excerpts of these mutilated diaries. I tremble as I reread them. I find them strangely tender; they speak with warmth of the victims, and with compassion of one another. According to these documents, the threat of death did not separate parents from their children, did not necessarily awaken the beast in man.

In the writings of Langfus and Gradowski there is an incomprehensible and secret kindness that is heartbreaking and, for me, miraculous.

In those days, everything was miraculous. Pursued by the omnipresent and omnipotent enemy, no Jewish child could count on pity or humanity. The killer killed without thinking, without feeling, almost without paying attention—as if he were destined to shoot down and burn human beings. Surviving within the mechanism, within death, was the exception rather than the rule. Surviving while remaining human was a miracle.

It must therefore be said over and over again: confronted by inhuman executioners, victims suffered and died without betraying their humanity. For every father who, at breaking point, stole from his son, there were 100 who sacrificed themselves for their children. For each man who, diminished by hunger and fear, thought only of surviving—even at the expense of those near to him—there were countless others who tried to help their unfortunate brothers and friends by offering a piece of bread, a spoonful of soup, a promise, a memory, a bribe of consolation, the trace of a smile drawn from a devastated world.

On this human level, the enemy lost. He did not succeed in reducing all his prisoners to the animal state. In the camps and ghettos, there were men who prayed, women who taught, doctors who healed, poets who sang and made others sing; there were warriors who fought, simple men and women who fasted on Yom Kippur, and refusing despair, drew on their faith or memory. And yes, there were human beings who rejected cruelty and brutality as instruments of survival: surely that is a miracle.

Shoah is not only about miracles, but also about what negates them. *Shoah* is about men and women and children, children above all, who lived and died in a universe of ashes. *Shoah* is not only about death, but also about something as stubborn as death: memory.

Out of Darkness

DAVID DENBY

Simon Srebnik, a Polish-born Jew, is one of exactly two survivors of Chelmno, the small, improvised, little-known killing center in northwestern Poland where the Nazis began the systematic gassing of the Jews on December 7, 1941 (that's right, the same day). By the time the camp was closed, in January 1945, about 400,000 men, women, and children had been murdered there—in gas vans, with carbon monoxide. At the beginning of Claude Lanzmann's extraordinary nine-and-a-half-hour documentary, *Shoah*, we see Lanzmann and Srebnik walking across the beautiful meadow in Chelmno where bodies were once incinerated; and we hear the villagers of Chelmno say how much they liked Srebnik, who was only thirteen when he lived in the camp and who was a graceful and jaunty boy with a beautiful tenor voice.

Later in the film Lanzmann reunites Srebnik with some of these villagers. They all stand together on the steps of a large church—the same church, as it happens, in which Jews were locked up, sometimes for days and without food, before being put into the vans. And we see that the villagers, laughing and nodding their heads, remember Srebnik and really do like him; they are glad that he is still alive. But then Lanzmann asks them why they think the Jews were exterminated, and even as the resurrected Srebnik stands among them, they say—can it be possible, so many years later, in *this* town?—they say that the Jews were all rich, the Jews murdered Christ, the Jews. . . . Not one says the word "Nazis."

I admit that even after reading the rapturous early accounts of Lanzmann's film in the *New York Times* and in *Newsweek*'s international edition, I was not eager to see it. Having absorbed my share of books and films on the Holocaust, I doubted I was capable of learning more, feeling more, understanding more. Numbness, I thought, was beginning to set in, a prospective fatigue that was, in its way, one of the intended side effects of the enormous crime. But now I've seen *Shoah*, and it turns out to be far more original in technique, far stranger and more obsessive than the early accounts suggested. Lanzmann has redeemed the catastrophe from banality. He has also made one of the three or four greatest documentaries in the history of the cinema.

Shoah (the word means "annihilation" in Hebrew) ranks with Marcel Ophüls's *The Sorrow and the Pity* as a moral inquiry. Lanzmann, like Ophüls, is a gently persistent but finally implacable interviewer who manages to coax astounding revelations from his subjects. Whatever else it is, *Shoah* is a collection of remarkable speech (the text has been published by Pantheon). From the lips of old Nazis, unconscious self-accusations fall gaily and shamelessly into the air, catalogs of lies, swindles, willful delusion, and forgetting. The Jewish survivors Lanzmann chose, who were among those forced to assist in the work of the camps, and hence in the destruction of their own people, appear to be consciously avoiding rhetoric and emotion; they are somber and impressive, and two of them reach a pitch of bitter anguish—despair and the elation of survival inextricably mixed—that leaves one shattered. Mere witnesses to the disaster calmly fill in details, but a few climb to levels of incomparable eloquence or stupidity. One of the former, Jan Karski, an aristocratic Pole who tried, and failed, to arouse the outside world to what was going on, gives a long, declamatory account of his experiences that bears comparison with one of the racked, climactic speeches of a Shakespearean tragedy.

Like Ophüls, Lanzmann uses a circular rather than a table-of-contents or merely chronological way of organizing the material. Themes are introduced, developed, momentarily dropped, then varied, recapitulated, all in a widening spiral of reference and emotion. The film is beautifully paced, with a kind of musical feeling for repetition, meditation, crescendo, release. One adapts to the slow unfolding, the obsessive circling; Lanzmann, like all great film artists, changes one's sense of time. (*Shoah* will be shown in two parts. . . .)

Shoah is a film about history, and yet Lanzmann flying brazenly in the face of convention and common sense, uses not a single moment of archival footage in his 561-minute work. No, not one foot of newsreel; not a single still photo; no music, no narrator, no artifacts of the period; no radio speeches by Goebbels or Hitler, no diaries of SS officers. This is a movie about history as it is remembered as well as made—an account, then, of memory and forgetting, in which the fog and distortion of time and untruth matter as much as the recovered moment and the actual record. As his survivors, executioners, and witnesses talk, Lanzmann moves his camera around the outskirts of the death camps as they look today. He approaches, gliding through the woods, and stops; approaches and stops again; and finally enters into their heart. The gigantic Auschwitz–Birkenau complex looks virtually the same as it did in 1945, when the Soviets liberated it. But the ruins of the other Polish camps that Lanzmann uses—Chelmno, Sobibor, and Treblinka—have been cleared away, the land covered with grass and trees (usually planted by the Nazis) and a variety of memorial monuments.

At first one experiences feelings of betrayal. Surely this is an anticlimax! One longs for a sulfurous photograph of the camp in operation. But then, as the horrifying testimony—the stories of people herded, stripped, gassed, burned—continues over the idyllic images, Lanzmann's point becomes clear to us. The Nazis tried to make the earth swallow up their victims. For instance, the Sobibor stationmaster, who today is a traumatized man, describes an uncanny experience: In 1942, when the camp was being built (right next to the station), "there were orders shouted in German, there were screams, Jews were working at a run, there were shots." But finally the camp was finished, and as he was riding his bicycle home one night, the first transport—maybe 40 cars—rolled in. The next morning he returned. Silence. Absolute silence. All the Jews had vanished.

Today the clearing next to the station is again silent, as are the forests at Sobibor and the rivers where the ashes were dumped. Lanzmann's camera violates the stillness; he cannot make the ground crack, heave, and yield up its dead, but he can at least disturb the insensibility of nature; he can end, by the mere act of remembering, the collusion of mass murder and "healing" time. As we watch these sequences, with their feral words and calm images, we have to re-create the Holocaust in our own heads; Lanzmann will not allow the familiar pictures, which have an almost pornographic appeal, to do the work for us. That is why this movie could bring about a change in consciousness even in people who have read and thought about these things many times before.

Lanzmann, 59, was a student leader in the French Resistance during the war and worked for years as a writer and editor at *Les Temps Modernes,* the intellectual quarterly founded by Sartre. His instincts are reportorial—and also topographical and archaeological. Again and again, he walks over the ground, pacing it off himself or with someone who was there: This is where the train stopped; this is where the ramp was; this is where the Polish peasants, whose fields abutted on the Treblinka station, stood and made signs of throats being cut for the Jews waiting in the cattle cars—according to the peasants, a courageous warning of what was to come. (Then why do they sound so jocular when recounting it?)

Lanzmann wants us to grasp the details *physically;* he's like someone going over a mugging or an accident, trying to make it real for himself. Posing as a French historian eager to "restore the balance of truth," he gained access to old Nazis who might not otherwise have talked. (He used a hidden camera at these interviews.) Franz Suchomel, a deputy SS platoon leader at Treblinka, is a kind of treasure trove because he remembers in shockingly vivid detail what Lanzmann wants—the exact movements and sufferings of the Jews, step by step, from train to gas chamber. By concentrating on what happened, and not on the participants' attitudes, Lanzmann gets people to talk freely. When Lanzmann feigns a kind of admiration, Suchomel exuberantly describes the technique of murdering 3,000 people in three hours; the elderly man is moved by this interest in his *work*. But Lanzmann's game falters a few times: He almost loses patience with the ineffable Walter Stier, a railway official who ran the eastbound train traffic during the war and who insists he didn't know the Jews in some of those trains were headed for death. Immersed in the glory of their old jobs—the moment when they were important—the Nazis continue to live as guilt-free, contented professionals. They will die happy.

Lanzmann shot 350 hours of footage and worked on the film ten years— plenty of time to gain corroborating or conflicting evidence. For instance, Raul Hilberg, the American historian of the Holocaust, produces a document—an order for four death trains and the empty returns—that makes it obvious railway officials must have known what was going on. The trains, Hilberg reveals, were booked through the same state travel bureau that handled routine group vacations; every train had to be paid for (children under four rode free). The SS handled the task, using confiscated Jewish funds—thus causing the Jews to pay for their own destruction. The trains become a recurring image for Lanzmann. Again and again, he shows freight cars rumbling through the Polish countryside; the melancholy sound of those wheels, which normally has such lyrical, nostalgic associations for us, becomes a kind of musical motif of despair. The rhythm of *Shoah* envelops and mesmerizes. Reading about this movie isn't enough: You must see it.

Closely Watched Trains

MARCEL OPHÜLS

Books have been written. In my line of work, I've read a great many more of them than I might otherwise have done, but not nearly enough ever to understand. Questions have been asked, in private conversations and at public meetings, in classrooms and in lecture halls, in panel discussions, some of which, in the course of the last twenty years, I've felt obligated to attend, either out of a sense of duty or because I needed the money. In the end, all the debates could always be reduced to one essential question: "How can the unspeakable horror, the memories of total evil and complete degradation that the survivors themselves feel cannot be communicated, be forced back into collective awareness, into the conscience of mankind?" No archival footage of bulldozers and mass graves, no expert testimony, no fictional transposition has ever provided a satisfactory answer. As for the survivors themselves, they have repeated endlessly, and in obsessively repetitive terms, that the experience of the camps "*also* is something that *probably* can't be communicated." I've still got those "alsos" and those "probablys" ringing in my ears; I can still mimic the exact tone of the voices, the helpless resignation, the self-interrogation, and sometimes the secret pride!

Shoah's survivors, too, keep repeating this leitmotiv, but Claude Lanzmann, with single-minded, stubborn, sometimes even brutal dedication, has overcome this obstacle. I consider *Shoah* to be the greatest documentary about contemporary history ever made, bar none, and by far the greatest film I've ever seen about the Holocaust. (A journalist, that is, a professional wordsmith, Lanzmann has expressed distaste for the term "holocaust." He points out that it refers to a natural disaster and this implies, therefore, that the destruction of the Jews was in some way inevitable, an act of God. His whole film is a passionate denial of that poisonous thought.)

When *Shoah* came out in Paris recently, Lanzmann was asked why he had undertaken such an arduous ten-year task. His immediate reply was, "Because I was asked!" How well I know the question and how often I've felt compelled to give that same answer. It is a truthful one, I suppose, perhaps the only immediately available truth. It's also part of a defense mechanism, the strategy of the Jewish filmmaker having to face an unpleasant innuendo: "Are you obsessed by concentration camps and Nazis because you are a Jew?" I've also learned how many misunderstandings such an answer can provoke, how many false assumptions and even suspicions it is meant to disarm, how much fatalism and resignation about anti-Semitism it reveals.

As far as I know, and contrary to what some specialists seem to believe, I've never made a film *about* the destruction of the Jews. I've made two films in which the most monstrous genocide of all time played, inevitably, a crucial and central role. One of them was about the Nazi occupation of France, and the other was about the inadequate but necessary attempt to deal with the crimes of the Third Reich in terms of human justice. I made these films "because I was asked." I've always moved on the periphery. I've never been faced with the staggering task of looking straight into the eye of the storm and reporting what I saw. Had I been, I can only wish that I could have mustered the intellectual and emotional discipline, the spiritual courage, the intense dedication, and the sheer will power that Claude Lanzmann placed at the disposal of his subject matter. It's like the old question about heroism in the face of mortal danger. You never really know until you have been tested.

When *Shoah* first came out, sometime in the middle of May, I must confess that I wasn't even aware of it. I was busy filming a fifteen-minute report for French television about Ronald Reagan's visit to Germany, to those SS graves in Bitburg (only a few miles away from the village in which Klaus Barbie, the infamous "Butcher of Lyon," grew up) and the belated, hurried presidential excursion to Bergen-Belsen, I had five days to edit the report, and when it was finished, we called it "All the President's Graves." A few weeks after my return from the Bitburg cemetery, I was off to Bolivia, retracing Barbie's footsteps with a camera for another film I am making about Barbie himself, and it was only after I had come back from that expedition that I got a call from the editor of this magazine. Without the phone call from Washington and the financial inducement attached, therefore, I might have taken my own good time about seeing *Shoah*, which usually turns out to mean, for most of us, not seeing a film at all. For one thing, while I had been suitably impressed by Lanzmann's previous film, *Why Israel?*, I hadn't been wildly enthusiastic, perhaps because it had struck me as a bit too derivative of my own work. For another, I've always shared to some extent Max Ophüls's distaste for film gluttony, which he liked to explain as follows: "Why should I go to the movies? If I think the picture is bad, I get restless and depressed, and if it's any good, I get jealous!"

Finally, as I've pointed out whenever and wherever I can, documentaries—or whatever their directors care to call them—are just not my favorite kind of movie watching. The fact is that I don't trust the little bastards. I don't trust the motives of those who think they are superior to fiction films, I don't trust their claim to have cornered the market on the truth, I don't trust their inordinately high, and entirely undeserved, status of bourgeois respectability. Most of all, I dislike the idea of the greatest of all popular art forms ever being shanghaied into the service of a cause, any cause. So it was with a good deal of trepidation that I entered the darkened Paris theater where the Lanzmann film was running.

A peaceful, crystalline river, flowing gently through an idyllic countryside—this is the first image of *Shoah*. A flat-bottomed boat is floating in the water. Two adult men are in the boat, but what we hear on the sound track is a child's innocent voice raised in song. In an opening roller title on a black background, Lanzmann has explained that we are in Chelmno, a village in Poland, which was the site of the first destruction of the Jews by gas. Carbon monoxide from the exhaust fumes of trucks was piped directly into the interiors of the vans. Four hundred thousand men, women, and children were thus destroyed. One of the two survivors, Simon Srebnik, then a boy of thirteen, was enrolled by the SS as a "work commando." His life was spared temporarily because he had a beautiful soprano voice. Several times a week, ordered to feed the rabbits at a nearby farm requisitioned by the SS, in chains and escorted by an SS guard Srebnik would head up the river Narew in a small, flat-bottomed boat. As the villagers remember, he would sing Polish folk songs, and the Nazis, in return, would teach him old Prussian military ballads, one of which, later in the film, the middle-aged Srebnik will remember and sing haltingly on camera in a deep baritone:

> When the soldiers go marching through the town
> All the girls open their windows and their doors
> Why? Just because . . . Why? Just because.
> Just because of the drums and the music and the razzmatazz!
>
> Wenn die Soldaten durch die Stadt marschieren
> Oeffnen die Mädchen die Fenster und die Türen.
> Hei, warum? Hei, darum! Hei, warum? Hei, darum!
> Hei, bloss wegn' dem Tschingderassa, Tschingderassa Boum . . .

(Just now, I checked the exact spelling of the words with my wife, who had to learn it as a child in a German school during the Third Reich. My Jewish father taught me the tune and the lyrics, which we sometimes sang together, first in Paris, later in Hollywood. Neither Régine nor I, as she pointed out to me, had to learn it from a guard in an extermination camp.)

In 1945, as the Nazis retreated from the Russian army, Srebnik was shot in the neck, like all the other Jews in the work detail, but he crawled into a Polish farmer's pigsty, and was nursed back to health by a Russian army surgeon. The conclusion of Lanzmann's introduction reads as follows: "I found him in Israel and persuaded that one-time boy singer to return with me to Chelmno. He was then forty-seven years old." This constant blending of past and present, rather than a mere juxtaposition, this constant effort to erase time in order to re-create a continuous reality is, as far as I can see, the basic principle on which the whole film is constructed. At the very end of the first part of *Shoah*, we meet Simon Srebnik again, standing among a tight group of Polish peasants who have just come out of Sunday mass. They crowd around the camera, volunteering a veritable torrent of information. One old woman, rather small, wearing a peasant's kerchief, constantly interrupts the others, thrusting her head over any available shoulder. All of them talk about the Jews, about the trucks, about confiscated Jewish gold. At the end of this incredible group sequence, one man, more respectably dressed than the others, a certain unmistakable air of authority about him, steps to the forefront and takes over. The Polish translator explains in French: "Monsieur Kantarowski is going to tell us what one of his friends has told him." There follows a long, violently anti-Semitic story about a rabbi who, after having obtained permission from an SS man, told the Jews arrested in a nearby village that 2,000 years ago they had been condemned because of Christ's death, and that perhaps the day of reckoning had now arrived. Lanzmann then asks in French whether Monsieur Kantarowski thinks that the Jews had to pay for the death of Christ. The translator translates, and the well-dressed man is quick to point out that he didn't say that, the rabbi did! And then someone adds, "It was God's will—that's all there is to it!" Throughout the whole scene, which probably lasts more than ten minutes, the former child soprano remains silent, almost motionless among the villagers who crowd around him, sometimes nodding his head politely, wearing a strange, embarrassed, apologetic smile. I remember wondering whom that soft, lopsided smile reminded me of. It came back to me after a while. It was the same smile I've seen on the face of German Jews of the same generation who are still living in Germany and whose lives were saved by German families during the war, whenever others around them talk about the Nazi years.

Coming out of the second part of *Shoah*, late in the evening, on the narrow sidewalk of the Rue Monsieur-le-Prince, I try to decipher in the display case of the theater some of the French rave reviews that are posted there. The light is dim, and I'm nearsighted. I try to take a few notes. One man, if I'm not mistaken, has written that *Shoah* is the mirror image of my film, which he describes as "a cold masterpiece." I take off my glasses and press my nose to the windowpane of the glass showcase! Cold? Well, just as long as they spell the name right! Standing right next to me, two young Parisians are indulging in the contemporary sport of instant analysis:

"I've read somewhere that it's supposed to be anti-Polish."

"Do you think it's anti-Polish?"

"Oh, yes, absolutely! It's very anti-Polish!"

"I've always heard that the Poles behaved very badly toward the Jews during the war."

"Yes, and that would explain why Lanzmann . . ." I never hear the end of that sentence, because I suddenly remember where we had parked the car. As I cross the Boulevard Saint-Michel, how could I help but be reminded of the endless, sterile, excruciatingly boring discussions *The Sorrow and the Pity* has never ceased to provoke in France over the past sixteen years, about whether it is pro-French, anti-French, or somewhere in between?

In the second week of August, there is a news item in *Le Monde*: "*Shoah* Is Going to Be Shown in Poland." It appears that the Polish authorities have modified their initial reaction to the film. When it first came out in France, they had summoned our chargé d'affaires in Warsaw to "demand the banning of the film on French television. . . . It contains outrageous insinuations for the Polish people concerning its alleged collaboration in bringing about the Holocaust." This is all Greek to me; it has always been Greek to me. Where else but in those Polish wheat fields, on those station platforms, and in front of those wooden houses is Lanzmann expected to have found nonparticipating witnesses to the arrival of the trains, to the herding of the Jews into the gas chambers, to the smoke rising from the chimneys, people who can testify to the stench invading the countryside? That some of these farmers profess compassion while obviously contemplating every detail of the proceedings with barely concealed relish is not the director's invention. These are real people, not actors. One obscene, potbellied farmer in a sweatshirt never ceases to smile in voyeuristic delight while explaining how he tried to warm the Jews by crossing his throat with the index finger of his right hand, a ritual gesture supposedly of sympathy, but in fact and unmistakenly a sign of collective sadism. In the same interview, this man tries to imitate awkwardly what he assumes to be the sound of excited Jews babbling on the station platform at Treblinka: "Ra, ra, ra. . . ." Lanzmann, who does not speak Polish but whose passionate anger burns like a cold, bright flame, immediately cuts in:

Lanzmann: What's he saying? "La-la-la-la"—what is he trying to imitate?

Translator: Their language.

Lanzmann: No, no! But ask him, ask him right now! Was this some kind of special noise, the noise of the Jews?

Potbelly [shrugs]: They spoke in Jewish. . . .

Lanzmann: They spoke in Jewish! Ask Monsieur Borowi if he understands Jewish.

Potbelly: No!

Without ever having met Lanzmann, I suspect that he must have felt much the same anger at the "anti-Polish" charges that I did. Sixteen years ago, while I was filming *The Sorrow and the Pity*, I confronted a shopkeeper in Clermont-Ferrand who, after the fall of France, had placed an ad in the local paper to assure his customers that, despite his name (Marius Klein), there were no Jews among his ancestors. A Jewish filmmaker is bound to be struck by such cynical lack of human compassion. If others don't feel this quite as strongly as we do, why should we be blamed for it? Admittedly, in that particular context, *Shoah* can be considered "anti-Polish," as my film was considered "anti-French." My advice to film producers and television executives: "Next time, get a non-Jewish Pole and a native Frenchman!" Come to think of it, they don't need my advice. That's what they've been doing anyway!

A little later in the first part of *Shoah*, a railway employee at Treblinka is being interviewed by Lanzmann:

Railroad Worker: They jumped out of the wagons; it was a sight to see. One day a mother with her small child in her arms . . .

Lanzmann [interrupts]: A Jewish mother?

Railroad Worker: Yes, with a child. She fled from them, and they shot at her heart; they shot into her heart.

Lanzmann: Into the heart of the mother?

Railroad Worker: Yes, into the mother!

There is an awkward pause. The Polish worker starts to cry, and these are precious tears, indeed.

Young Woman Translator: Monsieur has been living here for a very long time, one mustn't forget that. . . .

That's when, as I remember it, Lanzmann throws his arm around the man's shoulder. Here, as in many other parts of the film, we watch the interviewer becoming part of the action, see him involve himself completely, courageously, and logically in his own work of art. When, again in the very first minutes of the film, he questions Mordechaï Podchlebnik, the other survivor of the death trucks in Chelmno, who speaks in Yiddish and delivers a pat, self-rehearsed little speech about wanting to forget what is dead, about not even reading his own testimony at the Eichmann trial, about wanting to live and survive, Lanzmann intervenes just as I, just as we all, would want to:

Lanzmann: Ask him why he's smiling all the time?

Interpreter: What do you expect him to do, cry? "Once you smile," he says, "another time you cry. And when you're alive, it's better to smile."

While jotting these notes, after viewing the first part of *Shoah*, I feel the urgent need to drive out with Régine to the nearby small eighteenth-century Parc de Bagatelle. It has one of the loveliest rose gardens in the world. At first we sit on a park bench, enjoying the summer sunshine; a little later under the foliage of the tall chestnut trees, at a table in the park's café. The place is quietly bustling with prosperous Parisians and foreign tourists. I am still taking a few notes. Régine suddenly calls my attention to an old lady in a wide-brimmed summer hat, who has just walked past us, with a concentration camp number tattooed on her wrist.

In the same review of *Shoah* that caught my eye because my name was spelled right, Pierre Murat writes: "The immense difference [from Ophüls] is that Lanzmann does not only question, he interrupts, he digs, and keeps on digging. He hurts and bruises. He tears off the outer layers, and leaves evil naked. When in front of one of the men who has escaped from Hell, and who breaks down sobbing, covers his face, and begs him to stop filming, he insists, like a benevolent torturer, to go on filming, one feels the sudden urge *to reach out and slap him* [italics mine]."

That's absolutely correct. If being a gentleman is a documentary filmmaker's top priority, he'd better get into some other line of work. Lanzmann, however, never tries to ingratiate himself with the audience, hardly ever tries to charm or entertain. Perhaps this is no more than the difference between having been trained intellectually by Jean-Paul Sartre as opposed to having been sired and raised by a film and stage director, but I don't think so. Lanzmann, I'm sure, is fully aware of the seductive powers of the audiovisual medium. If he chooses not to ingratiate himself, it's because of the unique nature of his task. By that, I don't mean the sterile, solemn, more or less intimidated awe with which most people approach the subject of the Holocaust when it becomes unavoidable for them to do so. Lanzmann will have none of that, and in one of the interviews I've read, he denounces these attitudes in no uncertain terms.

But I think that for a Jewish filmmaker to ingratiate himself in this particular context would have been akin to the frantic, laughable, and eventually unsuccessful attempts of so many of our elders to blend into the landscape. It would have seemed too much like their vain efforts at assimilation, which we now realize were condemned in advance by the monstrous agents of history.

One of the most striking moments in *Shoah*, when Lanzmann demonstrates overtly that a filmmaker looking at total disaster and at total evil cannot and need not adhere to the rules of cricket on the playing fields of Eton, occurs when we suddenly see two young technicians fiddling around with the image of a black-and-white monitor inside a small van parked in front of a German apartment building. This is our first clue that a former Treblinka SS guard, Franz Suchomel, is being filmed without his knowledge by means of a hidden camera. Just as we realize this, we hear Lanzmann's voice, in German, promising the guard that not even his identity will be revealed! I can hardly find the words to express how much I approve of this procedure, how much I sympathize with it. This is not a matter of means and ends, this is a matter of moral priorities. Other criminals who participated in the Final Solution are interviewed by the same method, and every time this happens, it is shown happening. Most of the time, these criminals are asked very precise, technical questions about the details of their activities. Had Lanzmann asked any of these men about the state of their souls, they would have recoiled like rattlesnakes. Addressed as mere technicians of death, as experts in extermination, Suchomel and the others appear almost grateful to be able to tell "their side of the story" to a man whom their early training in Nazi racialism must have told them was Jewish. Gradually, from one sequence to another, they become more and more communicative until we actually see and hear, as in a monstrous real-life version of Bertolt Brecht theater, Suchomel volunteer to sing "The Treblinka Song":

> We look upon the world,
> Always brave and joyous,
> As we march off to work.
> For us, now, there's only Treblinka,
> Treblinka is our destiny!

Lanzmann has stated repeatedly that he considers all previous filmic accounts of the Holocaust to be woefully inadequate. I happen to agree with Lanzmann, but I do wish he could have been a bit less insistent in denouncing the American television miniseries *Holocaust*, which at least had the minor virtue of being artistically and philosophically unpretentious. Its attempt to render the abstraction of six million exterminated Jews emotionally gripping by letting us get acquainted with Mrs. Weiss before she steps into the gas chamber may have been deeply flawed, and doomed to failure in the long run, but it was not ignoble. Most of all, I dislike the idea of Lanzmann, whom I have come to admire more than words can say, coming down on the same side of the issue as all those German *Kulturmenschen* who condemned the series as American (that is, "Jewish") kitsch in order to try to keep it off their television screens. The German director Edgar Reitz, who has rehabilitated the word *Heimat* in a wildly successful and totally ambiguous manner, in a film lasting, not nine and a half, but *sixteen* hours, was at great pains to point out that his was a deliberate effort to defend the memories of his childhood against the foreign invasion of *Holocaust*.

I wish Lanzmann had seized the opportunity of *Shoah's* release to denounce the unspeakable vulgarities of Wertmüller's *Seven Beauties*, the neo-Fascist self-indulgence of Fassbinder's *Lili Marleen*, and the crass voyeurism of

Pontecorvo's *Kapo*. A pox on all night porters! They have been crawling out of the woodwork year after year. Lanzmann may not agree, but I don't think this is a matter of choosing between fiction and nonfiction. Every time "Concentration Camp" Ehrhardt, in Ernst Lubitsch's *To Be or Not to Be*, gets into trouble, he keeps yelling at his subordinate: "Ach, Schultz, trying to shift responsibility again!" This refrain, of course, has a direct bearing on the executioners' testimony in *Shoah*. They too keep shifting responsibility up and down the SS chain of command. Even the self-pitying, obscene "Treblinka Song," which the SS guards themselves composed, is a reflection of what Erich Fromm once called "the escape from freedom."

For whatever reason, Simone de Beauvoir, in the preface to the published version of *Shoah*, seems utterly spellbound by these very real culprits. Just as soon as she can get around to it, she goes sailing into those German criminals with a vengeance. Dare I confess that although I recognize the mere fact of their testimony having been filmed as a major achievement, I cannot quite bring myself to share Mme. de Beauvoir's fascination? This is not a matter of being pro- or anti-German. For me, one of the most truly horrible moments in *Shoah* comes when another of those nonparticipating witnesses to the Final Solution, an old German woman, wife of a Nazi schoolteacher, sent out to colonize that particular part of Poland, reacts to Lanzmann's questioning as follows:

Lanzmann: Do you know how many Jews were exterminated there [in Chelmno]?

Frau Michelsohn [a bit puzzled, hesitates]: Oh! Something with *four* in it . . . four hundred thousand? Forty thousand?

Lanzmann: Four hundred thousand!

Frau Michelsohn: That's right: four hundred thousand. I was *sure* about the four! Sad, sad, sad!

I must confess that I find the unfathomable mystery that this testimony brings to light far more absorbing than the pathology of any Nazi mass murderer. Hitler has long been the German people's fall guy; the Gestapo and the concentration camp guards have even been used to "rehabilitate" the Waffen SS at Bitburg, and "les Boches" are still the target of the spite of many who failed to resist them when the Nazis were triumphant.

On the Sunday afternoon following our viewing of *Shoah*, my wife and I go to spend the day with some good friends in the country, and I try to play the part of the recruiting sergeant. The more I let my enthusiasm get away with me, the more restless and fidgety my listeners become. One of them is a young television executive who has expressed interest in buying my film about the Nuremberg trials, another is a good friend and colleague who has made two films, one on the Dreyfus Affair, the other on Philippe Pétain. Neither of them can easily be suspected of anti-Semitic feelings. We are having lunch in a magnificent garden in Normandy. Food and wine, as usual, are excellent. Then suddenly our hostess, with a stubborn crease between her eyes, announces casually and definitely, "Well, I don't think I'm going to see *Shoah!*"

Her filmmaking husband tries to soften what he assumed, rightly, to be a blow to me by suggesting that they'll wait for it to be shown on television. Whereupon, in rapid succession, as if suddenly released from a major burden, all the others agree with her. Régine throws me a swift glance which conveys one message: "Drop it!" I obey.

Orwell once wrote, "It all depends on whose ox is being gored."

Is *Shoah* too long? Too long for whom, too long for what? Is *Shoah* too arid? On the contrary, it is rich, infinitely varied, constantly surprising, like any great work of art. Is it too strenuous, then? No, it is emotionally compelling and stubbornly relentless. I would like to quote a brief passage from my own film *The Memory of Justice*:

> *Dr. Kranzbuehler [former defense attorney of Krupp, Flick, and Grossadmiral Donitz]*: When lunch hour came around, Chief Justice Lawrence could become easily impatient . . .
> CUT TO
>
> *Edgar Faure [former French prime minister, former assistant prosecutor in Nuremberg]*: On the contrary! He was extremely patient. I remember one of my colleagues once saying to me, "How patient he is! All these endless stories of stolen art treasures." And then . . . there was all that harrowing testimony about the concentration camps. Necessary, no doubt, but, it must be admitted, tedious. . . .
> CUT TO archival footage of the Nuremberg courtroom.
>
> *Chief Justice Lawrence*: What did you say this witness is going to prove about those fifty thousand Jews?
>
> *U.S. Asst. Prosecutor*: Your Honor, please. . . .
>
> *Chief Justice Lawrence*: What is he going to prove?
>
> *U.S. Asst. Prosecutor*: If Your Honor please. . . .
>
> *Chief Justice Lawrence*: What is he going to prove with regard to the Final Solution?
>
> *U.S. Asst. Prosecutor*: Their ultimate disposition, sir, at Auschwitz.
>
> *Chief Justice Lawrence*: Well, let him go on to what ultimately happened to them, then.

One gets the feeling that Lanzmann would not have pleased the British magistrate. He does not restrict himself to "what ultimately happened to them."

There is a great difference between the effort to teach and the resolution to testify. In this respect, I'm almost sure that Lanzmann and I have lived through many of the same experiences. Whether filming on a Polish wheat field or among Barbie's friends and neighbors in Bolivia, the moral catastrophe we have discovered is not so much guilt as murderous indifference. Consequently, what started out as attempts to persuade others gradually changes into the stubborn effort to record and give shape to experience. This is not resignation, far from it! It is an affirmation of the self. If teaching, preaching, or persuading has ever been or still is at the center of Lanzmann's preoccupations, his choices and professional moves would have looked superficially similar to those of any show business professional pursuing commercial ends. Voluntarily and step by step, he would have brought his product down to more easily marketable proportions. It's not for any trivial reason, as far as I can see, that he has refused to do so. His is not the narcissistic modern urge for self-expression, avant-garde, hubris, not a secret wish to make non-Jews do penance. It's those hundreds of hours spent filming farmers on Polish fields. Beyond the urge to persuade, and even the need to testify, I suspect that a new state of mind has come to guide and sustain this magnificent achievement: *not resignation but defiance!*

Shoah

LEON WIESELTIER

Claude Lanzmann's *Shoah* is more than nine hours long; but long before you understand what is present in this visual account of Auschwitz you understand what is missing from all the others. The others—all the sickening photographs of the living corpses and the dead corpses that the Nazis made out of Europe's Jews—all the images of that inferno that has become canonical in our culture, that has, as if to complete the curse, become even clichéd—all have failed at full exposure of the enormity, at least by the standard of radical exposure that Lanzmann has in mind. A little reflection will reveal, indeed, that rather than exposing us, the famous photographs have protected us, by virtue of their being photographs, that is, frozen, fixed, false to the flow of time in which the sufferings were lived.

The photographs have an extracted quality. They are the epitome of the experience, the apotheosis of the atrocity. But this was an experience without epitome, an atrocity without apotheosis; so it was designed by its German innovators in inhumanity. It stretched on for years across a whole continent, it was long and wide enough to constitute for its victims not an event, but a second world. (A second world war.) The pictures that shock us, that would shock us again if we could see them again for the first time, would not have shocked the inhabitants of the Nazi world, because within the Nazi world they showed only stations in a sequence, points in a logic. I have observed survivors regard the pictures that made us weep without weeping, without almost any trouble at all. (Before pictures of their first world, which should have been their only world, I have seen almost all of them, in the final sanctuary of their third world, break down badly.)

Consider, moreover, the extra degree of protection provided by the photographs for their being black and white. Imagine the increase in horror and in fear that would result from the attempt to put these scenes—the little boy surrendering to the helmeted troops in the ghetto, the rows of broken bodies stretching across the compound of the camp—into color. That is probably as good a way as any to measure the gulf that divides those who were there from those who were not. Those who were there saw it in color. They saw the tones of the death. Those who were not still have innocent eyes, for which certain colors have not been forever compromised; and their innocence is protected by the shades of the photographs, which cannot show how the sun shone upon what was taking place in its light.

Lanzmann's film begins with shots of Chelmno, near the Narew river in Poland, which was the scene of the Nazis' first effort to destroy the Jews physically. These were the forests through which the gas vans rode, until the men, women, and children within them were dead. Lanzmann's camera lingers long over these trees, these meadows, these clay pits, these roads, as it will linger long over the other scenes (the *mise-en-mort*, if you will) of the Final Solution. And the colors are shocking. The trees are green. The meadows are brown. The clay is red. You realize, almost as if you never realized it before, that the Jews were murdered in a place on earth. Lanzmann's slow, sedulous panning across this lethal landscape marks the collapse of all verbal and visual rhetoric about "the Holocaust." It also inflames in a new way. I thought immediately of David's curse upon the ground where Saul and Jonathan were killed—"Ye mountains of Gilboa, let there be no dew, neither let there be rain, upon you. . . ."—and wished that the words had not yet been spoken, that they had been saved for the forests and the fields of Poland. "Ye banks of the Narew. . . ." But Lanzmann shows how futilely they would still be spoken. His film—a nine-hour proof of the proposition that all things human must bend or break before the supreme facticity of the world—shows neither wilderness nor wasteland. There appears to be no trace in nature of what men have done. The seeds sown by the wind have not been repelled by the soil soaked in blood.

Because there is not a single frame of documentary footage in *Shoah*, it is the most original restoration of its subject to consciousness that I have ever seen. Lanzmann has established how much can be accomplished when distance is acknowledged. His film is a profound meditation on the situation of those who came after. It sets out from the premise that, for the purposes of understanding, they are, fortunately for them, forever lost. They (that is, we) can never annul the difference in time and in space that separates them from the event. The presumption that they can, which is what much "Holocaust literature" and "Holocaust film" has presumed, leads only to sentimentality, or to arrogance, or to other kinds of inadvertent numbing. For those who were not there, the holocaust, strictly speaking, never happened. It is dead; always elsewhere. It is "the Holocaust." We cannot "remember" what the Germans did to the Jews, because we cannot remember what we never knew. It is not an unfamiliar predicament for Jewish sons and daughters—which is why it has been a primary intention of Jewish culture throughout the ages to invent precisely a new form of memory, a fortifying fiction that we now know as "collective" memory. ("In every generation every individual must regard himself as if he journeyed out of Egypt": the Jews have made much nourishment out of this philosophical nonsense.)

But there are people for whom there is no "Holocaust," for whom the holocaust is alive; and places where it is always here. Lanzmann's brilliance lay in his decision to find just those people and just those places, in his strict abstention from any other avenues of access. Not to fight against the condition of latecoming, but to seize the people who never, and the places where nobody, alas, came late. He would see them and hear them, to the exclusion of everything else; and, with a cruelty that only collective memory could justify, he would return some of the people to some of the places, so that not even their own healing would stand in the way of Lanzmann's record. In some sense Lanzmann has literally reassembled the catastrophe. We are shown the sodden woods of Chelmno, the rocky hill of Treblinka, the greening ruins of Auschwitz, as we are told by those who were there what happened there. The juxtaposition of these words and these images adds up to, or at least approximates, the lived experience of the end.

This project—the creation of presence by absence—required a very long movie. In some instances Lanzmann could even dare to reassemble the catastrophe in real time. The "operating vehicles" at Chelmno, for example, did their foul work sufficiently swiftly for Lanzmann's camera to reproduce the full span of the drive, as it follows the same rainy roads at the same remorseless pace. Similarly, in perhaps the most shattering segment of the film, the Jewish barber Abraham Bomba tells of barbering in the women's crematorium in Auschwitz while he barbers in his shop in Tel Aviv; it is not long before the cold, mechanical flexings of his scissors, then and now, in Auschwitz and in Tel Aviv, collapse into a single act, into a single story.

More generally, it was Lanzmann's aim to furnish the viewer with all the firsthand acquaintance that is still available. That meant details. The viewer would have to come to know not the stunning revelations of the history books, which take no time at all, but the texture of the event—to come to recognize individual trees and pits and platforms, the lines in the faces of the witnesses and the variety of their voices. It is a chilling measure of the film's success that by the film's end all these recognitions have been made. We have been taken to the catastrophe and left there for nine hours, and after nine hours, as Lanzmann expected, you remember things. *Shoah* has the duration not of spectacle, but of experience.

There is no more lasting effect of this film than the feeling it leaves for the trains. They were the enabling condition for the Nazis and the disabling condition for the Jews. The Final Solution, after all, required the transfer of whole Jewish populations to the killing centers. The trains, then, were everywhere, and they are everywhere in the film. The heavy, mindless, inexorable chugging of cattle cars runs through *Shoah* like the tormenting theme of a nightmare. For the Germans, the efficiency of the transports represented a triumph of bureaucratic rationality. For the Jews, as Lanzmann correctly grasps, the trains were where extermination began. They boarded them living; they left them dead or dying. It was on the trains that the victims were broken down. (Jorge Semprun has written an unforgettable novel about this.) For this reason it was entirely appropriate that the selection for the gas chambers should take place immediately at the end of the line, as the wretched Jews spilled out of the cars. The work of the murder had begun on the way.

Lanzmann's attitude is the opposite of the historical attitude. Not that he is uninterested in the facts; quite the contrary, he is obsessed by them, almost to the point of morbidity. What dissatisfies him about the historian is that he, too, is a latecomer, with a latecomer's aspiration to omniscience. Instead, Lanzmann wants to push the facts back to when they were not yet the facts, to restore them to the state of becoming the facts, when they were fresh to the senses and new to the mind, to reconstitute the ordering of what was happening into a world. Unlike the many writers and filmmakers on "the Holocaust" who seek to transcend history, Lanzmann seeks to precede it. He seeks a sense of contemporaneity.

It is a vain search. Contemporaneity is denied him. But between contemporaneity and history lies a third term, which combines the sentience of the one with the structuring of the other, and that is memory. There is an American Indian superstition according to which a man is not dead until the last man who remembers him dies. That is Lanzmann's feeling about the holocaust. The oxymoronic temporality of his film—the past seems like the present, the present seems like the past—is a perfect reproduction of memory's blurring of the dimensions. Except that, in the case of memory, the blurring has the result of vividness, of saving an existential kind of precision, like a soul saved from the underworld, from oblivion, or from the perfections of narrative. This strange placement in the interstices of the tenses makes it difficult to assign Lanzmann's film to a genre. It has been called a documentary, which it certainly is not. It is just as certainly not a docudrama. Perhaps it should be called a documemory, since it is upon that uncanny faculty for keeping dead things in life that it is entirely based.

There are errors of judgment in the film. Returning Simon Srebnik, forty years later, to the jolly, Jew-hating company of the villagers who tried to kill him is more cruelty than even collective memory can justify; the scandal of Polish anti-Semitism established by this long segment does not exceed the indignity that this survivor is made to endure. Similarly, there is something a little too Montparnassian about Lanzmann's repeated insistence that Abraham

Bomba recall his feelings at the sight of the naked women in the gas chamber. The most surprising mistake, however, is the inclusion of Raul Hilberg, the foremost scholar of the destruction of the Jews. With the exception of a riveting scene in which Hilberg decodes a Nazi train schedule for its full, rank, real-world meaning, Hilberg's mood of knowingness (won by immense historical knowledge, to be sure) and distance (the very condition of historical knowledge) is sharply in contradiction to the essence of the film.

Still, these are the lapses of a masterpiece. Lanzmann has gone where nobody has gone before. He has penetrated time, and the privacy of other minds. And, by means of his fanaticism for capturing the sensation of being murdered, he has captured, imperishably, with love and with truth, the inner life of the survivors. These are the heroes who live, like black suns, in our midst. Who will forget Abraham Bomba's face, as the full force of what he saw is restored to him, and he pleads for permission to stop remembering? His is a double hell, the hell of the experience and the hell of the memory of the experience. How much easier it might have been, for Bomba and all the thousands of others who were asked by fate to return from Auschwitz to the world, had the world, and not just their extraordinary part of it, really ended.

Ei Warum, Ei Darum

O Why

ANNE-LISE STERN

Translated by Stuart Liebman

In 1931 Stefan Zweig wrote of Freud: "Once again, as always, it is enough for a single man to have the will to truth in order for there to be more truth in the world." Among the psychoanalysts who have seen *Shoah*—and they are not that numerous—there are some who have not really been knocked off their seats. And those who were have only landed nearby and made themselves comfortable again. For a long time I believed this reaction to be an absolute scandal, then saw it as a form of resistance in the Freudian sense of the word. Nevertheless, since its release in the spring of 1985, the impact of truth from Claude Lanzmann's film has continued to spread. Among psychoanalysts, has it not most affected even those who, by refusing to see it, wished to make a statement?

In 1987 several psychoanalyst friends banded together in a group called "Psychanalyse Actuel," which they publicized in a leaflet entitled "Why." Their project spoke of preoccupations truly familiar to me, a German Jewish child who had become French, been deported to Auschwitz, and returned—though her grandmother and aunt did not—and who then had become a psychoanalyst: an "assimillionaire," as the painful witticism by Fernand Niderman puts it.[1] In their questions and answers, and in their questioning of my own responses, I recognized, in a different form, my most intimate concerns, concerns not really *unheimlich* at all, but rather ones so curiously familiar that I almost did not read their "leaflet." But that title "Why" obsessed me. It was as insistent as the start of a song, of a refrain—why, *warum*. It was the refrain of the song heard in *Shoah*, heard anew, that is, recognized by the Jewish German child. A song of a "*lansquenet*," a mercenary, as Lanzmann remarks in an interview. *Ei warum, ei darum . . . Ei warum?* O why?—*Ei darum!* Oh, that's why! *Warum*, why, a question beginning with W. *Weh-Fragen*, "woe-questions." *Warum*, why? *Wo*, where? *Was*, what? *Wann*, when? *Wer*, who? *Wie*, how? *Wem*, to whom? It is with such questions, and on all these questions, that Lanzmann has worked, that his film works; where, what, when, who, how, to whom?—but never on the first question: why? He leaves that question hanging, suffering.[2]

Shortly after *Shoah* aired on German television, a woman old enough to have been an adolescent in Nazi times—and it cannot be doubted that her family was not Nazi—told me about her joining, belatedly—but she did join all the same—the BDM, the *Bund Deutscher Mädchen*, the female branch of the German youth movement. "You know, it was just because of the . . . *Tschingdarassa-bum*! . . . You see what I mean." In her mind it was a matter of the outings in uniform, with trumpets blaring a regular, insistent onomatopoeic beat, of meeting the boys who were also in the troupe, of singing around campfires. Yet that very morning she had confessed to me how overwhelmed she had been by the screening of *Shoah*, and how profoundly her own relatives, her Jewish stepdaughters, had been shaken up by it.

O in German is spelled *ei* and is pronounced "aïe." *Ei* is also an egg. *Eia-Popeia*, an old-fashioned expression, was still used by the poet Heinrich Heine. In his "Deutschland, a Winter's Tale," one reads: *Sie sang das alte Entsagungslied, das Eia-Popeia vom Himmel* (She sang the old song of renunciation, the cuckoo from heaven.).[3] The little baby bird [*doudou-poupon*], the little egg cuckoo, *o*.

A stream, a verdant, tender landscape appears, and after this introduction situates the action, before any human being comes into view, one hears a nostalgic air, almost inaudible, in the distance. This is how the film begins. Then one distinguishes his words, in Polish: . . . "a little white house" . . . "in my memory." . . . The tune drifts closer as Simon Srebnik, today an adult, once the child-singer of that place, is borne toward us on a boat. A child then? An adult today? With a similarly soft, pure voice, he later sings another song, this one in German, the song of a "lansquenet," a mercenary. It is partially translated in the book *Shoah*, which records in French all the subtitles and words in the film, including the songs, except the last, which remains in Yiddish: "*weil azoï muss sein . . .* " (because that's the way it must be).[4]

But his refrain is not translated. *Ei warum, ei darum, ei bloss wegen dem tschindarassa-bumdarassa-sa!* (O why, oh that's why, just because of the boomalaka-boomalaka-boom!)—this is the *exact* refrain of the song sung by Simon Srebnik in his pure, sweet voice. But two little exclamations have fallen out of the text, and with them all the insolence of this hackneyed military air. In his mouth, subtitled by his gaze, it has become something completely different, an Other Thing. The song says (and a very fine recording of it by Marlene Dietrich exists):

Wenn die Soldaten	When the soldiers
Durch die Stadt marschieren	March through the town,
Öffnen die Mädchen	The young girls open
Die Fenster und die Türen.	Their windows and doors.
Ei warum, ei darum,	O why, oh that's why,
Ei bloss wegen dem	It's just because of the
Tschindarassa-bumdarassa-sa!	Boomalaka-boomalaka-boom!

So why do you think a young girl opens her door for a soldier? Only for this boomalaka-boomalaka-boom that strikes up the beat of the sexual act from which—why? *O, ei!*—the egg comes out: O this child who, coming of age, will pose all the "whys," the painful questions from birth to death. Why, when, how, who, where, what, to whom—needed to be done so that a child would once more come into the world with all these questions?

Questions about pleasure too. Why, in exchange for what, do the girls offer their soldiers:

Eine Flasche Rotwein	A bottle of red wine
Und ein Stückchen Braten	And a piece of roast meat?

Oh that's why! And just for that! For this boomalaka-boom. . . . A *Bumslokal* is a cheap dance hall, and nowadays they say *bumsen* for screwing. Even the face of the teacher's wife,[5] the one who knows how to count to four (forty thousand, four hundred thousand dead? Really?)—one of the most unpleasant characters in the film—lights up with the freshness of a young girl when Lanzmann starts with the words: "When the soldiers . . . , the young girls open their. . . ." But Simon Srebnik does not sing this gay refrain that way, the way his SS guard certainly must have taught him as he was floating down the Ner on the boat bearing sacks of ashes—or rather, in those days only grass for the rabbits. Simon Srebnik sings, or rather he murmurs in dulcet tones: *Warum–darum*, why–that's why (the *Ei* has disappeared), *wegen der Kinderrasse, Kinderhasser, Bum*. Indeed, he did not know German very well; but the words *Kinder* (children), *Rasse* (race), *Hass* (hate)—he had to know such words, if only because of the similarities between German and Yiddish. And thus he murmurs: Why—that's why, because of the child race, of hatred for children, of the hate for this race of children. At least in the film he reconstructs the refrain in this form. But in those days what did he think of all this?

> I was just thirteen years old,
> and all I had seen until then,
> were dead people, corpses [. . .]
> I had never seen anything else [. . .]
> I thought things had to be this way,
> that it was normal, that's the way it was. I walked through
>   the streets of Lodz,
> I would go, say, one hundred yards and there'd be two
>   hundred bodies . . .
> People were hungry,
> they walked and they fell, they fell . . .
> Sons took bread away from their fathers,
> And fathers took it from their sons.
> Everyone wanted to stay alive [. . .]
> I also thought: if I survive,
> I only want one thing:
> that I would be given five loaves of bread. To eat . . .
>   Nothing more . . .
> [. . .] But I also dreamed:
> If I survived, I will be the only one left in the world.
> No other human being, just me. Alone.[6]

Ei, the egg, has disappeared: why, that's why, because of the child race, of the hatred for children . . . *Warum-darum, warum-darum, wegen der Kinderrasse, Kinderhasser, Bum.* Why, that's why, why, that's why, because of the child race, the children haters, boom! Here one must restrain oneself, because once a child appears, the psychoanalyst dreams of being on the lookout for trouble. I simply want to underline that it was precisely this passage, not another, it was this murmuring that Lanzmann chose to include when editing his film. By never asking "why?" he shows *how* it happens; or rather he does not show it but makes it absolutely visible. By rejecting any psychoanalytic prying, any "interpretations," he in fact clarifies better than any psychoanalyst what clinical practice teaches us every day: the way in which the "how" nevertheless weighs on every "why." Why are there mothers and fathers, where do children come from, today? From down there, the originating source of their questions, in our day? It applies as much, in the crudest sort of way, to the virginal little girls of Chelmno. Their graceful genuflections in honor of the Madonna's birthday, on the steps of the church, expose gray tights under their short skirts that are accessible to the glances of boys of the same age as Simon was then, to their fathers and mothers, to the spectators of the film. Thus this scene in front of the church—the same one from which Jewish families were swallowed up by the gas vans in their grandparents' and parents' day—lays bare, with no way out, the ways in which a phantasmatic scene of origins (of children, of human beings, of the world, of God) and a primal scene (that of the ordinary parental boom-alaka) are imbricated with each other, woven together forever, in horror of the Real. Can psychoanalysis "cure" us of all this? Surely not by reestablishing our Father in Heaven, toward which, in one form or another, an increasing number of psychoanalysts, both Jews and non-Jews, are inclined, and this supposedly more for the "good" of those whose history seems particularly affected by this History.

Eia-Popeia, Heine said ironically, in order a bit further on to demand joys and liberties in the here and now, on earth: *Den Himmel überlassen wir / den Engeln und den Spatzen* (The heavens we leave / to the angels and the friars.) It is an irony difficult to sustain now that the heavens have been populated by ashes. Freud quotes this passage from Heine in *The Future of an Illusion*: "Then, with one of our fellow-unbelievers [*Unglaubensgenossen*], they will be able to say without regret, *Den Himmel überlassen wir*, the heavens we leave . . . ," and so on. But can we say this today? And what if we tried hard to push Lacan's[7] theoretical advances concerning the "question of the father" to their limits by taking a stand for his absolute rejection of any theological design, even if in reality he does not avoid the question of God, and by taking into account his concept of the *objet petit a* as a logical element? Why did he need to coin this term? one might ask. To this charge, Lacan gave this secular response: "The analysis of contemporary subjectivity which we have experienced, this something that we have baptized under the name of *totalitarisme*, may be applied by anyone as a function of the category of the *objet petit a*."[8]

And Lanzmann, why does he need to . . . ? Having come back from there, and having become (despite it? Or because of it?) a psychoanalyst, I will not prohibit myself—even if I am prohibited—from inquiring into this work's epic power, its ability to reach beyond itself. One can, it seems to me, locate its core in the tension between Claude Lanzmann, a man whose desire obliges him to explore these questions, even at the risk of his life (and it is not only a matter of the risks still to be confronted in reality)—and the Man-Lanzmann, the brother of all his people, of all human beings, a man from their "country."[9] He leads them into this country of yesteryear, heavy with all these "promises," this place that neither he nor any of his close relatives—some criticize him for this—ever knew firsthand. And what if he refuses to ask the question why but incarnates it most powerfully in his infernal questioning that offers no way out, as implacably as an infant; what if, in doing so, he thereby conveys, in truth, the answer, the answers?

I am convinced of this: "the question of the father"—hereafter—is situated by this work on the same side of the impasse that, at one point, silenced Lacan, forcing him to suspend his seminar "The Names of the Father." The International Psychoanalytic Association (IPA), largely composed of Jews not quite aware that they also legitimated themselves as such through Freud, did not permit Lacan to hold the seminar. Or rather, excluded by this community, which was his own, at the precise moment of his daring endeavor in 1963, Lacan was then not authorized to do so. When he restarted it in 1973, he called it

Les non-dupes errent.[10] After the release of his first film, *Pourquoi Israël,* in October of that same year, 1973, Lanzmann restarted his work on the Shoah, on his film that did not yet have a name. Between the seminars *Les noms du père* and *Les non-dupes errent,* there was a parenthesis, and during that time Lacan's ever more precise development of the *object petit a* and the category of the Real. *Pourquoi Israël* asks questions without a question mark. This was before *Shoah* had made its name. Lanzmann, as much as the psychoanalyst, would be duped by the Real for making it without asking "why?" But as someone not duped by the father, he would go astray and become as mad as the psychoanalyst by having to make himself the creator of this work, *Shoah,* which teaches us to what extent God cannot respond to that Why, and is not the answer.

Notes

1. The witty condensation of assimilation and millionaire works in both English and French. For the "famillionaire" which corresponds to this "assimilionaire," see Anne-Lise Stern, *Le Savoir-Deporté* (Paris: Éditions du Seuil, 2004), p. 157. In Book V of *Les Formations de l'Inconscient,* Lacan comments at length on the joke discussed by Freud in *Jokes and Their Relation to the Unconscious:* one of Heine's characters, Hirsch-Hyacinth, a poor lottery agent, tells how he was treated by the wealthy Solomon Roth-schild "quite famillionairely."

2. Claude Lanzmann, "Hier ist kein Warum," *Nouvelle Revue de Psychanalyse* 38 (Autumn 1988): 263. Reprinted in *Au sujet de "Shoah," le film de Claude Lanzmann,* ed. Michel Deguy (Paris: Belin, 1990), p. 279, and translated in this volume. For the *Weh-Fragen,* see Stern, *Le Savoir-Deporté,* p. 155.

3. See Heinrich Heine, "Germania, a Winter's Tale," trans. Gérard de Nerval, in *Poèmes et légendes* (Paris: L'École des loisirs, 1995), p. 124.

4. Claude Lanzmann, *Shoah,* with a preface by Simone de Beauvoir (Paris: Fayard, 1985), pp. 17–19.

5. Stern refers to Frau Michelson, the wife of the German teacher in Chelmno and a colonizer of the region, who observed the operation of the gas vans during the first period of gassing.–Tr.

6. Lanzmann, *Shoah,* pp. 115–116.

7. The French psychoanalyst, psychiatrist, and physician Jacques-Marie-Émile Lacan was born on April 13, 1901, and died on September 9, 1981. In 1963, he founded the "École freudienne de Paris," a breakaway group from the French psychoanalytic organizations and the dominant neo-Freudian ego psychologists. Claiming a return to Freud as the central inspiration for his work, his key concepts stress the centrality of language to the functioning of the unconscious and the role of the "mirror stage" in the origins of consciousness. Among his major works are a series of *Seminaires. The Four Fundamental Concepts of Psychoanalysis* was the first to be published in an English translation by Alan Sheridan (New York: Norton, 1981). –Tr.

8. Jacques Lacan, course notes for the seminar "La Logique du Phantasme," held on November 16, 1966.

9. Stern is here punning on Lanzmann and *Landsmann*, a Yiddish word incorporating *Land* (region or state), which refers to someone who comes from the same geographical area.–Tr.

10. Lacan is here exploiting a protracted pun in French. *Les non-dupes errent* (those who are not fools err) rhymes with *les noms du père* (the name of the father). The latter is one of Lacan's key theoretical constructs. See his *Écrits*, translated by Alan Sheridan (New York: Norton, 1977).–Tr.

Shoah's Absence

FRED CAMPER

I.

At the core of *Shoah* lies an absence. Claude Lanzmann's nine-and-one-half hour film on the Nazi extermination of Europe's Jews is haunted by those images that we never see. Witnesses of the time speak and recall the past, and Lanzmann's camera films camp sites in the present day, but there is no footage photographed at the time of the events discussed. Lanzmann has spoken of the Germans' attempts to destroy the records of their genocide, and of having to make his film out of "traces of traces," but it is clear that the exclusion of images from that time, perhaps the filmmaker's single most important decision, is rooted in an aesthetic as well as a moral choice.

In *Shoah*, as is the case with many avant-garde films, length is used as a formal element. Noncommercial filmmakers most commonly try to determine the length of their films on the basis of the amount of time needed to explore their subject matter properly, rather than on any arbitrary limits such as feature format. Simply based on that criterion, *Shoah* is clearly not a minute too long. But the very length of a film can be part of the statement it makes as well. For instance, certain very short avant-garde films may use their brevity to heighten a certain fleeting, poetic elusiveness inherent in their imagery. *Shoah*, by contrast, affects the viewer in part through its extreme length. The film proceeds slowly, piling detail on small detail in the way that the historian who appears within the film describes his own researches as beginning first with tiny facts, hoping thereby to build on them till reaching the whole. For this method to succeed in a film on this monstrous subject, one of great length would seem mandatory. But more to the point is the way in which *Shoah*'s slow, almost languorous rhythms, rhythms based on this steady accretion of detail, form a monumental jeremiad. Lanzmann's use of repeated imagery, repeated locations, and a steady stream of facts, which, while not identical in detail, are very close to each other in their specifics, indeed recalls that greatest of laments, also based on repetition and near repetition, on a piling-on of imagery, the *Lamentations of Jeremiah*, which also intones sorrow and loss again and again in a hundred different ways, through numerous images, each a variation on the same theme.

In *Shoah* the endless recounting of detail introduces an ineffable sadness. But as the film progresses, its length gains another significance: the viewer begins to feel the way in which the film is taking a large chunk of time out of his day, out of his life. The standard two-hour feature format is something to which we are all accustomed, and a two-hour film tends to enclose or encapsulate itself as an object, its duration a thing we are used to accepting as part of the rhythm of daily living. But a very long film, even one of only four or five hours (*Shoah* is generally shown in two parts, though I prefer to see both parts together, in order, on the same day), carves a significant space out of one's temporal field. We attend to it differently; it intrudes more directly into our thoughts and lives, an intrusion thoroughly appropriate to *Shoah*'s subject.

What do we see in the film's nine and one-half hours? There are interviews with Jewish survivors, those who actually witnessed the killing; with apparently unreconstructed Nazis, including a Treblinka SS guard; with Poles who remember, not entirely positively, the years when Jews lived in their villages; with others who played a role in the events of this time, such as a bureaucrat whose job was to route trains to and from the camps. There is also present-day footage of sites such as Auschwitz and Treblinka: empty ruins, devoid of life. And there are occasional images of the contemporary landscapes of Germany and Poland. We see the buildings of prosperous German companies that contributed to the Nazi war machine and used its slave labor in their factories. We see empty fields. Everywhere there are moving trains.

The seemingly interminable pans over the empty field and the piles of stones of what once was Treblinka are among the film's most powerful and haunting images. On a primary level, they constitute a documentary record of the site today. The absence of people in this field of stones suggests that absence which haunts every moment of the film, from its very title (which means "annihilation" in Hebrew): the absence of those generations that number six million. When we eventually see the stones in closer shots, we realize that some are memorial gravestones with place names of whole nations or communities, and the sense of emptiness deepens.

Lanzmann has said that he wishes to lessen the sense of a difference between past and present, in fact, to make the past present. The contemporary landscapes suggest that the memory and ever present possibility of the genocide still lives. The trains course across the landscape, apparently unexceptional freight transports for modern Europe, while the editing configures them as awful ghosts of the long-past trainloads of Jews referenced in the banal technical descriptions of train routing given by the bureaucrat. Indeed, in this film of long takes and no rapid montage, Lanzmann as editor provides one of the most extreme moments in his final image. We cut from a long, extremely slow, and indescribably moving description of the end of the Warsaw Ghetto to one more shot of a train, moving forward through an indeterminate landscape, lumbering anonymously and inhumanly, an unstoppable mechanism, a final metaphor for the Nazi death machine.

But it is Lanzmann's knowledge of the limits of representation, his willingness to acknowledge the impossibility of full cinematic mimesis of his subject, that is at the heart of the film's aesthetic and moral position. The film's first witness, a Treblinka survivor, says at *Shoah*'s outset, "This is an untellable story," and Lanzmann has structured his film around the idea that its subject is too vast, and ultimately too other-than-human, to be enclosed in a series of film frames. Near the end of the film the camera slowly zooms in on a grayish pond while a voice-over explains that the ashes of thousands of cremated Jews were dumped here. The zoom expresses beautifully the impossibility of ever measuring, in cinema or in the mind, the scale of genocide. As we get closer and closer to the colorless water, we see only blankness, an utter void. It is this void that lies at *Shoah*'s heart, and one's sense of the film's having unaccountably vast dimensions stems in part from such moments. The blank gray surface, seen through the mechanical movement of the space-compressing zoom, denies entry. It is at once the absence of the civilization that was exterminated, that almost unfathomable historical fact, and the impossibility of ever representing that absence with anything other than emptiness. At this, as at many other moments in the film, the historical impossibility of recovering an annihilated past coincides with the filmmaker's utter and absolute inability to depict anything as enormous as the genocide, and with the inevitably similar failure of the viewer's imagination.

The effect of this zoom is paralleled in many other moments earlier in the film. Once the viewer realizes that Lanzmann's rhetorical method will be to use his film to describe that which he cannot show, a central issue becomes the extent to which one can form mental images of what one hears described. Technical details of the layout and routine at Treblinka, supplied by a former SS guard, encourage us to try to construct a mental map. His revelation that naked female Jews were "undoubtedly" beaten at the entrance to the gas chamber horrifies, and one wants to recoil from creating a mental image of such a scene, but the possibility of an image has in fact suggested itself in the mind, if only to be immediately suppressed. But when the same guard indignantly denies Lanzmann's claim during the interview that 18,000 Jews per day were exterminated there, insisting that it could have been no more than 15,000, the mind's ability to encompass this statement with an image, or to cope with the ludicrousness of this guard's argument, is utterly destroyed. It is not merely the hugeness of the extermination but the absurdity of the debate about numbers that denies all imagery. Similarly, when a historian recounts that since the Nazis had no budget for genocide, they financed it by seizing the property of those to be exterminated, so that the Jews paid for their own destruction and made the operation self-financing, any initial mental movement toward images of household valuables being seized and sold dissolves before a contemplation of the awesome amorality that made such an operation possible.

Throughout the film Lanzmann repeats an image of the main entrance gate at Auschwitz, shot from a train car approaching it on railroad tracks, the camera thus assuming, as it were, the position and view of an entering prisoner. In each successive view we move closer to the entrance gates on this moving train, and thus the shot serves as a metaphor for the film's attempt to try to understand some small piece of the lives of the Nazis' victims, to try to bring the viewer a bit closer to what they might have experienced. But when Lanzmann finally fulfills the expectation he has built up over many hours, through the repetition of these moving shots, and brings the film image through the gates, so that we now see the surviving buildings no longer enclosed by that entrance-frame and are in effect "inside" the camp, he effects this final passage not through a camera movement with the camera passing under the gate, but via a zoom, the camera remaining obviously outside. Zooms tend to appear mechanical, artificial. As the contents of the image grow closer, the spatial ordering and depth of the image alters, flattening. If camera movement tends to suggest movement through space, as of a human body, the zoom tends to represent the movement of the mind, a shift in human perception. Lanzmann's use of the zoom here is his acknowledgement that neither he nor we can truly pass through the gates of Auschwitz as its inmates did; that no one can recover lost time: we have only our mind's eye, which too must finally fail. Here, as throughout his film, Lanzmann is avowing not only the practical limitations of the medium—Hollywood costume dramas notwithstanding, it cannot recreate the past—but also the deeper impossibility of *Shoah*, that we can never recover the dead, that we can make no images that would be true either to their lives or to their dying. It would be an utter violation of Lanzmann's profound respect for those dead for him to move his camera physically through the gates, and so he must hold back and acknowledge that he cannot live their loss.

In an interview Lanzmann remarks that the Nazi functionaries who carried out the genocide avoided naming it: "Had they named this act, they couldn't have accomplished it." In his utter refusal to attempt depiction, in his decision to construct a film that is about the impossibility of such depiction,

Lanzmann has created a work that is the inverse of the mainstream tradition of the documentary, which relies on the use of the film image to represent the presentness of the time of its taking. *Shoah* is in fact the only documentary I know of that bases its aesthetic on the absence of any direct images of its principal subject. While acknowledging the impossibility of imagery, Lanzmann does indicate, with the quotation from Isaiah 56:5 that begins his film, the desire to give an "everlasting name" to the Jews who were exterminated. But how does one name an absence? How can one imagine, let alone represent, that lost future, the unconceived and unborn children of those who were killed, those future generations that never were? Around this terrible impossibility *Shoah* swirls.

II.

Whereas the best of the so-called structural films of the American avant-garde are surprisingly total works, films that despite their often "minimal" appearance managed to include much of human consciousness in their making, many derivative academic works, empty exercises in camera movement or montage, followed in their wake. *Shoah* is a film that should be of particular interest to independent filmmakers. While on the one hand it has none of the expressionistic gestures of much of the "non-structural" avant-garde tradition, and its long takes and repeated shots do indeed bear certain superficial similarities to the structural film, it is an awesomely emotional work, a film whose canvas is broad enough to include grief and loss, the filmmaker's own aggressive rage, historical fact, along with meditations on the possibilities and impossibilities of representation through imagery, the latter a subject of much avant-garde work. But in *Shoah*, all these themes are presented as an inextricably connected skein of thought: emotion, intellect, time, and imagery are restored to the interconnected wholeness drained from them by academic filmmaking. Lanzmann's investigations of the limitations of imagery are as profound as any in cinema, and they gain rather than lose in power through being connected to the Nazi genocide. Filmmakers need not exclude the messiness of life even while meditating on the properties of the medium. Indeed, it might be worth asking whether a useful—in the sense of having any potential value to anyone except film academics—film could be made whose near-exclusive focus is on exploring the properties of the medium. Many have tried, but to my knowledge none has succeeded.

Lanzmann has also chosen to include himself in the film, in a gesture also worthy of—but of course not limited to—the avant-garde film: witness, for instance, Rouch and Morin's *Chronique d'un Été*. We hear his voice as the interviewer on the sound track; we learn his biases; we come to feel his aggression. Rather than pretending impartiality, as documentary filmmakers are wont to do, Lanzmann expresses his own feelings and depicts his own deceptions, including his own lies within his film, as well as the reason for them. Thus in his interview with the Treblinka SS guard, an extraordinary document in itself, we see the deceptions that Lanzmann used to get it while at the same time appreciating the interview's value. We see Lanzmann approach another former Nazi, using his camera as an instrument of confrontation. Indeed, in response to a question as to whether he hates the Nazis he interviewed, Lanzmann responded, "Hate! I was beyond hate. The point was not to kill them, but to kill them with the camera, which was much more important." But while using his camera as an aggressor in certain specific ways, ways that are acknowledged within the body of the film, Lanzmann also constructs a much deeper implied critique of human aggression. Again, the film does its work through its form.

It can be argued that the photographing of any cinema image of a part of the actual world is an act of aggression. The photographer wrenches a specific part of reality from the context with which it makes a whole, then places that fragment in a rectangular frame, and thereby further delimits it in time. As if all that were not enough, the filmmaker frequently feels the need to exercise control over what is in front of his camera, even to the point of creating, or at least "directing," it. Indeed, our medium remains under the invisible spell cast by its progenitor, the one-minute film long said to have been the very first motion picture. Louis Lumière filmed his workers leaving his factory, which he described years later as an "easy subject," presumably meaning both convenient and controllable. His film begins at quitting time, the blowing of the factory whistle constituting the medium's first directorial call for "action," the workers departing at the owner-assigned time from doing the owners' bidding are once more, albeit mostly unwittingly, doing his bidding before his camera. In subsequent years, in documentaries, home movies, travelogs, feature-length narratives, erotic and pornographic films, and "art" films, the film image has more often than not, while doing the bidding of its creator, the filmmaker, sought to seize, possess, and transform those objects that fall within its space. In the home movie, the film functions as a way of possessing the child or other family member in past time. In the Hollywood melodrama, the audience is encouraged to feel empathetic, even erotic, involvement with the stars. In "porno" films, bodies and organs and orifices are laid bare and open for the viewer's fantasy-possession. In all cases, the filmmaker creates a film image, through what could be considered violent acts of framing and editing, that serves his own expressive ends above all else, even to the point of expressing the maker's self.

It is natural that such a use for film would evolve, given the intense illusionistic power of the medium. The viewer is encouraged, in the darkened theater, to feel that the images are in some sense his own. The brightness of the image, the precision with which it is enclosed in the frame's rectangle, the seductiveness of the constantly flickering light source—all build empathy between viewer and screen. A feeling of possession is even more natural to the filmmaker, who has photographed and edited the image as well. I find I cannot think of a good film that acts in a totally condemnatory fashion toward one of its images. Seized by the camera's eye from their context in the world, film images are then somehow inevitably glorified by the projector's beam. It is hard to imagine how it would be possible to construct a complex and expressive film that contained images of utter evil and for which images the film expressed univocal hatred. In most cases, films that include morally questionable material, such as films dealing with violent crime, display either perversely positive or at best ambivalent attitudes toward what is depicted. In a good film, each image is charged with a certain aesthetic beauty, or at least a kind of energy, and it is hard to imagine such energy being utterly controlled by condemnation. To take one example: as much as Eisenstein may have felt he was condemning Tsarist violence in *Potemkin*, it is hard not to feel the filmmaker's visionary, even erotic energy infusing the electric harshness of the editing, the violent angularity of the compositions. In an indifferent or bad film, the filmmaker may appear to be taking no clear attitude, or an overly simplistic attitude, toward the subject matter, but in most accomplished works it would be hard to imagine the imagery as representing the unequivocally reprehensible.

These considerations return us to *Shoah*, and to its avoidance of images of its time, of its primary subject. Lanzmann's film made me realize more clearly how problematic the images of starving prisoners and piles of corpses are in other films. Lanzmann has remarked that there is no footage of the actual killing; surviving footage was taken by the Allies after Liberation. But *could* he have used footage of the actual killing, if such existed? I think not. Every representational film image in some sense must name and endorse the things that it shows; every image encourages some form of viewer empathy. To use an image in one's film is to acknowledge one's possession of it, even control over it; in placing it in an edited framework, one declares an understanding of its significance. Images of emaciated corpses may represent death, but they cannot represent the lost life that is as much a part of the present as the fact of death. In an essay Lanzmann quotes a sentence by Emil Fackenheim: "The European Jews massacred are not just of the past, they are the presence of an absence." But an image of a corpse cannot possibly suggest anything other than a corpse, and to use such images is somehow, however unwittingly and unwillingly, to identify oneself with their true creators, the Nazi murderers. To show death on film is inevitably to traffic in it. The great moral lesson of *Shoah* is in its rejection of the filmmaker as autonomous artist, free to choose his imagery on emotional or aesthetic criteria alone. Lanzmann instead, by his careful consideration of what is and is not shown, by his use of techniques such as the zoom, and by his inclusion of his own feelings and subterfuges in the body of the film, has infused image-making with a renewed ethical dimension, with a deep respect for his seen and unseen subjects. When he feels the need to try to direct and control his witnesses, he lets you hear what he is doing; when he wishes to step back and let a witness speak at his own pace, the film is filled with long and terrible silences. The film never relies on imagery as its main source of expression or meaning, for every image is incomplete, and is so presented in the film. Lanzmann's images have the opposite effect to that of images of corpses, which are so overwhelming that they become complete in themselves, irrefutable facts about which no other image can speak, and ultimately reek only of death. Lanzmann's meditation is instead a dual one: on death, and on the life that was lost, the life that might have been, and to achieve this, his imagery must be open, his shots must refer to the imagination, to each other, to the unimaginable rather than to the closure of a corpse. In making a film about our century's great death, he has, through his survivors as well as through his filming and editing, made a film that is also about life, and this is his great triumph.

Lanzmann has wondered why he filmed the stones of Treblinka "from every angle, using every possible technique"; he then observes that his film is a "resurrection." But the more one sees of the stones, the more silent they become. As with the two zooms referred to above, the closer one comes to this graveyard, this terrain of the dead, the more one feels the presence of death, the silence, a silence no human can hope to represent, because it is something no living human has ever known. In most great films the aesthetic expression results from a kind of cinematic space that one may abstract from the images-in-time and that we may view as the filmmaker's unique and special vision. In the evolution of the Hollywood film, for instance, composed, classical, community-oriented landscapes of John Ford give way to the utterly malleable and intensely physical spaces of a Welles film noir. *Shoah*'s great achievement is to leave us with no such single abstractable image, which we might carry with us like an object as we leave the theater, our distilled essence of the filmmaker's expression to be filed away in the mind for future reference. *Shoah*'s refusal to participate in cinema's mainstream aesthetic tradition of an art based on the qualities of image-making is a result of the way in which it organizes its materials expressively, to point not toward the concrete but rather toward the construction of an emptiness, the null set.

Shoah's great act of respect for the dead, which one might also choose to call a kind of resurrection, consists of the filmmaker's stepping back from what he cannot show and cannot know. As the film proceeds, its accretion of detail makes the fact of the Nazi genocide all the more undeniable while at the same time rendering its meaning and consequences ever more unfathomable. Though the film is well photographed, its images well composed, the compositions are rarely if ever expressive in themselves. The interviews in particular, despite striking backgrounds provided for some of the witnesses, are filmed in a relatively impassive fashion. Even when filming Treblinka from "every angle," Lanzmann's camera never becomes expressionistic. But these forms of impassivity come from the same principle that prevents Lanzmann from showing footage of corpses: he knows that no image, no film technique, nor any unimaginably large plenitude of images or techniques could ever describe and delimit his subject. Instead, he piles images that do not emotionalize their subject matter through composition and that are in a way haunted by their own peculiar neutrality, itself a kind of absence, upon interviews that discuss for hours what is never seen, and with each passing minute the film's chasm becomes ever more yawning, its unimaginably inhuman heart ever more incomprehensible.

But then would one wish to be able truly to "comprehend" the enormity of the Nazi crimes? Films that include images of the camps take a step, if only a small one, in the direction of pretending comprehensibility: if one thinks one is seeing the facts, one begins to take their measure and makes them one's own. By presenting his subject not only through its facts but through a form that gives that subject a life in film, through its haunting vision of an unseeable and unhealable wound, a void that can never be filled, Lanzmann has given the most profound and everlasting of names to those who were lost.

The Site, Despite Everything

GEORGES DIDI-HUBERMAN
Translated by Stuart Liebman

The Return to the Site

The history of cinema is filled with all sorts of *possible places*. The invented, reinvented, reconstructed, or transfigured locations in films impress themselves on
our memories and are offered as indelible frameworks for our recollections.
This is what we might call "making the site magical." Recall the immense Baby-
lonian walls in *Intolerance*, the oblique roofs of *Caligari*, the subterranean
spaces of *Metropolis*, the skyscrapers of *King Kong*, the glass labyrinth of *The
Lady from Shanghai*, the oppressive palace in *Ivan the Terrible*, or the black
monolith in *2001*. Even so-called natural locations—the gigantic statues in
North by Northwest or the Rome Fellini surveyed in *Fellini Roma*—assume, in
great films, the fascinating quality of *transformed places*, rendered magical and
open to all that is possible, that is, open to the apparently limitless, glistening,
exuberant power we call the imaginary. In this sense the cinema offers us something like a perpetual celebration, a perpetual feast of possible spaces.

But when I take up the question of sites as well as other things, I am
obliged to come back to other kinds of issues that are never to be forgotten,

issues more difficult to bear. These issues forced a man to begin making a film twenty years after the events it evokes, based on the rejection, on the essential impossibility, of resorting to the sparkling scenic and cinematic rules of the game. He rejected "sets" and their magic—that is, the way a place is used by a tale—not because of an aesthetic decision, such as the one Straub made, but rather because of an ethical constraint at the very center of his intentions,[1] one central to the truth he was obligated to take into account. Common-sense logic would hold that he could have made many things other than a film in order to achieve the truth for which he had taken responsibility. Moreover, he was not a filmmaker by profession. But the cinema was an indispensable *recourse* for him, somewhat in the way writing was for Robert Antelme, who had never been a professional writer but who one day turned to writing as an indispensable means of expression.[2] For this man, the cinema was a means and at the same time an obligation—and not a way to celebrate anything; it was the indispensable way to render visible the *real but impossible sites* that were humanly and ethically impossible to conceive of as, or that could be transfigured into, sets.

These sites were the camps, the death camps. But in what way—in the most far-reaching sense of the word—are the camps "sites" for us? What sorts of thoughts and what kinds of visualizations do the camp sites require of us? Such questions, among many others, Claude Lanzmann had to answer over the length of his film *Shoah*, a cinematic response that remains admirable and, of its kind, one that absolutely cannot be bettered. What, then, to do with these sites—these sites of destruction, which had themselves been destroyed since the end of the war? What should one make of them cinematically? During the eleven years of work on this harrowing film, the question was often this: what was the point of *returning to the sites*? Paula Biren, a survivor of Auschwitz whom Lanzmann went to interview in Cincinnati, tells him, "But what would I see? How can I face this? . . . How can I return there, to visit?"[3]

And this woman also says that the cemetery of Lodz in which her grandparents were buried is itself in the process of being destroyed, and therefore that the dead from before the war who once could still be "located" will soon no longer be. Lanzmann films her speech and uses editing to align it with the unfathomably brutal statement by Mrs. Pietyra, a citizen of Auschwitz (Oświęcim), who explains why the Jewish cemetery of her village is "closed." "They do not bury anyone there any more."[4] Then why return to these sites? What can they "tell" us if there is *no longer anything there to see*? Lanzmann, who started on his journey in 1978, had from the start thought of Poland and the entire geography of the camps as "the imaginary site *par excellence*."[5] His quest somewhat resembles those of children who come back to *a place* because they absolutely want to see *the place* where they were born, even if *it* no longer exists or has been irreparably changed into something else, a highway or a supermarket. But the cineaste's quest was of a different sort, of course. Lanzmann returned to the sites because he absolutely wanted to see, and to make others see, *the places where millions of his fellow men and women were destroyed by other human beings.*

This *return despite everything*, despite the fact that there was nothing left, nothing at all left to see, this return via the agency of cinema, has given us access to the violence of something that I will call *the site, despite everything*, even if, at one point Lanzmann himself only came up with the expression "non-site" to refer to it.[6] Why are these sites of destruction the sites despite everything, the sites *par excellence*, the essential sites? Because Lanzmann, by filming them according to uncompromising rules that must be analyzed in detail, discovered in them a terrible power that went far beyond the "imaginary *par excellence*" he had thought about from the start of his work. It is the power of that which, whether destroyed or effaced, nevertheless *had not changed*: "The shock emerges not only from the ability to assign a geographic reality and even a precise topography to names—Belzec, Sobibor, Chelmno, Treblinka, etc.—that have become legendary, but also from the perception that nothing has changed."[7]

The essence of the project lies in the fact that Lanzmann was not afraid to film precisely this: that nothing has changed. Its essence lies in the fact that Lanzmann found the correct *form* to make this power, this paradox, visible so that this paradox confronts us in both an immediate and a lasting way. In his film the destroyed sites maintain, despite everything, despite themselves, the indestructible memory of their agency in the destruction to which history led them and of which, in this film, they will remain the site forever. Like the railroad tracks, the sign telling travelers that they have arrived at Treblinka is still *there*. Treblinka is still *there*. And this means that the destruction is still *there*, or rather—this is the work of the film—that it is *here* forever, close enough for us to touch, looking out at us from the depths, even as the place seems to present itself to us only as a completely "exterior" thing.

That is why the austere way in which Lanzmann filmed the sites has nothing imaginary, metaphorical, or idealist about it.[8] He does not seek the essence of places, as Plato tried to do in *The Timaeus*—and one should recall how the philosopher purified places into something like oneiric apparitions: "It [space] is apprehended without the help of sense, by a kind of spurious reason, and is hardly real; which we, beholding as in a dream. . . ."[9] What is sought in the film is precisely the opposite: sites are not "purified," simply because history has already altered or "razed" them; no "spurious reason" produces them. Instead, they are offered in a conspicuously blunt way that, far from excluding sensation, precisely imposes a simultaneous sensation of distance and closeness, a sensation mixing strangeness and something even more unbearable: the familiar. Finally, these sites are not at all "imaginary" or oneiric, because they are imposed as documents, always specific (never presented in general terms) and always as incarnations (but never resulting from any mollifying) of the collision between a past destruction and a present in which this very destruction, even if later altered, has "not changed." No one, or almost no one, is there any longer, they say; nothing or next to nothing is there. Nevertheless the film shows us discreet vestiges of how much *every-thing, here, remains, in front of our very eyes*. Lanzmann's work has been to construct, irrefutably, visually, rhythmically, this site *there, in front of our very eyes*.

The Silence of the Site

"I filmed the stones like a madman," Lanzmann has said.[10] How strangely reso-nant this phrase is for the spectator of the film, who leaves the screening over-whelmed by so many speeches, so many firsthand accounts, so many faces. This phrase may permit us to understand the difficulty *Shoah* confronted from the start. It was a matter of producing a radical form of reminiscence, one that would oppose the evocation of already established memories. Even before sur-vivors of this destruction could be understood, it involved allowing surviving victims and the torturers who were still around to speak with such precision that the speeches filmed by the camera's eye were made into something like a wager against all odds—to make the stones speak through an insane but necessary violence, one rooted in *respect* for them. Every person in this film is constrained, by the film's categorical imperative, to deliver a speech always proffered with a similar cadence—miracle, symptom, lapse, breakdown, withdrawal—because insofar as he or she is a survivor, everyone in the film, for reasons that are unique to each, seems like a madman, or a stone.[11] Each has been made mad by pain, or remains trapped inside his or her individual story like a stone lying in a riverbed.

Lanzmann thus tried to break open the stones, and the film did just that. But in order to do so, he had to come back to the sites, to *their silence*, in order to render this silence visible cinematically so that the site would truly speak. This was the case, for example, with Simon Srebnik, one of the two who escaped from Chelmno, with whom the film begins. Lanzmann has clearly explained the problem: what Srebnik could say was at first little more than nothing: he was confused, mad, unable to speak, silent as a stone.

> First of all, it was difficult getting them to speak. Not that they refused to speak. Some were crazy and incapable of conveying anything. They had lived through experiences so extreme that they could not commu-nicate anything. The first time I saw Srebnik, the survivor of Chelmno, who was thirteen during the period—these were very young people— he gave me an account that was so extraordinarily confused that I un-derstood nothing at all. He had lived through so much horror that it had destroyed him. I therefore proceeded by trial and error. I went to the places, alone, and I perceived that one had to combine things. One

must know and see, and one must see in order to know. These two aspects can't be separated. . . . That is why the issue of the site is so important.[12]

The filmmaker understood that as he was faced with the inability to record an account in the normal way, the *question of the site* is to be understood simultaneously as a place that raises questions about what is said and the conditions of its enunciation. The site is also a question that must continually be posed anew, especially during the filmed dialogues, that is, as a crucial dimension of all film utterances. It was just this question that the film had above all to take responsibility for, by constructing and shaping it to a nearly impossible degree. It is enough to recall the minutes at the beginning of *Shoah* to begin to understand how demanding the logic and the aesthetic of this entire, immense filmic construction is.

We remember, first of all, *a written name*: it is the title of the film—*Shoah*—a foreign word that is not translated and whose epigraph, contained in the same shot, says only one thing: that it is an imperishable name because for us the destruction of human beings is an imperishable fact.[13] The name is written in silence, as are the titles, and silent also is the text that immediately follows: it is *an account that unfolds*, recounting without emotion the place known as Chelmno "in Poland that was the site for the first extermination of Jews using gas." "Of the four hundred thousand men, women, and children who went there," the text continues in silence, "only two escaped." The first is Simon Srebnik, whose story is briefly presented: his father killed before his eyes in the Lodz ghetto, his mother asphyxiated in a gas van at Chelmno while he, a boy of thirteen, was assigned to maintaining the camp and, no less than the others, was slated for death. But the account informs us of his strange fate, which "spared him from death longer than the others" thanks to his voice, the melodious voice of an innocent. "Several times a week, when the rabbits kept by the SS needed fodder, Simon Srebnik, under guard, rowed up the Narew River in a flat-bottomed boat to the alfalfa fields at the edge of the village. He sang Polish folk tunes, and in return the guard taught him Prussian military songs. Everyone in Chelmno knew him." Just before the arrival of Soviet troops, Simon Srebnik, like all the other "work Jews," was executed by a bullet in his head. But "the bullet did not touch his vital brain centers," and he survived.[14]

This terrible bit of history, whose ending is graced by a miracle as strange as one in an oriental tale, is conveyed in silence. Lanzmann did not demand that Srebnik tell his story (as almost any maker of documentaries would have done). His story is told, of course, but it will remain in Srebnik as the ungraspable touchstone of his youth and its silence. Lanzmann wanted only one thing, but it was something radical: Srebnik was not to *tell* his story, but would rather *revisit* it. So Lanzmann returns with him to the sites, above all to this river where he sang, so that from now on he remembers and will forever transmit, in this film of memory, his song of Scheherazade that was also a small fragment of human history. The first *image* of the film would therefore lie between allegory and truth, between past and present: a man sings gently (and, at first, imperceptibly) in a flat-bottomed boat gliding on the river. The first image of the film pictures a *faraway song*, a song that is remote in time and space and distant from the camera but that nears us by gliding over the water, while a Polish voice, a peasant from Chelmno, tells what he remembers.

And then we find ourselves at the edge of the site: at first a *blank face*, that of Simon Srebnik, appears, timid, too impassive, softly coughing a bit, not knowing where to look in this site whose past destructiveness has itself been destroyed. He marches along the forest's edge. He stops and looks again; then, in German—the most difficult choice he could have made to convey his words—he pronounces the first phrases of what will become, during the entire film, a sort of infinite conversation about the reality of the destruction: "It's hard to recognize, but it was here. They burned people here. Many people were burned here. Yes, this is the place. [*Ja, das ist das Platz.*]"[15]

What place? It is *an open space*, absolutely empty, marked by a line defining the foundation of a structure already overgrown by grass, which the camera encompasses in a slow pan. Srebnik's voice continues over the site, even as each phrase sounds as if henceforth it will be impossible to say anything ever again: "No one ever left here alive."[16]

This is the site of *Shoah*, the place for us today of the Shoah. We will necessarily explore the irremovable vestiges of this "void" as we will this "character's" countless fates and the lasting meaning of the word "never." In order to explore these questions, Lanzmann had to "return to these places, alone" as he himself says. Then he had to return to these sites with the survivors for whom he had searched everywhere, demanding from them a single requirement: the ability to communicate their ordeal, if only by naming the site: *Ja, das ist das Platz.* Lanzmann therefore accompanies Simon through the open field that never changed, through a camp that has disappeared even as it had caused so many to disappear. Then he leaves Simon on the site, moves the camera back, and entrusts to Srebnik's voice, sad and astonished, both intimate and emerging almost from inside him, the task of saying: today's silence (the "calm" of the visible countryside) is comparable to yesterday's (the "unimaginable calm of the dead"). "I do not believe that I am here. No, I can't believe that. It was always this peaceful here. Always. When they burned two thousand people— Jews—every day, it was just as peaceful. No one shouted. Everyone did his job. It was silent. Peaceful. Just as it is now."[17]

This is the site of *Shoah*. Its silence refuses to render visible an event without a witness and engages in dialogue only the witnesses who bear this silence.[18] It *shows silence* and also augments it, that is, gives it form, constructs it, giving to the site the power to return our gaze, thereby in some way "telling" us what is essential. That is why such a silence is so heavy to bear for everyone in the film (those in front of the camera as well as those behind it, those who are on screen as well as those in the theater who sit before the projected images of their fellow men). This silence is *laden with the unimaginable*.

For Lanzmann, the film has obstinately, literally, and visually constituted this terrible weight constantly evoked by the words: destroyed bodies that were disintegrating, bodies seen "from below," crushed, "drifting along with the current," "piled up" on the ramp, "fallen" as if they were things, with violet crystals embedded in them, disfigured, bodies become ashes or shaped into blocks like basalt cliffs, etc.[19] In *Shoah*, some have said, the silence of the faces and sites filmed *contains* the destruction of the bodies, transmits this fact and simultaneously preserves them. It thereby encompasses them, but because *Shoah* was made not merely to satisfy a journalist's curiosity, and is even less an agreeable dramatization of events—it contributes to knowledge by explaining, disclosing, and proffering it openly through its singularly detailed and overwhelming form. Its form inheres in its specifically cinematic nature. Its cinematic qualities become means to recount this impossible story in the "normal" manner;" its filmic qualities are visual and rhythmic means to convey the paradox of the sites and the reality of death: everything was destroyed, nothing has changed.

The Present Site

This is the site of *Shoah*, with its infinite play of cross-references (because each site, however singular or self-contained, evokes memories of all the others); its infinite paradoxicality, its infinite cruelty are brought to light at every point by the questions, in the accounts and images the film continuously presents. There is, for example, "the charm" of the forest at Sobibor, where, a Pole says, "they still hunt."[20] There is the border between the *camp*, where men by the thousands agonized, and the *field*, where other human beings continued to farm, because it had to be done and also because they "got used to it."[21] There are Lanzmann's unrelenting, intolerable, but necessary questions about the *dimensions* and the *limits* of the camps, the size of the gas vans and the gas chambers, how cramped the undressing rooms were—precise details required by a destruction process that was mathematically precise; and all the questions about the topography and the kind of sand at the "selection point" at Treblinka, on the ramp at Auschwitz or in the camouflaged passageways that led to death as well as the organization of rail traffic, and the collaboration by industrial companies—Krupp or Siemens—in the death factories.[22]

There are also the cruel comments more or less spontaneously uttered by the witnesses at the sites or by the bureaucrats who organized the destruction. One example: a Pole runs his finger across his throat in a gesture provoked by the situation in which Lanzmann placed him. These expressions are also aroused by a *memory of the sites* and can be said more easily than memories of what these sites were made for: "We realized that what the Germans were building would not aid mankind." Or, in the mouth of Franz Suchomel: "It stank for kilometers . . . everywhere. It depended on the wind." Or again, in the mouth of Franz Grassler, who was the adjutant to the Nazi Commissioner of the Warsaw Ghetto: "I recall my excursions in the mountains more clearly."[23]

These sorts of cruelties have also not changed. Like the foundation lines in the empty space that is Chelmno, the words that have been censured or confined beneath a will to forget have stayed alive and continue to flourish. In the responses given to Lanzmann's questions, however, the unforgettable *names of the sites* are enough to produce something like the inconceivable figure for all this destruction, all that is unnameable. We know that death itself could not be referred to as such by the camp administrators where it was forbidden to utter what they did there, and where they instead developed precisely a *figural* substitute—"resettlement"—to describe it. One knows that the Germans baptized the perimeter of the extermination area at Majdanek the *Rosengarten* or *Rosenfeld* ("the rose garden" or "the field of roses") even though, obviously, no flower grew there. But the human beings who died there were sometimes called "Rosen."[24] Lanzmann's film itself explores all the paradoxical parlance and cruel comments used at the sites. We learn that the cinemas in Warsaw were open while the ghetto was burning.[25] And Madame Pietyra, a citizen of Auschwitz [Oświęcim], explains the "resettlement" in her own way:

What happened to the Jews of Auschwitz?

They were expelled and resettled, but I don't know where.

What year was that?

It began in 1940, which was when I moved here, and this apartment also belonged to Jews.

According to our information, the Auschwitz Jews were "resettled"—that is the word they used—nearby, in Benzin [Będzin] and Sosnowiec, in Upper Silesia.

Yes, because those were Jewish towns.

And does Madame know what happened afterward to the Jews of Auschwitz?

I think they all ended up in the camp.

That is, they came back to Auschwitz?

Yes, all kinds of people from everywhere were sent here. All the Jews came here, . . . to die.[26]

We are now better able to comprehend the ways in which this "geographical, topographical film," as Lanzmann calls it, had to make the sites into the figures, objects, and "things" of his project. A *figure*, because he often makes a detour so that a truth incapable of being conveyed in signs comes to light as a symptom, if only in a pan shot of an empty clearing in the forest. And what Srebnik is unable to describe adequately—telling how they burned his own people—he brusquely indicates at the site (we understand that his detour is not really a detour) by recognizing, even as he doubts what he says, that "it was here."

The sites are also *objects*, because continuously interrogating them in counterpoint with the faces of those who escaped are essential moments in the film. But the film also treats them as *things*, because the visual field that Lanzmann simply presents, always using desperately empty pan shots or tracking shots that are too slow to be manipulated in the ways that Spielberg or the "tracking shot of *Kapo*"[27] do, this open visual *field* only traces a border in the present around this unimaginable thing (one, moreover, that should not be "reconstituted") that the *camps* were. Lanzmann's cinematic "field" is therefore very much the opposite of the Polish field that was Treblinka; its frame, even if constructed forty years later, does not refuse to testify but rather is one through which the site is interrogated in the present; once it is filmed, it succeeds in bringing us to face the worst, close to the survivors' faces and to *what took place*. Looking at the sites, working on them in *Shoah*, was for Lanzmann undoubtedly the only possible way, the only possible form for "facing the horror."[28]

If there are no archival images in this "documentary" on the Shoah, that is so also because Lanzmann always conceived the site of destruction in the dialectical manner I have already mentioned. "Everything is destroyed" (how can we *approach* these historical images?), but "nothing has changed" (is it not essential to see and understand *these sites that are so close to us*?). That is why *Shoah* corresponds exactly, it seems to me, to the critical requirement formulated by Walter Benjamin for the work of art in general: that it constitute itself as a *dialectical image*, that is, it produces a collision between what is Now and what is Past, without transforming the past into a myth or reassuring the present:

> It is not that what is past casts its light on what is present, or what is present its light on what is past; rather, image is that wherein what has been comes together in a flash with the now to form a constellation. In other words: image is dialectics at a standstill. For while the relation of the present to the past is purely temporal, the relation of what has been to the now is dialectical: not temporal in nature, but figural (*bildlich*). Only dialectical images are genuinely historical—that is, not archaic— images. The image that is read—which is to say, the image in the now of its recognizability—bears to the highest degree the mark of the critical, perilous moment on which all reading is founded.[29]

Here is a film, evidently *figural* in nature, that took up the *dialectical* challenge of being a "film purely in the present,"[30] one whose sole aim was to develop the "critical, perilous moment" making it an ensemble of "genuinely historical images," that is, a work of "recognizability." It is significant that, in this "fiction of the real,"[31] Pierre Vidal-Naquet was able to recognize how memory was brought "into play" and how it would work on historical consciousness itself, in a decision equivalent to what Marcel Proust did in novelistic form.[32] This "Proustian" decision is sustained by the displaying of a truth that permits *the time of the return to the site*; it is maintained in Srebnik's posture when he says, "It was here." The "it was" forbids us from forgetting the terrible "past time" in the camps; it forbids us from believing that the present has accounts to settle only with the future. The "here" forbids us from mythifying or sacralizing this "past time" in the camps, which would amount to distancing us and, in a certain way, getting rid of this past. This is the dialectical image of *Shoah*, its insistence on the Now:

> The worst moral and artistic crime that can be committed in produc-ing a work dedicated to the Holocaust is to consider the Holocaust as past. Either the Holocaust is legend or it is present; in no sense is it a memory. A film devoted to the Holocaust can only be a counter-myth. It can only be an investigation into the present of the Holocaust, or at least into a past whose scars are still so freshly and vividly inscribed in certain places and in the consciences of some people that it reveals itself in a hallucinatory, timeless moment.[33]

Undoubtedly, the counter-myth of *Shoah* was certainly not interested in the history of cinema, because it had to confront a History much more threat-ening than those in our ordinary feasts of images. But the *form* of this con-frontation, in the nine hours of its images and speeches, will change the very course of the cinema through its conscience, that is, the story it tells.

Notes

1. But one quickly understands that every appropriate constraint constitutes a choice and that every aesthetic choice invokes an ethical rule (and I do not mean a morality).

2. Robert Antelme, *L'espèce humaine* (Paris: Gallimard, 1957). See the dossier de-voted to this essential book in the review *Lignes*, no. 21 (1994): 87–202. [An English translation of the former exists: *The Human Race*, trans. Jeffrey Haight and Annie Mahler (Evanston, Ill.: Marlboro Press/Northwestern University Press, 1998).–Tr.]

3. C. Lanzmann, *Shoah* (Paris: Fayard, 1985), p. 27.

4. Ibid., p. 29.

5. "J'ai enquêté en Pologne" (1978), in *Au sujet de "Shoah," le film de Claude Lanz-mann* (Paris: Belin, 1990), p. 212.

6. "Les non-lieux de la mémoire" (1986), in *Au sujet de "Shoah,"* pp. 280–292.

7. "J'ai enquêté en Pologne.," pp. 213. See also "Le Lieu et la parole," in *Au sujet de "Shoah,"* p. 299. [See translation of the latter in this volume.–Tr.]

8. "Les non-lieux de la mémoire," in *Au sujet de "Shoah,"* p. 287: "I have not made an idealist film. No big questions, or any ideological or metaphysical answers. It is a geographical, a topographical film."

9. Plato, *The Timaeus*, 52b. [Jowett translation–Tr.]

10. "Le Lieu et la parole," p. 299. [See translation in this volume.–Tr.]

11. This is, for example, what one could call the "stony smile" of Mordechai Pod-chlebnik at the beginning of the film: the overwhelming smile of the survivor. ("Every-thing is dead, but one is a human being.") Franz Suchomel, the SS *Unterscharführer* of Treblinka is another sort of stone, who watched people fall "like potatoes."

12. "Le Lieu et la parole," p. 294. [See translation in this volume.–Tr.]

13. "And I will give them an imperishable name." Isaiah 56: 5. On imperishability and the destruction, see Maurice Blanchot, "L'indestructible," in *L'entretien infini* (Paris: Gallimard, 1969), pp. 180–200.

14. C. Lanzmann, *Shoah*, pp. 15–17.

15. Ibid., p. 18.

16. Ibid.

17. Ibid.

18. See S[hoshana] Felman, "À l'âge du temoignage: *Shoah* de Claude Lanzmann," in *Au sujet de "Shoah*," pp. 55–145.

19. C. Lanzmann, *Shoah*, pp. 24–27, 66–69, 71–72, 139–140, etc.

20. Ibid., p. 21. And he continues: "There are lots of animals of all kinds . . . Here, at that time, there were only manhunts."

21. Ibid., pp. 36–37.

22. Ibid., pp. 43, 49–51, 53–62, 76, 92, 124, 126–127, 137, 147–151, 163–166.

23. Ibid., pp. 68, 80, 196.

24. Raul Hilberg, *La Destruction des juifs d'Europe* (1985), trans. M.-F. Paloméra and A. Charpentier (Paris: Fayard, 1988; new edition: Folio-Histoire, 1991), pp. 762–763.

25. C. Lanzmann, *Shoah*, p. 218.

26. Ibid., pp. 31–32.

27. See S[erge] Daney, "Le travelling de *Kapo*," in *Persévérance* (Paris: POL, 1994), pp. 13–39. [*Kapo*, an Italian film made in 1959, was directed by Gillo Pontecorvo and starred Susan Strasberg.–Tr.]

28. C. Lanzmann, "Hier ist kein Warum" (1988), in *Au sujet de "Shoah*," p. 279. [See translation in this volume.–Tr.]

29. W[alter] Benjamin, *Paris, capitale du 19e siècle. Le Livre des passages*, ed. R[olf] Tiedemann, trans. J. Lacoste (Paris: Le Cerf, 1989), pp. 479–480. [This English version is taken from Walter Benjamin, *The Arcades Project*, trans. Howard Eiland and Kevin McLaughlin (Cambridge, Mass.: Belknap Press, 1999), pp. 463.–Tr.]

30. "Le Lieu et la parole," p. 297. [See translation in this volume.–Tr.]

31. Ibid., p. 301.

32. P[ierre] Vidal-Naquet, "L'Epreuve de l'historien: réflexions d'un généraliste" (1988), in *Au sujet de "Shoah*," p. 208. [Translated by David Ames Curtis as "The Shoah's Challenge to History" in Pierre Vidal-Naquet, *The Jews* (New York: Columbia University Press, 1996), pp. 142–150.–Tr.] "Between lost time and time rediscovered lies the work of art. The challenge to which *Shoah* subjects historians lies in the obligation it places on them to be at once scholars and artists. If they do not face up to this challenge, historians will lose, irremediably, a portion of the truth they are pursuing." Also see Vidal-Naquet's *Les Juifs, la mémoire et le présent* (Paris: La Découverte, 1991), p. 221: "It concerns bringing memory into play, doing for history what Proust did for the novel. It is difficult, but *Shoah* has shown that it is not impossible."

33. C. Lanzmann, "De l'Holocauste à *Holocauste*, ou comment s'en débarrasser" (1979), in *Au sujet de "Shoah*," p. 316. [See translation in this volume–Tr.]

The Aesthetic Transformation of the Image of the Unimaginable

Notes on Claude Lanzmann's *Shoah*

GERTRUD KOCH

Translated by Jamie Owen Daniel and Miriam Hansen

> *For instance, if the image of a dead loved one appears to me suddenly, I have no need of a "reduction" to feel the ache in my heart: it is a part of the image, it is the direct consequence of the fact that the image presents its object as not existing.*
>
> JEAN-PAUL SARTRE, *The Psychology of Imagination*

If we recall the debates that have revolved for several decades, with greater or lesser intensity, around the question of an aesthetics after Auschwitz, we find that they divide along the lines of a moral and a material question. The moral question would be whether, after all hope for the stability of the human foundation of civilization had been destroyed, the utopia of the beautiful illusion of art had not finally dissolved into false metaphysics—whether, generally, art is still possible at all. The second, material question concerns whether and how Auschwitz can and has been inscribed in aesthetic representation and the imagination. In his "Meditations on Metaphysics," which conclude his *Negative Dialectics*, Theodor W. Adorno provides a succinct response to those who tried to construct a normative moral taboo upon his earlier aperçu that, after Auschwitz, poetry could no longer be written. "Perennial suffering has as much right to expression as a tortured man has to scream; hence it may have been wrong to say that after Auschwitz you could no longer write poems."[1]

But, Adorno continues, the question that arises after Auschwitz is not only that of the survival of art, but also the survival of those marked by the guilt of having survived: "[Their] mere survival calls for the coldness, the basic principle of bourgeois subjectivity, without which there could have been no Auschwitz; this is the drastic guilt of him who was spared."[2] The moral question cannot be isolated as an aesthetic one, but we can determine where aesthetics degenerates into bad metaphysics: wherever the aesthetic imagination extorts metaphysical meaning from the mass annihilations. This tendency manifests itself early on, in the first literary testimonies dealing with mass annihilation, in theological or metaphysically oriented, existentialist interpretations. Even independently of the concrete aesthetic structure of individual works, the metaphysical anchor is cast wherever mass annihilations become a subject. The fact that the majority of these early literary works were written by authors who had themselves escaped or evaded the machinery of annihilation appears to be of central importance here. Thus the "screams of the tortured" are indeed expressed in their works, but so in fact are the feelings of "the drastic guilt of the survivor[s]." This entails a manic search for "innocence" and transfiguration, whether in a theological or a moral sense. These manic attempts to find confirmation of the moral substance of the human in the very hell organized by human beings, as if the perspective of survival could thereby be brought into a meaningful context free of the universal feeling of guilt, have not diminished. Thus Sami Nair, in his essay on Claude Lanzmann's film *Shoah* in *Les Temps Modernes*, can still allow himself to get carried away by metaphysical tropes when he writes that Lanzmann "rehabilitates the survivors from the Jewish work commandos who assisted the Nazis in murdering their [Jewish] brothers and sisters . . . and transfigures them here into saints by revealing their inner *innocence*."[3]

What makes Nair's argument so unfortunate is its implied assumption of an *inner* margin of moral choice within the framework of which someone could become guilty or remain innocent. To be sure, the moral dimension of human action is based on the capacity to decide and on the decision to do what one considers right. Yet, where the possibility of making a decision is destroyed to the extreme degree that it is within the terroristic confines of a concentration camp, the celebration of minimalized processes of consciousness can only appear as metaphysical. Even if one considers this "inner" margin as a relevant factor, as Bruno Bettelheim does, it still does not offer a sufficient standard by which one could *morally* rehabilitate or, by the same token, discredit the victims of the concentration camps. This is not to deny that there were actual differences in behavior; but the individual's "inner" potential for resistance cannot be used to infer that everyone conducts him- or herself morally in situations that eliminate every human measure of freedom. No doubt Nair owes this implicit idea of an intact "inner" freedom to the premises of a one-sided, dogmatically construed existentialism, which has its foundations in Sartre's fatal paradigm that freedom of choice exists even under torture—a paradigm that accompanied the above-mentioned debates.

In the aesthetic realm this paradigm, which was influential in the debates of the 1950s, has led to an affirmative transfiguration even of terror. As Adorno notes in a rejection of Sartre's concept of engaged literature—a rejection that is not always fair to its object—this transfiguration

> implies, whether intentionally or not, that even in so-called extreme situations, indeed, precisely in these situations, humanity flourishes. Sometimes this develops into a dismal metaphysics which does its best to pare down atrocities into "limit situations," which it then affirms to the extent that they reveal human authenticity.[4]

At this point I would like to suggest that Nair's comments may apply to the general tone of the 1950s and to the topos of the limit situation in particular, but not to the aesthetic construction of Lanzmann's film. The film takes up neither the constricted situational context nor the theological variation of those literary treatments of the death camps which attribute affirmative meaning to them, a meaning that—even at the highest aesthetic level—still permeates the poetry of Nelly Sachs. Besides, the various patterns of meaning inscribed in the representations of the death camps cannot be distinguished according to literary forms or genres. Just as purely autobiographical, documentary literature is not free of the compulsion to search for meaning, aesthetically wrought works like Paul Celan's do not necessarily lapse into affirmative idealization because of their aesthetic stylization. In his discriminating study *Versions of Survival*, which includes literary as well as documentary and psychological testimony pertaining to the mass annihilations, Lawrence L. Langer concludes,

> We need to measure the various versions of survival by their fidelity to the ethical (and physical) complexities of the death camp experience, not by their success in repairing the ruptured connection between human will and human fate until it is restored to its pre-Auschwitz condition. If our age of atrocity has taught us anything, it has taught us that the certainty of that connection will never be as firm.[5]

Authenticity as a criterion indeed encompasses many forms and genres. Yet it unmistakably opts for a modernist aesthetic which aims at expression rather than communication. If the affirmative aspects of the metaphysical and/or theological imputation of patterns of meaning to mass annihilation can be linked to a premodern aesthetic, there are, on the other side of the scale, the unresolved aporias of autonomous art. The latter obtains its power from the theory of the imagination, the notion of art as idea or image (*Vorstellung*) rather than representation (*Darstellung*), expression rather than illustration. The imagination claims its own autonomy; it can project, annihilate social existence, transcend it to become radically other, while allowing the speechless, hidden substratum of nature in the mute body to reappear. At first glance the autonomous freedom of the imagination, which does not allow itself to be confined by any concept of meaning, seems far less burdened with the tendency to suffocate, through affirmation, the claims to expression made by the oppressed and tormented.

The autonomy of art, however, is itself not unlimited. In a certain sense it finds its limits in the capacity of the human imagination. It is therefore appropriate that Langer places a quotation from Samuel Beckett at the beginning of the first chapter of his book: "I use words you taught me. If they don't mean anything anymore, teach me others. Or let me be silent."[6] The increasing silence, the hermetic character of modern art is itself already a reflection on this limit. The following passage from Adorno's "Meditations on Metaphysics I: After Auschwitz," cited earlier, also touches on this aesthetic nerve of the imagination: "The earthquake of Lisbon sufficed to cure Voltaire of the theodicy of Leibniz, and the visible disaster of the first nature was insignificant in comparison with the second, social one, which defies human imagination as it distills a real [*reale*] hell from human evil."[7]

The limits of the imagination of a human evil are those of society, which allows what can still be conceived of by the imagination as human evil to become a *real* hell. This accounts for the difficult and tenacious struggle for "inner innocence," the desire to push the outer limits of the imagination back within. Alas, in the face of this historical dimension of an insurmountable difference between what can be humanly imagined and what has been proven to be socially possible, even the attempt to posit evil as an absolute category, at least within aesthetics, as Karl Heinz Bohrer has recently attempted to do, seems almost touchingly antiquated. The satanic evil of the imagination is just as incapable as the Beelzebub of theology or the negative absolute of metaphysics of surpassing real hell through aesthetic illusion. In order to be able to maintain his theory, Bohrer must conjure up the "disquieting step into the namelessness of an unlimited power of imagination which can no longer be controlled by any familiar discourse,"[8] whereas historically the limits of imaginative power have long since been delineated, and not in terms that are defined by aesthetic content, but rather socially.

But the argument—itself not entirely free of false pathos—that the attempt to imagine the annihilation aesthetically should therefore be discontinued altogether is even more misguided, directed as it is against legitimate claims to expression. The desire to establish a normative aesthetics of content from an objective social limit is an authoritarian longing; rather—and above all—we should investigate how this limit is reflected and re-marked in art itself. What nonetheless constitutes the *skandalon*, as the irreducible condition of the aesthetic, is the pleasure contained even in the most resistant work of art—a pleasure culled from the transformation into the imaginary that enables distance, the coldness of contemplation.

In the following I would like to show how a radical aesthetic transformation of this problematic is achieved in Claude Lanzmann's film *Shoah*. The debate about this film, especially in West Germany, has in most cases refrained from aesthetic criticism and instead has presented the film as a "stirring document" from which we can extract various historical, political, and moral dynamics. The fact that it is also a work of art is acknowledged only in passing and almost with embarrassment. Purists of the documentary form came closest to acknowledging the problem, since they were struck by the fact that long stretches of the film are not "documentary" at all.

Lanzmann himself has left no doubt that his conception of the film extends far beyond the portrayal of eyewitnesses. He would argue that the people in his film are acting; they are playing out what they have lived through, *le vécu*. But this implies something other than "remembering." To remember can mean, "Oh, yes, I remember, it was a hot day, I found myself in such and such a situation," etc. Such a statement of memory need not contain anything of how I experience this situation. For this reason Lanzmann must insist that the people in his film do not narrate memories but rather reexperience situations. What this entails can be illustrated by a crass example. In a long sequence of the film, the exiled Polish politician Jan Karski says that he has never spoken about his experience of the Warsaw Ghetto. As a memory this is questionable—historians know that Karski reported on his visit to the ghetto immediately afterward, that he even published such a report. But what is expressed in his formulation is the feeling of being able to speak only with difficulty about what he had experienced—the shock he felt in the ghetto that rendered him speechless when he saw what was to be seen there.

It is crucial to Lanzmann's strategy that he encourage a certain margin for play. He allows entire scenarios to be played out in a borrowed railroad car, challenging his protagonists to reenact particular gestures and actions. This strategy is no doubt indebted to the concept, central to Sartrean existential psychoanalysis, that there is a physical materiality even prior to the symbolizing process of language—an impudent laugh, the barely repressed sadistic glee over a threatening gesture. Such materiality breaks through only when gestures, physical movements, are repeated. In playing these, everyone again becomes who he is—that is *Shoah*'s criterion for authenticity, that is the immense visual power of this film, which so clearly sets it apart from other "interview" films. The smiling mask that covers the petrified inner world of the former *Mussulman*, who could survive in the concentration camp only by adopting an expression that anticipated rigor mortis, is no less an authentic expression than a dramatic breakdown. It is precisely this transformation into play that determines the seriousness of the representation (*Darstellung*).

Indeed, Lanzmann seduces, lures, and cajoles the protagonists into doing and saying things that would otherwise have remained silenced and hidden. This strategy has made Lanzmann the target of a moral criticism which reveals much of the old resentment against everything aesthetic, that the stolen image entrapped the soul of whatever it portrayed. To some extent, every aesthetic image contains the spoils wrested from social existence, but it is therefore no less legitimate. This is in no sense an example of aesthetic coquetry or the vain presumption of a director who does not want to give up control over his production. What Lanzmann is aiming at here is precisely the problem of the imagination—whenever something is narrated, an image (*Vorstellung*) is presented, the image of something that is absent. The image, the imaginary—and here Lanzmann is a loyal Sartrean—is the presence of an absence which is located outside the spatiotemporal continuum of the image.

Lanzmann remains strictly within the limits of what can be imagined: for that which cannot be imagined, the concrete industrial slaughter of millions, he suspends the concrete pictorial representation. There are no images of the annihilation itself; its representability is never once suggested by using the existing documentary photographs that haunt every other film on this subject. In this elision, Lanzmann marks the boundary between what is aesthetically and humanly imaginable and the unimaginable dimension of the annihilation. Thus the film itself creates a dialectical constellation: in the elision, it offers an image of the unimaginable.

But the film also approaches the problem from another angle: it begins quite literally with the aesthetic transformation of the statement that the annihilation "took *place*," in that it projects this statement into spatial visibility. It travels to the locations of the annihilation. The spatialization occurs in the present; what remains absent is what is temporally removed, the annihilation itself. The latter is narrated (often from off-screen) only fragmentarily from the imaginations of the protagonists. The length of the film may have obscured, for many viewers, its complex montage structure, which plays on multiple levels with real and filmic time. The juxtapositions, on the same temporal plane, of real events separated by very distant locations—such as, for example, the voice of the narrator from Israel on the soundtrack and a walk through the forested terrain of a death camp—are designed to irritate our realistic sense of spatiotemporal certainty: the presence of an absence in the imagination of the past is bound up with the concreteness of images of present-day locations. Past and present intertwine; the past is made present, and the present is drawn into the spell of the past. The long pans that realize the real time of the gaze remain trapped in historical space. What many of these shots convey is a sense of not being able to run away, of being closed in. Whenever the camera does not assume the subjective gaze, it may, for instance, move in such a way that, as in one particularly extreme long shot, a group of people approaching us from a distant edge of the woods are never really able to come closer but are again and again kept at a distance in the field by the camera. The camera's movement is aesthetically autonomous; it is not used in a documentary fashion, but imaginatively.

This method is at its most radical when Lanzmann uses camera movement for fictive scenarios of reenactment into which he manipulates not only the protagonists, but himself and the viewers as well. As the railroad car enters Treblinka, it does so in a subjective shot. The viewer is driven along with the train: this is also an insidious seduction. First Lanzmann has the former engineer of the train reenact his run once again, then it is Lanzmann himself who is doing so, and, after a delayed second of horror, the viewer finally realizes that he or she too is sitting in the train that unremittingly follows the tracks into the enclosure of the death camp. Yet the subjective camera never exceeds the limit; it takes us just far enough to allow us to sense, on the edge of the imagination, the reality of the annihilation, the frictionless matter-of-factness of its implementation—without lapsing into the embarrassments of gruesome shock effects.

In the montage of space and time described above, Lanzmann aesthetically organizes the experience of the most extreme discrepancy between what there is to see and the imagination (*Vorstellung*) triggered by that seen. It is the experience of the discrepancy between the indifference of the first and the horrors of the second. Thus Lanzmann resumes representational strategies which appear early on in literary treatments of the annihilation. I am reminded here above all of the stories of Tadeusz Borowski, in particular the following passage from a story entitled, "This Way to the Gas, Ladies and Gentlemen":

> A small square; ruins surrounded by the green of tall trees. In former times, this was a tiny little train station somewhere in the provinces. Somewhat off to the side, close to the road, there is a tumble-down shack, smaller and uglier than the smallest, ugliest shack I've ever seen. A little farther on, behind the wooden shack, entire hillsides of railroad ties are piling up, mountains of tracks, enormous piles of splintered boards, bricks, stones, and well rings. This is the loading dock for everything destined for Birkenau. Materials for building the camp and human material for the gas ovens. It was a working day like any other: trucks drive by and load up with boards, cement, and people.[9]

If we substitute "today" for "former times" and read what follows in the past tense, Lanzmann's scenario emerges. This effect is even more pronounced in other passages of the same story:

> We pass by all the sections of Camp II B, the uninhabited Section C, the Czech camp, the quarantine, and then we plunge into the green of the apple and pear trees that surround the troop infirmary. This green, which has burst forth in these few hot days, seems to us like an unfamiliar landscape on the moon.[10]

And even the church, to which Lanzmann cuts from the Jewish cemetery, is present in Borowski:

Idle and indifferent, their eyes followed the majestic figures in the green uniforms, drifting to the near and yet unattainable green of the trees, to the church steeple, from which a late Angelus rang out.[11]

This is not to say that Lanzmann has filmed Borowski's story. Rather, the comparison is meant to emphasize that there is an aesthetic transformation of the experience of the annihilation that does not permit itself to become ensnared in the pitfalls of the usual indictments and paradigms. Claude Lanzmann's *Shoah*, I would argue, is part of this tradition of the aesthetic transformation of the image of the unimaginable. Without question, the film also contributes significant material to the necessary political and historical debates. But the fascination it exerts, its melancholy beauty, is an aesthetic quality that we cannot afford to suppress or displace onto subliminal resentment against the character of its author.

Notes

1. Theodor Adorno, *Negative Dialectics*, trans. E. B. Ashton (New York: Seabury, 1973), p. 362.

2. Ibid., p. 363.

3. Sami Nair, "*Shoah*, une leçon d'humanité," *Les Temps Modernes*, no. 470 (1985): 436.

4. Theodor Adorno, "Commitment," trans. Frances McDonagh, in Ronald Taylor, ed., *Aesthetics & Politics* (London: Verso, 1977), p. 189 (translation modified).

5. Lawrence L. Langer, *Versions of Survival* (Albany: State University of New York Press, 1982), p. 216.

6. Ibid., p. 1.

7. Adorno, *Negative Dialectics*, p. 361 (translation modified).

8. Karl Heinz Bohrer, "Das Böse—eine ästhetitische Kategorie?" *Merkur* 39 (June 1985): 472.

9. Tadeusz Borowski, "Die Herrschaften werden zum Gas gebeten," in Marcel Reich-Ranicki, ed., *16 polnische Erzähler* (Reinbek, 1964), p. 111. [An English translation appeared in the collection *This Way for the Gas, Ladies and Gentlemen*, trans. Barbara Vedder (New York: Penguin Books), 1967; since this English translation deviates radically from the German version quoted in this article, however, the translations here and following are our own.–Trans.]

10. Ibid., pp. 110–111.

11. Ibid., p. 113.

Photo Gallery

Shoah is a film of the faces and voices of witnesses to the worst systematic mass murder in history, fixed forever by an implacable camera's gaze. It is also and equally a filming of innocent-looking landscapes burdened by a terrible, unseeable past–what Lanzmann has called "non-sites of memory"–relentlessly surveyed and interrogated by his movements through and across them. These are the traces of an unfathomable destruction of almost an entire people–the Jews of Eastern Europe, their homes, their culture, their ways of life and death–as well as of countless others from every nation of Europe.

The following portfolio of images from *Shoah* highlights some of the men, women and places we come to know, as they have been revivified through the agency of Lanzmann's camera. The order is, in part, conceptual, as it follows the course of the destruction process from the trains that transported the victims, through the camps and crematoria that swallowed them up, to the memories and memorials that abide. The images of the witnesses have been arranged approximately in the chronological order in which we meet them in the film.

Locomotive at Treblinka Station. (Courtesy of New Yorker Films)

Birkenau, entrance gates. (Courtesy of New Yorker Films)

Birkenau, site of ramp where Jews were unloaded for selection.
(Copyright *Shoah*/Claude Lanzmann)

Simon Srebnik, survivor of Chelmno, with Polish villagers.
(Copyright *Shoah*/Claude Lanzmann)

Henrik Gawkowski, Polish locomotive driver.
(Courtesy of New Yorker Films)

Polish peasant, Grabów. (Copyright *Shoah*/Claude Lanzmann)

Polish peasant, Grabów. (Copyright *Shoah*/Claude Lanzmann)

Abraham Bomba, former barber for women at gas chambers of Treblinka.
(Courtesy of New Yorker Films)

Richard Glazar, survivor of Treblinka.
(Copyright *Shoah*/Claude Lanzmann)

Raul Hilberg, historian, University of Vermont.
(Courtesy of New Yorker Films)

Rudolf Vrba, survivor of Auschwitz. (Copyright *Shoah*/Claude Lanzmann)

Filip Müller, survivor of five liquidations of *Sonderkommando* at Auschwitz. (Courtesy of New Yorker Films)

Dr. Franz Grassler, adjutant to Dr. Auerswald, Nazi Commissioner of the
Warsaw Ghetto. (Copyright *Shoah*/Claude Lanzmann)

Jan Karski, courier for the Polish underground government.
(Copyright *Shoah*/Claude Lanzmann)

Simha Rottem ("kazik"), one of the leaders of the Warsaw Ghetto uprising. (Courtesy of New Yorker Films)

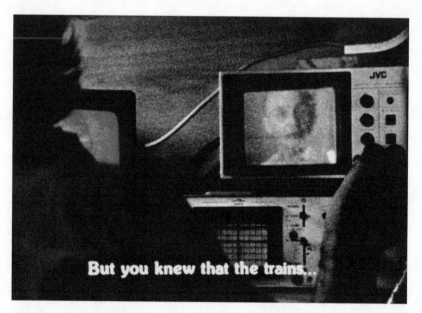

Walter Stier, former chief of Office 33 of the Reichbahn, secretly filmed and seen on closed-circuit television. (Courtesy of New Yorker Films)

Claude Lanzmann (left) interviews Franz Suchomel, former
SS *Unterstürmfuhrer*, Treblinka. (Courtesy of New Yorker Films)

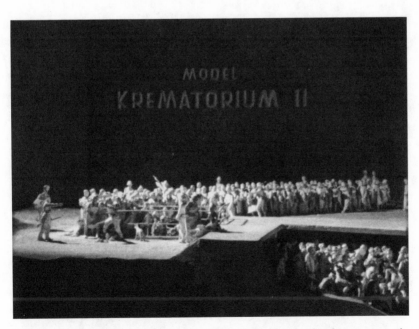

Model of Crematorium II, Birkenau. (Copyright *Shoah*/Claude Lanzmann)

Greek survivor from Corfu holds images of relatives killed at Auschwitz.
(Copyright *Shoah*/Claude Lanzmann)

Treblinka memorial monument.

PART III
Controversies and Critiques

The Life of Death

Shoah—A Film by Claude Lanzmann

TIMOTHY GARTON ASH

An enormous film about a subject central to the history of our time, Claude Lanzmann's nine-and-a-half-hour-long film about the Holocaust, has already opened in New York, after winning tremendous critical acclaim in France and stirring controversy in Poland. . . .

Shoah is a film about memory. Memory plays tricks. So does *Shoah*. But the tricks of *Shoah* are quite different from those of [Edgar Reitz's] *Heimat*.[1] Reitz allows the Germans their forgetting. Claude Lanzmann compels everyone to remember. *Shoah* has been described by a French critic as "a monument against forgetting"; beside it, *Heimat* looks like a monument *to* forgetting. Reitz's position is deliberately amoral ("We try to avoid making judgments"). Lanzmann is fiercely moral. "I am deeply convinced," he has explained in an interview with *L'Express*, "that there is identity between art and morality." The tricks of *Shoah* are those of art: but art in the service of morality.

Lanzmann's unique artistic achievement is to have re-created the life of the death camps. The life of death. Re-created out of nothing—no, out of less than nothing, out of nothingness, *le néant*, as Lanzmann himself says. There were not even the ashes. Re-*created*, not merely reconstructed. *Shoah* is not a documentary. It has none of those familiar black and white sequences: hysterical crowd chanting *"Sieg Heil"* CUT to pile of corpses at Bergen-Belsen. No Hitler, no corpses. Instead we have nine and a half hours of interviews with surviving Jewish victims, German executioners, and Polish witnesses (spectators? bystanders?—every word anticipates a judgment), long, harrowing, astonishing interviews, intercut with one another and with slow, lingering camera shots of the extermination camps as they are today, and the railway lines leading to them, of the surrounding countryside, and the railway lines again, of the cities where the survivors now live, and again the railway lines. Germans, Jews, Poles: Lanzmann requires, cajoles, and, if need be, bullies them all to recall in minute physical detail their experience of the death camps. "You have to do it," he insists when a Jewish survivor breaks down. "Please. We must go on." "Can you describe this 'funnel' precisely?" he presses the SS officer from Treblinka. "What was it like? How wide? How was it for the people in this 'funnel'?" And by the end of Lanzmann's film I felt that I began to know what it seems by definition impossible to know: "How it was" for the people in the "funnel" that led to the gas chamber at Treblinka.

No other film that I have seen about the subject has haunted me as *Shoah* does: images and voices returning, unasked and, so to speak, unwanted, when I awake in the night or as I play in the park with my baby son. Some written witness, some literature, has come close to it—I think of André Schwarz-Bart's *The Last of the Just* or the stories of Tadeusz Borowski.[2] But there is a particular compulsion that results precisely from *Shoah*'s being not a book but a film. "I couldn't put it down," says the book reviewer's cliché. Well, you literally can't "put *Shoah* down." You can't stop on page 43, after reading the description of a mother disowning her own child before the gas chamber, and walk out into the garden to regain your composure. Unless you walk right out of the theater, and, as it were, miss the next fifty pages, you just have to go on sitting through it. You lose your composure. You get thirsty. You get exhausted. Perhaps you even get angry when the camera takes you once again, for what seems like the hundredth time, slowly, oh so slowly, down the railway line to the ramp. But this deadly repetition, this exhaustion, this *having* to sit through it, is an essential part of Lanzmann's re-creation. He deliberately uses the dictatorial powers of the director to lock you in a cattle wagon and send you for nine and a half hours down the line to Auschwitz.

Lanzmann is a supremely self-conscious artist. At a discussion organized by the new Institute for Polish-Jewish Studies in Oxford, after the first showing of the film in England, he analyzed, explained, and commended his own achievement with an obsessional artistic self-interest that recalled accounts of Wagner or Joyce. ("He is a monster," a friend commented afterward, "a *golden* monster.") Lanzmann talked about his film as of a symphony, a great work of architecture, a Shakespearean play. Asked why he had not used interviews with this or that famous survivor, he said they were "weak" as characters, they were incapable of truly *reliving* the experience before the camera, they did not fit into his play. In this film, he went on, every protagonist becomes an actor, it "is a fiction of reality." Asked about his criteria of selection, he replied, "The film is made around my own obsessions, it wouldn't have been possible otherwise." "The film can be something else than a documentary," he said. "It can be a work of art—and it can be accurate too." Accuracy is the second extraordinary feature of his work. Behind the nine and a half hours are some 350 hours of recorded film and eleven years of research across the globe. In Oxford, faced with some of the world's leading experts on Jewish and Polish affairs, he answered every criticism on points of factual detail with what seemed to me overwhelming knowledge, conviction, and something more: the justified sense that he had done what none of these historians had done. Why had he not included anyone from the *Einsatzgruppen*—the specially constituted Nazi mass-execution squads? There are very few survivors of the *Einsatzgruppen*, he replied. He tried to interview them. It was very difficult. In one case the camera concealed in his shoulder bag (which he used for secretly filming most of his Nazi interviewees) was discovered. "I spent one month in the hospital. I was severely, . . . extremely beaten. All my material was stolen."

Yet as he talked, it became clear that his criteria of selection were not only those of the artist's truth ("my obsessions") but also those of the historian's truth. He argued for his interpretation of the long-term causes of the Holocaust, and the nature of the extermination process, as a historian debating with historians. In large part, Lanzmann's interpretation follows that of Professor Raul Hilberg, who appears in *Shoah* as the key professional witness. There was a "logical progression," says Hilberg, "because from the earliest days . . . the missionaries of Christianity had said in effect to the Jews, 'You may not live amongst us as Jews.' The secular rulers who followed them from the late Middle Ages then decided, 'You may not live among us,' and the Nazis finally decreed, 'You may not live.'" However, there was no one clear order that stated "now the Jews will be killed." The Final Solution was rather "a series of minute steps taken in logical order," at the end of which the "bureaucrats became inventors"—a "bureaucratic destruction process" that Hilberg has done more than anyone to reconstruct in scrupulous detail.[3] One may question parts of this interpretation, as Professor Israel Gutman did most powerfully in the Oxford discussion, but there is no doubt that on this central theme *Shoah* makes a clear and cogent historical argument.

Challenged more closely on his interpretation of Polish responses, Lanzmann said, "I think I have shown the real Poland . . . the deep Poland," and, crucially, *nothing essential* about the Poles is left out. In that last comment he again explicitly offered up his work as a historian inviting a historian's judgment. For this criterion of fairness, representativeness, completeness, this claim that "nothing essential" is left out, is always central to the judgment of what historians do but is generally peripheral to the judgment of art. To say that a novelist, dramatist, or painter has "left something essential out" is not usually to say anything meaningful or important. (Why did Leonardo leave out the Mona Lisa's feet?) To say that a historian has "left something essential out" is always important. We expect historians at least to declare their principles of exclusion.

Lanzmann thus applies to his own work two standards of judgment; not to say, a double standard. If I now proceed to question the historical comprehensiveness of the Polish part of *Shoah*, to suggest that here something essential *is* left out, then I shall at once be open to two criticisms: first, that the *artistic* completeness of the film is far more important than its historical completeness, or incompleteness; second, that the Polish part is anyway, historically speaking, the less important part of a film whose subject is the extermination process. I agree. Its artistic completeness *is* more important. The unique and unquestionable achievement of *Shoah* is that it brings home to us what no other documentary film has brought home: it makes us imagine the unimaginable, it re-creates the life of death.

Using the exact opposite of Brecht's "alienation effect," Lanzmann succeeds in eliminating the distance between past and present. In so doing, "he wanted to aid the human conscience to never forget, to never accustom itself to the perversity of racism and its monstrous capacities for destruction." This moral drawn from Lanzmann's art is the more striking because of the person who drew it. I am quoting Pope John Paul II, who thus singled out *Shoah* in an audience given to veterans of the French and Belgian resistance. Whether Lanzmann himself would agree that what he wanted to do was precisely this, or this above all, I do not know. But I have no doubt that this is one of the things he succeeds in doing. His work of art has a great moral effect.

Second, I agree that the Polish part is historically secondary. The Poles were neither the executioners nor the main victims in the extermination camps—Lanzmann's subject. They were only (only?) the train drivers and switchmen, the farmers who worked the fields around the camps, the local population who sheltered, ignored, or denounced the Jews. One Israeli participant in the Oxford discussion privately compared Polish criticism of the depiction of the Poles in *Shoah* to Jewish criticism of the depiction of the Jews in Andrzej Wajda's *The Promised Land*: both criticisms, he said, miss the main point of what the director is trying to show; the depiction of the Poles and Jews, respectively, is largely irrelevant, a backdrop, not the play.

Yet Lanzmann himself is obviously fascinated by the Polish backdrop— indeed he gives it more prominence in the film than its strict historical relevance to his main theme might dictate. (It is also striking that the image the American publisher of the subtitle texts has chosen for his dust jacket is that of the Polish train driver who drove the transports into Treblinka.) Moreover, Lanzmann asks that his treatment of the Polish backdrop be judged with the same historical rigor as the main play. The political controversy surrounding *Shoah* has largely concerned the Polish part. The history of Polish–Jewish relations may not be so important to the Jewish nation today (*may* not be), but

I have no doubt that it is still of vital importance to the Polish nation: to the Poles' proper understanding of themselves. For all these reasons, I think it is worth devoting the rest of this review to what is—I repeat—*not the most important* part of the film.

Contemporary Polish reactions to the Polish–Jewish question are a mess. This is not an issue where there are clear dividing lines between regime, opposition, and Church. After *Shoah* opened in Paris, the Polish government's first reaction was to fire off an official protest at the Quai d'Orsay. But the government subsequently bought the film for showing (in part) on Polish television and (in full) at a few movie theaters. There were stupid and ugly articles about it in the official press, mostly by journalist-propagandists who had never seen it. But there were subsequently intelligent assessments by critics who had.[4] Moreover, both categories of article could also be found in the Catholic and in the underground press.

The debate is hopelessly distorted by the extraordinary degree to which anti-Semitism has remained an issue, and an instrument of political manipulation, in postwar Poland. This was notoriously so in the 1968 "anti-Zionist" pogrom, led by factions in the Party and the security services, which resulted in the expulsion of most remaining Polish Jews from their jobs, but also in the crisis period between 1980 and 1982, when a few anti-Semitic voices could once again be heard in all camps—Party, Church, Solidarity—although this time they were truly marginal. Every politically conscious Pole writing about this subject therefore has a voice in his ear asking: What political use will be made of what I write? How will *Znolnierz Wolnosci* (the Army newspaper that played a leading role in the 1968 campaign) misquote me? Whom will this serve? Indeed, I can almost hear this voice myself, since the last essay I wrote about Poland for *The New York Review* has been made the subject of a charming little attack in *Znolnierz Wolnosci*, signed by one Colonel (!) W. Zielinski. But this voice is a voice of self-censorship.

Such fears are everywhere and always the bane of free discussion. In Poland they are reinforced by another complex. Every Pole is brought up to believe that his country is one of history's victims: the generally innocent and righteous victim of the predatory nationalism of more powerful neighbors. Then he is confronted with a bitter and sweeping indictment of his nation by an American or British or French or, indeed, Polish Jew—an indictment (and who has not heard it spoken?) that places the Poles right there in the dock between Barbie and Mengele. Brought up to see himself as a victim, he is suddenly told: "You were the executioner."

We recognize the nationalism of the conqueror. But there is also a nationalism of the victim. The nationalism of the victim is one of the many things that Poles and Jews have (or at least have had) in common. Characteristic for the nationalism of the victim is a reluctance to acknowledge in just measure the sufferings of other peoples and an inability to admit that the victim can also victimize. In his famous "Notes on Nationalism" Orwell writes that "if one harbors anywhere in one's mind a nationalistic loyalty or hatred, certain facts, although in a sense known to be true, are inadmissible," and he goes on to give examples of "intolerable facts" for different kinds of "nationalists": British Tory, communist, pacifist, and so on. I cite below one "intolerable fact" for the Polish and one for the Jewish nationalist—using the word "nationalist," I stress, in Orwell's peculiar, broad, and pejorative sense.

For the Polish nationalist: There was virulent and widespread anti-Semitism in Poland during the Second World War.

For the Jewish nationalist: The conditions of German occupation were worse for the Poles than for any other nation except the Jews.

To any reasonably detached observer who knows even a little of the evidence, these are both statements of obvious fact. "Please accept it as a fact," the commander of the Polish underground Home Army (AK) wrote to the Polish government in London in September 1941,

> that the overwhelming majority of the country is anti-Semitic. . . .
> Anti-Semitism is widespread now. Even secret organizations remaining under the influence of the prewar activists in the Democratic Club or the Socialist Party adopt the postulate of emigration as a solution of the Jewish problem. This became as much of a truism as, for instance, the necessity to eliminate Germans. [Quoted from Jan Gross's excellent book *Polish Society Under German Occupation* (Princeton, N.J.: Princeton University Press, 1979), pp. 184–185]

But equally, as Gross and Martin Broszat and many others have amply documented, the Nazi occupation of Poland was special and extreme. Churchill was not using mere hyperbole when he declared, "Monday [Hitler] shoots Dutchmen, Tuesday—Norwegians, Wednesday—French or Belgians stand against the wall, Thursday it is the Czechs who must suffer. . . . But always, all the days . . . there are the Poles." And consequently, as Nechama Tec soberly observes in her remarkable book about Christians who sheltered Polish Jews, "obstacles and barriers to Jewish rescue were the most formidable in Poland" (*When Light Pierced the Darkness: Righteous Christians and the Polish Jews* [New York: Oxford University Press, 1985]).

To present these two "intolerable facts" is not to imply any symmetry or moral equivalence. It is only to suggest that unless you are able to acknowledge such basic facts—and most of the people who have spoken or written about this subject over the last forty years do seem to have been unable to acknowledge either one or the other—then you cannot begin seriously to answer the real historical questions, such as: What is the connection, if any, between the fact of Polish wartime anti-Semitism and the fact that the German extermination camps were located in Poland?

Lanzmann's own answer to this central question, in newspaper interviews and in the Oxford discussion, has been confused. "The film, you are aware, is an act of accusation against Poland?" he was asked by *L'Express* (in an interview published in May). "Yes," he replied, "but it's the Poles who accuse themselves. They mastered the routine of extermination. No one was troubled by it." But in the Oxford discussion he said: "It's not an accusation . . . against the Poles, because I don't think they could do much." Yet a minute later, speaking of the Polish village of Grabów, which features prominently in the film, he exclaimed, "A small village like this just let go of half its population . . . knowing absolutely that they were going to be gassed, because everybody knew." To say they "just let go of " the Jews surely implies they could have done something about it. Subsequently Lanzmann revealed that his whole family was saved by French peasants during the war, and he declared categorically, "There could not have been extermination camps in France."

But never trust the artist, trust the tale. What does the film actually show us? Most memorably, it shows us long extracts from some of the extraordinary conversations which Lanzmann had in the Polish villages and farms near the death camps. In these conversations, old Polish peasants describe what they saw of the extermination process, how they reacted then, and what they think now. A farmer laughingly tells how as a young man he used to walk down the line of carriages, drawing a finger across his throat to indicate to the Jews that they were going to be killed. The foreign Jews came in passenger cars, he says; they were beautifully dressed, in white shirts . . . they played cards. The foreign Jews, oh yes, "they were this fat," repeat his friends, and "we'd gesture that they'd be killed." And they laugh into the camera. But the same farmer also says, "When people began to understand what was happening, they were appalled, and they commented privately that since the world began, no one had ever murdered so many people that way." The Poles feared for their own safety. Weren't they afraid for the Jews too? Lanzmann asks. Well, replies the farmer, it's like this: if I cut my finger, it doesn't hurt you, does it?

Later we meet the villagers of Grabów, living in houses that once belonged to the Jews. (Notice the beautiful wood carvings on the doors.) They describe how the Jews were herded into the church—the Polish Catholic church—and then transported to Chelmno, just twelve miles away. "The Germans threw children as small as these into the trucks by the legs. Old folks too." "The Poles knew the Jews would be gassed in Chelmno?" Lanzmann asks. "Did this gentleman know?" "Yes."

Then a group of old women. "The Jewish women were beautiful," they say. "The Poles liked to make love with them." "It's crazy how the Poles liked the little Jewesses!" What made them so beautiful? "It was because they did nothing. Polish women worked. Jewish women only thought of their beauty and their clothes." "The capital was in the hands of the Jews." "All Poland was in the Jews' hands." And a group of men. Are they glad there are no more Jews here? "It doesn't bother [us]. As you know, Jews and Germans ran all Polish industry before the war."

Then the most eerie scene of all. A group of villagers in front of the church in Chelmno. Sounds of prayer and hymns. What's being celebrated? "The birth of the Virgin Mary. It's her birthday." And as the old Marian hymns ring out behind them, the villagers describe how the Jews were herded into this very church, how the Jews moaned and cried in the night, before the gas vans came to take them away, to kill them. Why did it happen to the Jews? "Because they were the richest! Many Poles were also exterminated. Even priests."

Then a self-important-looking man steps forward. He obviously considers himself a cut above the rest, and the rest seem to agree. "Mr. Kantarowski will tell us what a friend told him. It happened in Myndjewyce [*sic*], near Warsaw." "Go on," says Lanzmann.

> The Jews were gathered in a square. The rabbi asked an SS man: "Can I talk to them?" The SS man said yes. So the rabbi said that around two thousand years ago the Jews condemned the innocent Christ to death. And when they did that, they cried out: "Let his blood fall on our heads and on our sons' heads." Then the rabbi told them: "Perhaps the time has come for that, so let us do nothing, let us go, let us do as we're asked."

And when Lanzmann questions this fantastic tale, an old woman shouts, "So Pilate washed his hands and said, 'Christ is innocent,' and sent Barabbas. But the Jews cried out, 'Let his blood fall on our heads!' That's all: now you know!"

The reaction of one of Poland's most respected Catholic intellectuals to all this was both symptomatic and rather shocking. (Speaks the self-censor in my ear: "Here comes a passage *Znolnierz Wolnosci* might want to quote out of context.") Jerzy Turowicz is editor of the leading Catholic weekly, *Tygodnik Powszechny*. Turowicz got up early in the Oxford discussion and said approximately this: The film is one-sided. These peasants are simple, primitive people such as you could find in any country. Lots of Poles helped the Jews. There are 1,500 Polish trees in Yad Vashem. Polish Catholicism has precious little to do with Polish anti-Semitism—and anyway Polish anti-Semitism has nothing to do with the Holocaust.

Now with the greatest respect to Mr. Turowicz, this really will not do, it will not do at all. This reaction is pure "nationalism," in the special sense in which, after Orwell, I am using that term here. Lanzmann's presentation of Polish peasant Catholic anti-Semitism is a challenge and an implicit rebuke to Polish Catholic intellectuals. It says, in effect: for God's sake, here is a *problem*, a raw, bleeding, horrid problem, and why has it taken forty years and my provocation for you to address it? And all Mr. Turowicz could reply was: We see no problem.[5]

Is Lanzmann's presentation of this problem in the film unfair? Yes and no. No in the sense that everything he shows is obviously true. These people exist. They said these things. To be sure, his questioning is aggressive, even angry. "They've gotten rich," he says of one Grabów couple who have moved into a Jewish house: that is to say, a wooden cottage in a poor farming village in one of the most backward corners of Europe. Rich! Lanzmann is clearly shocked and amazed to find himself talking to real, live Christian anti-Semites who could almost have stepped out of the pages of a textbook on anti-Semitism (a textbook that should exist in Polish). But he does not attempt to flatten out the human, all too human, complexities, the bizarre mixture of superstition and earthy common sense in the peasants' mental world. The Jews stank, says one peasant. Why? asks Lanzmann, and we expect an ideological answer. "Because they were tanners and the hides stank." An old woman says she is now better off than she was then. "Because the Jews are gone, or because of socialism?" asks Lanzmann. No, because before the war she picked potatoes and now she sells eggs.

He shows us their callousness, but also their compassion. A leathery old railway worker bursts into tears as he recalls a Jewish mother and child being shot. "Shot her through the heart. Shot the mother. This gentleman [explains the interpreter] has lived here a long time; he can't forget it." A mother and child, the central image of Polish Catholicism: Mary and Jesus. (A *Jewish* mother and child.) These "primitive" Poles are so much more human than the "civilized" Germans who would not dream of laughing on camera about the death camps—*man weiss, das tut man ja nicht.*

In the end, Lanzmann himself obviously developed, almost despite himself, a kind of affection for "simple" Poles like the little train driver, Pan Gawkowski, who actually drove the transports into Treblinka; an affection no one could conceivably develop for "civilized" Germans, like the unspeakable Herr Stier, former head of Reich Railways Department 33, who merely organized those "special trains" from afar and still insists he "knew nothing" about the nature of destinations "like that camp—what was its name? It was in the Oppeln district. . . . I've got it: Auschwitz!"

In these ways, the Polish part of *Shoah* is not only profound and moving, but also fair and true. However, its truth is not the complete historian's truth which Lanzmann claims for it when he says, "nothing essential in what regards the Poles is left out." Essential aspects of the Polish–Jewish relationship *are* left out, as can be seen by comparing it with the scrupulously fair account in Nechama Tec's book, *When Light Pierced the Darkness*, in which she examines all the published evidence and case histories of more than five hundred Poles who helped Jews. *Shoah* gives no example of a Pole who sheltered Jews, although it does include a powerful interview with a courier from the Polish government-in-exile, Jan Karski, who vainly tried to alert world leaders to what was happening to the Jews in Poland.

Tec concludes that the only sociological generalization that can safely be made about people who helped Jews is that *peasants* were the class least likely to do so. In *Shoah* one sees almost exclusively peasants. On the few occasions where Poles mention the penalties they had to fear if they helped Jews in any way, Lanzmann seems to cast doubt on this by his own questioning and crosscutting. In Tec's book, for comparison, we find a reproduction of a German poster announcing the sentencing to death of fifty-five Poles in one region

(Galicia) in one day in December 1943, eight of them for the crime of *Juden-beherbergung*—sheltering Jews.

At the very end of the film, a survivor of the Warsaw Ghetto uprising describes how he escaped from the ghetto by a tunnel into "Aryan Warsaw," where, to his stupefaction, he found that "life went on as naturally and normally as before. The cafés operated normally, the restaurants, buses, street-cars, and movies were open." "The ghetto," he concludes, "was an isolated island amid normal life." Lanzmann accompanies this statement with a long film sequence showing Warsaw *today*. Now, as Leszek Kolakowski pointed out in the Oxford discussion, Warsaw in 1943 may well have looked "normal" to someone who had just emerged from the indescribable hell of the ghetto, but the Polish capital under Nazi occupation was certainly not "normal" in the way that Warsaw *today* is "normal." It was a city living in terror.

This fact Lanzmann does not mention. But he also does not mention the merry-go-round just outside the ghetto wall, in "Aryan Warsaw," the merry-go-round that went on playing even as the ghetto burned, the sound of gunfire from the last desperate fight inside the ghetto mingling with the fairground music, while "wind from the burning houses/lifted the girls' frocks"—as Czeslaw Milosz describes it in his great poem "Campo di Fiori." He also does not mention what some people in "Aryan Warsaw" were saying—as Kazimierz Brandys memorably recalls in his *Warsaw Diary*: "The nice woman who weighed my meat in the grocery store said that Hitler had disinfected Poland of Jews (the Warsaw Ghetto was still in flames at that time)." He also does not mention the criminal Poles who blackmailed Jews (the *szmalcownicy*) or the role of the prewar Polish police (the so-called *Granatowa Policja*) in helping to round up Jews. Are these not also "essentials"?

The real point is that (*pace* Lanzmann) *Shoah* does not make a historical argument about the Poles and the Holocaust in the way that it clearly does make a historical argument about the extermination process. As we have seen, Lanzmann's own statements, outside the film, about the connection between Polish wartime anti-Semitism and the working of the death camps on Polish soil are quite confused. Inside the film there is no coherent statement—no historian's argument—about this connection. On this point too there is no key professional witness, such as Hilberg is for the main subject. (Partly, perhaps, because there *is* no Hilberg for Polish–Jewish relations during the Second World War.) This is not at all to put in question Lanzmann's achievement; only to define it. Just as it stands—vivid, personal, raw, and partial—the film within the film about the Polish role should be compulsory viewing in Poland. One would like to think that its very rawness and partiality could provoke Polish intellectuals and, above all, Polish historians into beginning a serious scholarly examination of the entire subject—so that, for the next film, there might be a Polish Hilberg to argue with.

With the Jaruzelski government permitting and apparently even encouraging Polish–Jewish studies in Poland (a political fact to be welcomed, whatever the mixture of motives behind it), and—equally important—with the support of the Pope, the external conditions for such an intellectual and moral effort would seem to be more favorable (or at least less unfavorable) than at any other time since 1945. But alas, one can equally well imagine it producing an opposite effect: yet another sterile, bitter clash of intellectual nationalisms—the (Polish) nationalism of the victim against . . . the (Jewish) nationalism of the victim.

Shoah is so obviously a larger film than *Heimat*—more complex, difficult, profound, and important—that one wonders if, after all, there is much point in reviewing them side by side. But on reflection, I think a real point emerges precisely from the very difference in quality between them. Why is Reitz's film about German memory so much "easier," lighter, more superficial than Lanzmann's film about Jewish and Polish memory? Not because Reitz is a lesser director, but because *the German memory of this period is itself "easier."* I do not, of course, mean the memory of those historically sensitive and morally anguished Germans who have shaped the Federal Republic's *public* attitude to the Nazi past, and who currently have a fine spokesman in the Federal President, Richard von Weizsäcker. I mean the popular and private memory of most ordinary West Germans which is Reitz's subject—the memory, as it were, of Herr Kohl at home. And in comparing the two films we discover the last monstrous injustice: it is the victims, not the executioners who suffer most in remembering. It is the victims who break down, while the executioners bask in the happy memories of *Heimat*.

Both films together remind us: Memory is treacherous. Memory is amoral. Memory is also forgetting. There are things that memory cannot look in the face. If German, Jewish, and Polish survivors try to remember exactly the same event, they simply cannot remember it the same—almost physically cannot, as a paralyzed man cannot lift a pen. And both films together also say: Beware the tyranny of the director. For both *Shoah* and *Heimat* are ultimately shaped, and bent, by the partiality of the directors' own attitudes and biographies. Reitz's America, Lanzmann's Poland—these too are the products, the inevitably distorted products, of one man's memory.

The one conclusion to which they both lead me is this: Thank God for historians! Only the professional historians, with their tested methods of research, their explicit principles of selection and use of evidence, only they can give us the weapons with which we may begin to look the thing in the face. Only the historians give us the standards by which we can judge and "place" *Heimat* or *Shoah*. Not that any one historian is necessarily more impartial than any one film director. But (at least in a free society) the terms of the historians' trade make them responsible and open to mutual attack, like politicians in a democracy, whereas the film director is always, by the very nature of his medium, a great dictator. So the historians are our protectors. They protect us against forgetting—that is a truism. But they also protect us against memory.[6]

Notes

1. The section on Reitz's *Heimat* has been omitted.–Ed.

2. *This Way for the Gas, Ladies and Gentlemen* (New York: Viking, 1967; Penguin, 1976).

3. Raul Hilberg, *The Destruction of the European Jews*, Revised and Definitive Edition (New York: Holmes and Meier, 1985; originally published 1961).

4. An example of the latter is Artur Sandauer, "'*Shoah*' a sprawa polska," in *Polityka* (August 3, 1985).

5. In fairness it must be said that many younger Catholic intellectuals are already keen to address these problems: see, for example, the April 1983 special issue of the Catholic monthly *Więź*. *Tygodnik Powszechny* itself has apparently been described by the Polish government spokesman, Jerzy Urban, himself Jewish, as "idolatrously philosemitic." In the November 10, 1985, edition of *Tygodnik Powszechny*, which reached me just as this article was going to press, Mr. Turowicz devotes a long leading article to "*Shoah* in Polish Eyes." He there repeats the basic lines of defense that he presented in Oxford, but he does also write that there was widespread anti-Semitism in Poland *between* the wars, that this had partly religious roots, and that it was a "social sin" for which the "reckoning of conscience" has not yet fully been made in Poland.

6. Direct quotations in this review are from the text of *Shoah* published by Pantheon (New York, 1986). Some small caveats must be noted about this edition and the publisher's bold description of it as "the complete text" and "an oral history of the Holocaust." In fact, as Lanzmann points out in his short introduction, many of the English words we have here are in fact the English translation of the French *subtitles* based on the (often hurried) simultaneous interpretation into French from Polish, Hebrew, or Yiddish, languages Lanzmann "did not understand." As Lanzmann observes, "the subtitling . . . has determined the way in which this book reads: the subtitles reflect very closely the spoken words, but they never express the entirety of what is said." What is "unessential" in the film becomes "essential" in the book.

Unfortunately, at least in the Polish passages, small mistakes that the interpreter understandably made in her haste, or that crept into the subtitles, have also been reproduced in the book. For example, on page 33 the train driver apparently gives the distance from Treblinka station to the ramp as four miles, but I am fairly certain he actually said "eight" in Polish, and surely he would reckon in kilometers anyway. On page 99 "Myndjewyce" is an orthographical impossibility as a Polish place-name. On page 174 Karski's pseudonym must be "Witold," not "Vitold," as printed, and it should be "Plac," not "Platz," Muranowski.

These points might seem too trivial to mention, were it not for Lanzmann's own magnificent obsession with accuracy in detail. It does seem a pity that after Lanzmann has spent a decade in scrupulous research, it has not been thought worth getting competent language readers to spend a few days checking the English text against the Polish, Yiddish, and Hebrew actually spoken on film. Moreover, the final published text does not contain the rider I found in the uncorrected proof to the effect that "a small number" of Lanzmann's questions "have been eliminated in the English-language edition to allow for a clearer flow of the narrative." Yet in at least one place, on page 88, it seems to me that this has in fact been done, and a tiny but not unimportant nuance lost.

Finally, one should note that much of the film's power comes precisely from the *clash* of languages—the appalling bureaucratic euphemisms of the executioners' German, for example, put against the survivors' plain English or Polish peasant crudities—and this is inevitably lost in translation. Still, it is probably better to have an incomplete and one-dimensional text than to have none at all.

Shoah

From the Jewish Question to the Polish Question

JEAN-CHARLES SZUREK

Translated by Stuart Liebman

More than forty years after the war, twenty years after the last massive exodus of Jews from Poland in 1968, the "Jewish question"—or, rather, that of "Jewish–Polish relations"—long buried beneath the complex strata of Polish communism, seems finally to have entered an era of analysis and stock-taking.

Until now, many opposed approaches to this problem have coexisted. There may be legitimate reasons for the very formulation of a "Jewish question," at least for the postwar period. However, if one admits, in principle, that such a question exists, then the most common kinds of responses should be briefly listed. Analyzing them here is not my principal purpose, and the way I portray the setting will inevitably suffer from the simplifications inherent in any schematization.

From the Jewish side, the most widely held opinion, above all for the evaluation of the postwar and Occupation periods, portrays Poland in terms of an exclusive, ontological nationalism incapable of encompassing the political projects of national minorities. This thesis is supported in all the more or less important works.[1]

The Polish point of view often insists on the difficulties Poland encountered in its national and economic construction and derives from this the presence of divergent interests and an inevitable clash of nationalisms.[2] When it treats the Occupation, Polish historiography habitually takes into account the specific horrors of the war as it was conducted in Poland as well as the praiseworthy aid offered by the Poles to the Jews.[3]

Aside from these "common-sense" arguments, which cannot be critiqued in a succinct presentation, a multitude of other versions exist, often linked with different actors. Certain Jewish ex-Communists, for example, speak about how their struggle for socialism collided with Stalinism and nationalism, without seeing that they themselves created the basis for a politics that would eliminate them as Jews, as well as others under other rubrics. On the other hand, the nationalistic Communists held views that were widespread in certain circles in Warsaw and, as paradoxical heirs of the prewar national democrats, their accession to power was rooted in ethnic *parti pris*. The Church and related institutions certainly had one, if not many, positions. The institutionalized opposition will certainly give rise to different stances.

In an effort to get away from these simplifications and inaugurate a dialogue both frank and friendly, more and more frequent international gatherings between Jews and Poles have taken place. That is why a colloquium gathering the most prestigious names of the university and literary worlds from Israel (Professors E. Mendelsohn, I. Gutman, C. Schmeruk), the United States (C. Miłosz, L. Dobroszycki), Great Britain (L. Kołakowski), France (M. Borwicz), and Poland (Professors Bartoszewski, Kloczowski, Gierowski) was held at Oxford in September 1984, launching a dispassionate and scientific exchange between the two sides.[4] Each phase of the millennial history of Jewish–Polish relations was analyzed, and it was obvious that the period of German occupation raised the most lively controversies. Note as well that in Poland certain signs of interest in Judaism, notably among the Catholic intelligentsia, have been perceptible for several years. That is how a "Committee for the Monitoring of Jewish Cultural Monuments" was born on November 2, 1981, in Cracow with the explicit goal of "bringing Jewish culture closer to Polish society," and the Catholic journals *Znak* and *Więź* (the "tolerated" opposition) published in 1983 and 1988 two voluminous dossiers dedicated to Polish Judaism.[5] Might one associate this movement with the government figures who authorized the release of the film *Austeria* (inspired by the novel of J. Stryjkowski, which almost exclusively portrays a Hasidic community) and the publication of the *Diary of Adam Czerniakow* (President of the Jewish Council [*Judenrat*] in the Warsaw Ghetto), or the republication of Emmanuel Ringelblum's diary? Malevolent lips insinuate that these measures helped to unblock certain Western loans. . . .

Claude Lanzmann's film *Shoah* erupted into this context, immediately probing the most delicate areas of the Jewish–Polish problematic and simultaneously revealing different points of view within Poland, respectively, of those in power, the Catholic milieus, and the opposition.

Shoah: An Innovative Anthropology

Is Poland at the center of the film? Not really. *Shoah* is, *more than anything,* a work exclusively devoted to the extermination of the Jews, and if Poland had to be mentioned, it is because the extermination took place there.

But the film has caused certain surprising ideas about Poland to emerge. In the French press, for example, numerous newspapers have begun to modify recent representations by replacing Wałęsa's Poland with that of the peasants from 1942, as if one historical truth necessarily had to erase another.[6] This sort of position conveys a misunderstanding of Polish society as much as a certain French complex that has appeared about *Solidarnosc.*[7] By starting off on the wrong foot as it focused its argument on the assistance provided to the Jews by the Poles, the official Polish press (see below), has tried to redirect the film toward issues that are not those it deems essential.

What Is Shoah?

The visual anthropological investigation of this film—nine hours long—leads via an original epistemo-methodological approach to historical understandings incommunicable in written form.

If it is true, as François Furet writes in his introduction to a collective work dedicated to the Jewish genocide, that "Nazism still poses, forty years after its collapse, a sort of enigma to historical reason"[8]—a remark made notably as a result of the rejection flaunted by a few individuals of the very instruments of death—Lanzmann's film, using sociological techniques, provides, by the quality of the witnesses it assembles, a new and meticulous awareness of the way the "genocide worked." Who could have imagined that Jewish survivors, German perpetrators, and Polish witnesses—all those who *most closely* lived the *moments* and inhabited the *places* of the extermination—were still alive and, by offering a mass of unprecedented details, could bring to life once more the process of death for us? The film, therefore, more than anything else, valorizes oral testimony, or rather returns it to legitimacy in historical research. Who, except those either intellectually dishonest or politically manipulative, would dare to deny the convincing depositions of the German Suchomel about a "day at Treblinka," confirmed at every point in a parallel account by Abraham Bomba, the Jewish barber of the camp? The cardinal value of the investigation, conducted on the basis of different and opposing sources, lies in the way it has captured the memory of the drama for all time by its actors themselves.

But this process of remembering would never have attained the heuristic value I have described had the author not adopted a methodological language, a methodology of method, that restored the evocative power of the past to different actors. Lanzmann's approach ought to make specialists in social science who work on historical issues reflect on what they are doing. It is through restaging, through a sort of theatrical technique, that the past is reintroduced into the present, brutally conferring on it a dramatic intensity and a precision that cannot be achieved by other means. Using this procedure, the author obtains striking results. Having discovered that the village of Treblinka still exists and that one of the locomotive drivers still lived there, he rented a locomotive and reconstructed with him, hour by hour, his itinerary of forty years ago, allowing us to catch a glimpse of and imagine what is unrepresentable. It is the same with the barber Abraham Bomba, one of the rare living witnesses of the final stage of the extermination process (he cut the hair of those in the gas chamber). A very controlled character, Abraham Bomba reveals the most essential details of his story only when, in a moment demanding for all concerned, and because Bomba was already retired, Lanzmann places him in a situation once again as a barber in a salon. Finally, by means of a coolly executed ruse and feigning a false intimacy, Lanzmann also succeeds in eliciting details from Franz Suchomel, a former SS man at Treblinka, that only his relaxed manner could elicit (for example, the Treblinka song hummed by Suchomel: "It is unique. Not one Jew knows that").

The exceptional character of *Shoah* as an anthropo-sociological document should therefore be attributed not solely to the exceptional historical importance of the actors subjected by Lanzmann to methodical interrogation, but also to their collective exercise of memory produced within a "reconstructed" psychodramatic framework. Like a sociologist, but without any preconceived theory, this author has had to *familiarize himself* with the assumptions behind such research, and these also required him to *see*: "one must know and see; one must see and know," Lanzmann says.[9] This global approach, it seems to me, has enlarged the horizons of historical sociology. As Simone de Beauvoir has written, the fact that there is magic in the film may be attributed to the author's talent.

This is the central thrust of *Shoah*. Every interpretation that does not take into account the twofold primacy of its exclusive focus on the mechanism of extermination, and its original approach that allows it to do so successfully, misses what is essential.

Nevertheless, a Polish problematic figures equally in the film. A notable part of it was shot in Poland because witnesses could be found among its populace, peasants for the most part, who lived near the extermination sites. It is therefore also a film about the Polish peasants of today, their values, their manner of speaking, their environment, and, naturally, their relation to the Jews. It was these "rural" sequences of the film that so horrified the French press, which saw in them the traditional expression of a Christian anti-Semitism still alive today, and therefore which must have been even more terrifying in earlier times.

The reality is more complex. In fact, there is a communication problem, in every sense of the term, between Lanzmann and the Polish peasants. If his powers of investigation and perception are wholly present when he speaks directly to his interlocutors in either English or German, the mediating translation [from the Polish] does not always—even at important moments—allow him to grasp the nuances of the peasants' discourse. In a more general sense, there is no communication between the director's universe and the peasants' because, however important it is to comprehend their relationship with the Jews, when their words are translated, they have been emasculated as they crossed the language barrier. Finally, constantly present in their encounter is the prejudice that associates Christian anti-Semitism with the peasants' indifference to—that is, their stake in—the genocide.

Despite this problem, Lanzmann's sometimes provocative questioning of the Polish populace—where nothing can be assumed and where every testimony must be confirmed—always leads to astounding insights into the German Occupation. The peasants' discourse highlights the fact that in these regions there were three *distinct* "actors": the Jews, the Polish peasants, and the Germans. For those in Poland today who would rather forget, the peasants recall this distinction by their use of the pejorative word *Żydek*, or "little Jew" (a word that never had as negative a connotation as the word *youpin* [Yid] does in French) that they *all* employ. One also notes that the houses they occupy today formerly belonged to their Jewish fellow citizens, a "detail" frequently overlooked by the younger Polish generations today. The suspicion that these peasants helped to hunt down Jews because of their greed is present in the author's questions, even if he offers no proof. Finally, if one haphazardly throws together the idea advanced at Chelmno that the Jews paid for the death of Christ with their own, and the famously ambiguous gesture of cutting the throat present in the film, not to mention the statement [by a Polish peasant] that "all Poland was in the hands of the Jews," one has an image of contemporary rural Poland that is like that of the earlier period—archaic, backward, and at the very least indifferent to the misfortunes of others.

Polish Reactions

The Official Press

The first Polish response to *Shoah* was indignation. The official press vigorously denounced "the anti-Polish accents" of the film, raising objections to the presence of François Mitterrand at the first screening of the film. The Polish government went so far as to submit an official note of protest to the Ministry of Foreign Affairs, since they believed the French authorities had paid for the film. The cry screamed in Warsaw was such that one might have thought that this was an exclusively Polish problem.

The articles in the French press, supplied with certain statements made by Lanzmann himself, contributed to the situation. For example, in the previously cited article in *Libération* (April 25, 1985), Lanzmann went beyond his film and said, "The extermination camps were concentrated in Poland . . . also because the Germans knew that they could count on the approving silence of the population. . . . The rare Jews who escaped were most often denounced to the authorities. Because of the gold taken away from the victims, the villages surrounding the camps are today richer than the average."

After having criticized the film without screening it, the Polish authorities decided after several months to show incriminating sequences on television, even as they authorized screenings in their entirety in a cinema in Warsaw, in Cracow, and then in Lublin.

At first the official press supported the government's indignation: "They used to say in Nazi propaganda films that the Poles and Jews killed the Germans; now it is the Poles and Germans who killed the Jews. In one case as much as in the other, it's a matter of smearing the Poles."[10] The government spokesman Jerzy Urban, using the pseudonym Jan Rem, set the tone in the weekly *Polityka*: "In this film one does not see contemporary houses and clothes, the cars and television antennas, the people of our civilization. One only sees houses in bad condition, horse-drawn carts, primitive faces."[11] And he treacherously concludes that the Church has always fomented anti-Semitism but that it today permits itself "to accuse the communists of anti-Semitism, when the Left has always fought against it."[12]

It has been clearly established that this staging was above all a *political manipulation* designed to discredit the Church. While the entire official press, with minor variations, echoed these positions, certain newspapers attempted to distance themselves from it. Thus *Sztandar Młodych*, the newspaper of youth organizations, produced an original report on Treblinka, finding other railway workers and making use of witnesses in a way that did not invalidate Lanzmann's film.

The weekly *Polityka*, which played an important role in supporting the ideology of the Jaruzelski clique, took this stage-managing abroad, for example to the Federal Republic of Germany, in the form of an article by one of its best journalists, Daniel Passent, in the newspaper *Die Zeit* (March 3, 1986). The article, entitled "Die Fahne beschmutzt" (The Sullied Flag), presented itself as liberal-minded and distanced from Polish reality. For Passent, by wounding Poland, Claude Lanzmann succeeded for the first time since December 13, 1981, in uniting "the socialist government, the Catholic Church, and almost the entire nation against him." On what German chord did he play in this instance?

There were limits, however, to the manipulation. As if they sensed that a simple political operation was not able to encompass the gravity of the question, and concerned perhaps—at least some were—not to portray themselves exclusively as political schemers, the journalists of *Polityka* "dived" into the dossier. Thus the writer Artur Sandauer, while situating *Shoah* in the West's global politics against Poland, called on his countrymen to come to grips with themselves: "even though they handed over the Jews and enriched themselves with their property, one cannot make a comprehensive reckoning."[13] Another journalist, A. Grzegorczyk, in a series entitled "The Jewish Question,"[14] after having pointed to the respective responsibilities [of each side] for the "ethnic conflict," openly repented for the past. "We who lived as adults under the Occupation, we are all responsible. . . . Neither the schools nor the Church prepared us to resolve social, ethnic, or civilizational conflicts. . . . Our current system of education has the same failings. . . . If we had been educated differently before the war, perhaps the peasants of Treblinka or Grabów would at least have prayed in their church with their priest for the murdered or tortured Jews, even though this would have been brought to an end by the Gestapo and the death of the priest."[15] Raising a general outcry, this author proposed (on television as well as in his article) a mutual pardoning, following the example Polish bishops made in 1965 toward their counterparts in Germany. The article was unfocused, was argumentative, and angered the opposing parties. For the ex-leader of K.O.R., J. Kuron, it was shocking that one would "pardon in any way the Jews dying on Polish soil."[16] And for Z. Kaluzynski, another journalist at Polityka, the Poles were not responsible for the facts of the war and they had nothing to be pardoned for except "when they demand that we pardon, the principal candidate for this task is the Church, and she does not do so."[17]

Though crude, this maneuver—orchestrated by at least fifty articles that appeared in different newspapers and periodicals—quite underhandedly claimed that the Church, which was actually a target [of the campaign], had been wounded in order to stir up national pride.

The Catholic Press and the Oppositional Press

The oppositional press was still entirely clandestine during the discussion of Shoah, which was not the case for a notable segment of the Catholic press. If I group these two kinds of press under the same rubric, it is because I have chosen the tolerated Catholic opposition around the weekly Tygodnik Powszechny, for which many opponents of the regime wrote. As for the oppositional press, it had proliferated so much and had attained such a high degree of pluralism that it would be illusory to pretend to present an exhaustive picture of what it contained. Nevertheless, the opinions conveyed here illustrate the diversity of the "clandestine Republic" established since December 13, 1981.

To tell the truth, the oppositional press was generally situated on the same terrain as the official press, in that they accepted the Polish aspects of Shoah as the centerpiece of the debate. The "universal dimension of the film," "beyond all particularisms," was mentioned in only one of the articles signed by Tadeusz Szyma devoted to Shoah in Tygodnik Powszechny.

> Shoah is too rich a work . . . to be able to reduce the complexity of its expressivity to an accusation against the Polish nation of having

participated in the extermination of the Jews. The Poles are, in fact, involuntary victims of the location of the Holocaust on our territory. The accusatory aspect of the film is of an entirely different dimension, much larger and more profound: it calls out to the conscience of every spectator and leaves no one in peace.[18]

All the other statements denounced the operation led by the government against *Shoah*—this way of "accumulating capital through the death of the Jews," declared J. Kuron[19]—and opened the Jewish–Polish dossier. Regarding accusations by the film and by *Polityka*, the Catholic response came from the pen of J. Turowicz, who had been editor-in-chief of *Tygodnik Powszechny* since 1945. In his article "*Shoah* in the Eyes of Poles," he reproaches Lanzmann for his "tendentious" questions, his choice of witnesses, and when all is said and done, an anti-Polish attitude—"according to a simplified and unfair stereotype of Jewish–Polish relations that the West generally employs." The essential argument, however, consists in detaching the Poles' Christian anti-Semitism (thereby admitting it as a religious and national factor) from the extermination process. "Polish anti-Semitism, whose importance we do not minimize and which we do not justify, has nothing to do with the extermination of the Jews. The racist anti-Semitism of the Third Reich . . . was very simply a peasant anti-Semitism." If the situation of a Jew and a Pole under the Occupation was not comparable, says Turowicz, one can at least affirm that the cruelty of the war created a community of fate "that liberated" attitudes of solidarity on the Polish side. If 100,000 to 120,000 Jews were able to be saved in Poland, it was thanks to Polish society, he continues. "The assessment of the Polish reaction to the extermination of the Jews is better than in many countries occupied by Hitler. Lanzmann is French and he knows very well that 75,000 French Jews were handed over to the Germans by the French police and the Vichy government."

About Polish and Catholic anti-Semitism, J. Turowicz is, however, not gentle: "It is a fact that anti-Semitic attitudes were, before the war, very widespread in Catholic society in Poland, including the clergy. . . . The Polish Catholic witnesses of the terrible fate of the Jewish nation on our lands, seeing how far anti-Semitism can lead, should have been led to a profound examination of their consciences with respect to the sin of anti-Semitism. I emphasize this strongly, as much as with sorrow that, in my opinion, this examination of conscience has still not been pursued as far as it should have been."[20]

If the majority of clandestine publications expressing views about *Shoah* certainly conveyed their emotions regarding the Jewish question,[21] certain ones, such as the review *K.O.S.* (The Committee for Social Resistance), close to the ex-K.O.R., nevertheless adopted clearly political positions: "The truth is such that the immense majority of Poles did nothing to save the Jews. We must scrutinize our own past to establish the truth, however bitter it may be, in a public debate. Our silence is the best argument of those who regard us as co-responsible for the extermination. We should not wait for this debate to be undertaken by the regime's press. Let us do it ourselves."[22]

The defense of a Catholicism whose tone recalls the prewar nationalist Right came from a newspaper in Lodz.[23] According to the author, Christian doctrine does not generate anti-Semitism. "It fights against it, proclaiming the equality of all men before God." As for doctrinal anti-Semitism, he continues, one can find the source in the Old Testament, where it appears as camouflage for political stratagems. A strange attack against Lanzmann follows: "The organizers of political conflicts use different means to mask their real goals. Anti-Semitism is not the only device. Class-ism (read: "class struggle"–J.C.S.), invented by Karl Marx, is perhaps the most frequently used, at least in the twentieth century. By the way, the author of *Shoah*, the destroyer of anti-Semitism, is at the same time a communist, a partisan and an adept of class-ism."[24] Defined in these terms, Lanzmann is then enjoined to indicate if he accepts or justifies the Cambodian genocide and, if his response is positive, whether he would affirm that all genocides are not equal. Strange conclusions, and a strange logic in which another kind of manipulation is deployed.

The case of Jews and Poles is regularly subject to manipulation in the absence of a real debate. Lanzmann, a communist? Such a statement, according to the *New York Times*, should make one smile given the Shakespearean dimensions of his work. But in affirming that "the screening of *Shoah* should smash to pieces an artificial consensus that was established between the government in Warsaw, the Church and Solidarity" (*Le Matin*, August 9, 1985), Lanzmann laid himself open to critical interpretations that have needlessly harmed the impact of his film. For these statements undeniably pleased the regime's ideologues (see above the citations of the slightly abridged statement by D. Passent) who advanced the notion that "the entire nation" had been offended by *Shoah*. Conversely, the opposition denounced what they believed to be a political operation. In effect, what consensus is being referred to? That of all the Poles "on the backs of the Jews"? Actually not: even before the *Shoah* affair, Solidarity and the opposition were on the way to new reflections about the Jewish question. Note, too, that Jews are to be found in *both* camps and took on visibly active roles. In the final analysis, neither during the first legal period of Solidarity nor today was the Jewish problem the union's first concern. Did Lanzmann wish to provoke the Church by making such statements? In the eyes of some, he seems to have played the government's game, since his attacks on the Jaruzelski clique seemed much milder.

Two other journals, among the most important in the clandestine press, must be mentioned. Although on the margins of the *Shoah* debate, they must be considered when one thinks about Judaism in Poland. The tenth issue of the journal *Arka* was almost entirely devoted to nationalism and anti-Semitism. In this journal from Cracow to which researchers and university figures regularly contribute under pseudonyms, the article by Marek Leski grabs one's attention.

It constitutes a response to the English historian Norman Davies, who is considered one of the best historians of Poland and who in his work *God's Playground: A History of Poland* (1981) devoted a chapter to the Jews in Poland. Leski believes that in the historiographical debate opposing Poles and Jews, Davies sides too much with the Poles.

After having demonstrated the anti-Jewish attitude of the prewar Catholic hierarchy in an astounding pastoral letter by Cardinal Hlond in 1936, Leski notes the Poles' indifference to and their pillaging of their "fellow citizens" during the period of the Occupation. He derives from this "a false interpretation of the situation of Jews during the war. Contemporary opinion, confirmed by manuals, books, the media . . . believes that the Jews were in a somewhat worse situation than the Poles and that they constituted the principal, but not exclusive, object of extermination of the nations of Eastern Europe. Alas, to a certain extent this point of view is equally advanced by N. Davies." The author continues, "The fact of being Polish was not automatically equivalent to a death sentence, but that was the case for Jews." The other problem, if one "wants to reconstruct the Republic" is to know what status to give to Poland's anti-Semitic past, above all for the generations that are in no way responsible. In fact, says Leski, "in the case of Polish–Jewish relations, as for that of every minority," it was a matter of Polish society's ability to assimilate pluralistic mechanisms. A reflection about the Jewish question is therefore necessary for the opposition, both in and for itself, and because it also poses the problem of pluralism, which would permit it to adhere to "cultures of liberty."[25]

One may certainly doubt that the categories of Western multiculturalism explicitly championed by the author are applicable to Polish society, which, thanks to the communists' nationalist stance, has become almost monoethnic. But the fact of posing the problematic in these terms, that is, *also* by *proceeding* from the Jewish question, certainly allows an approach to "the Polish question" that is drawn toward a modern, cosmopolitan form of reasoning and smashes the at times narrow framework—however inevitable for Poland—of its geographic and cultural frontiers.

The interview that Marek Edelman, former leader of the Warsaw Ghetto insurrection and honorary member of Solidarity, accorded to two young editors proceeds from the same desire for clarification.[26] If for the first time in public Edelman levels specific accusations against his Polish fellow citizens during the Occupation, these young researchers' implacable will to probe this *knowledge* as far as possible and then to publish their results was perhaps even more astonishing. Here are some significant excerpts.

Question: Do you think that the assistance from the Aryan side was sufficient?

Answer: First, there was none; second, they did not want to.

Question: You did not respond to my question.

Answer: How so?

Question: If someone cannot do something, then nothing can be changed, but if someone does not want to, then the situation is different.

Answer: It is difficult to respond, it is hard to assess. To what extent there was ill will, or how much theft occurred, cannot be measured either during the period or today. Those were different times. Every boy wanted to have a revolver. They had perhaps given five hundred, and fifty reached them. Whether they stole them or something else happened with them cannot be known. Facts are facts.

Question: For the Jews in the ghetto, how did the world outside the walls exist? Was there hope?

Answer: It was the enemy. You cannot understand. For an enemy isn't only the one who kills you, but also the one who is indifferent. Today Bujak [the leader of clandestine Solidarity at the time] has no place to stay. How many people offered him one? Ten out of a hundred. If death threatened him, each of these hundred would be his enemy. You do not understand this?

Question: I understand. . . .

Answer: That's it. An enemy in the sense that when you leave here and go outside and say who you are, they will kill you.

Question: Where they would not help you.

Answer: It's the same thing. Not to help and to kill are the same thing. Today one can still walk around the streets. But during the period, if they did not help you they would kill you on the next street corner. They are incomparable situations. Today Bujak could cross ten streets and no one would accost him.

Question: Can you say what happened to you after the revolt?

Answer: That's not important. All these details are of no importance.

Question: We want to say that, for us, they are.

Answer: Afterward, I was on the Aryan side. It's written somewhere in the books. You are annoying me.

Question: Afterwards you fought with the *Armia Ludowa* [the communist resistance]?

Answer: Afterward, I was in the Warsaw Rising. I was in the A.L. Because the A.K. [*Armia Krajowa*, the Home Army, the non-communist resistance] wanted to shoot me. They said that I had a false *Kennkarte* [identity card], that I was a Jewish spy. I succeeded in slipping a note to the outside and Kamiński [Head of the *Bulletin of Information*] got me out of there. I did not go around with those who wanted to kill me to amuse myself . . . that's why I was with the A.L. . . . You see that it's not as simple as it seems.

Conclusion

For a long time the "Jewish problem" in Poland was a problem only for Jews. It is now in the process of becoming a Polish problem, notably through the impetus of the younger generation that created *Solidarność*. *Shoah* accelerated this emerging awareness: that Polish historiography, oriented around its own sense of martyrdom, had never admitted the genuine differences [in the situation of Jews and Poles] during the Occupation, nor the extent of the Polish population's "indifference." More than that: these same Jews, formerly treated as a foreign minority, could—once they were dead—become part of the "six million Polish victims" of the war.[27] This kind of manipulative accounting can more than anything else be attributed to the particular government in power during the period of the Gomułka-Moczar clique. Recall that it has been almost conclusively established that all the manifestations of anti-Semitism since the war had political origins—that is, that they were provocations—and not religiously based.[28] But it must also be said, as M. Borwicz has observed, that the three known pogroms in Poland during 1945–1946 had accusations of a ritual crime as pretexts. Did not Cardinal Wysziński say at the time that "the question of the use of blood by the Jews had not been clearly resolved"?[29] Some expect that the Church, because of its moral stature, will express its views on the "Jewish question." But the institution does not usually respond to direct pressure. It is a response more difficult to make, since its power and legitimacy are rooted in its relationship to the nation, which has never had to deal with the "Jewish problem." This "Jewish problem" has even been considered an obstacle to national "fulfillment," something that holds even more true during the postwar period when the Church collectively reproached "the Jews" for their participation in the government, even when it was only communist activists who were involved. Heir to a cultural tradition that, above all during the darkest hours of Polish history, had always preserved national identity, the Church did not know how to easily abandon the ideological attributes that constituted the foundation of its power. The "conservatism" that one ascribes to it in the West is very real in many respects, and this stance has allowed it to occupy the strategic position of the Church-Nation, a historical bulwark of Catholicism facing the East. Doesn't every [historical] revision threaten the essential elements of its position? Certainly, it could always be claimed that the Church had protested (however timidly) the official anti-Semitism in 1968 or that, through the voices of the intellectuals in *Tygodnik Powszechny*, the Church had tried to *explain Shoah* in Poland.[30]

In pointing his camera at the church and toward the peasants of today, Lanzmann is behind the curve described by historians such as David Engel, who recently uncovered the history of the two reports made by Karski [to the Polish government in exile]. After six months of war, the Polish government, still in exile in Angers, received a report from one of its first couriers, Jan Karski, a key witness in *Shoah*. Karski's description of the effects of the German occupation on Jewish–Polish relations terrified those responsible in the Polish government. Karski notably wrote:

> the Jews will be grateful to the Poles if they understand them, if they admit that the two peoples are unfairly harried by the same enemy. This understanding does not exist among the large masses of Polish society. Their attitude with respect to the Jews is, in general, unbending, often pitiless. They profit to a large extent from the advantages that the new situation affords them. They often utilize these advantages—and even abuse them. This brings them closer to the Germans to a certain extent.[31] "The solution to the Jewish question" by the Germans—I state this with all the requisite responsibility—is a dangerous instrument in the hands of the Germans to "morally pacify" large segments of the population. . . . The nation hates its mortal enemy—but this question [of the attitude toward the Jews–J.C.S.] draws only a fine line between the spaces that the Germans and a large part of the Polish population inhabit.[32]

Fearing a hostile reaction from the Allies, the Polish government asked that Karski rewrite a version of the report favorable to Polish–Jewish rapprochement. Thus there exists two versions of this report composed in February and March 1940 (in which Karski relates the situation from October through December 1939). Other reports also reflect such ideas, but no more comprehensive investigation of Jewish–Polish relations under the German Occupation yet exists.

In the dialogue between deaf people that the two historiographies still conduct today, the Jewish communists have also assumed their share of responsibility. When they were in power, they contributed to downplaying the Jewish genocide by associating it with Polish martyrology. This fraternization in death was not accidental: Weren't passages about the Poles from Ringelblum's diary, published in 1952, cut by B. Mark, the director of the Jewish Historical Institute in Warsaw? Having come back with the Red Army, they tried, by using communism as a means, not only to build a communist society—which was their primary goal—but also to subscribe to a new way of assimilating. This was a situation that justified different kinds of manipulation, beginning with the manipulation of history.

Make way, therefore, for the historians, the "historiographers." Historical research has already begun to integrate arguments shared by both sides.[33] Concerning the Occupation, new works have avoided apologetics in order to approach this period in a more factual way.[34] The famous work by Ringelblum about Jewish–Polish relations under the Occupation, of which only the English version by Yad Vashem was known, has finally been published in Poland.[35] Jewish–Polish exchanges have continued to intensify in the last few years: Oxford has been succeeded by other meetings, notably a memorable congress held in Jerusalem in 1988.[36]

Shoah perhaps influenced Jan Błonski, the first Polish author to pose bluntly the question of Polish co-responsibility for the genocide, inciting a polemic in 1987–1988 as furious and passionate as the one following the broadcast of Claude Lanzmann's film *Shoah*.[37] If the latter certainly contributed to an important process of *remembering* the Jews of Poland—a process sometimes verging on a suspect modishness—it must be noted that a similar approach characterizes two works that are the most interesting created since that time in Warsaw: the film *Witnesses*, produced in 1987 by Marcel Łozinski and devoted to the [1946] pogrom in Kielce, and the book *Umschlagplatz* (1988) by Jaroslaw Rymkiewicz, in which the author follows the traces of the Warsaw Ghetto step by step. Both seem inspired by *Shoah*.

The taboo surrounding the question of Jewish–Polish relations during the Occupation finally seems to have been lifted. To clarify the presence or absence of Jews on their soil has been imposed as an essential task for the generation of young Poles. A praiseworthy task, one very much the order of the day, but one that is probably impossible to complete, since, despite the refinements brought by all sorts of new ways of thinking rationally [about the topic], can one really explain the inexplicable, the collapse of an entire society into nothingness? That is why *Shoah*, even in the eyes of its director, "remains in many respects opaque and mysterious."[38]

Epilogue

The preceding lines were written at the end of the 1980s. Today, more than fifteen years later, what does the landscape of Jewish–Polish relations look like?

In a short text written in 1978 after he returned from his first trip to Poland and published in *Au sujet de "Shoah*,"[39] Claude Lanzmann asked a question that arises with equal urgency today, namely, that of *Poland as a witness-country to genocide*. Perhaps the violent and accusatory character of his comments about "the Poles" has obscured this dimension—about which one hardly spoke at the time—and thereby shifted the debate to one between detractors and supporters of Lanzmann's vehemence.[40] In the light of the debates begun in 2000, this premonitory comment about Poland during the Second World War has become a key question. It was indeed premonitory; for example, the work of Raul Hilberg, *Perpetrators, Victims, Bystanders*,[41] deals with it relatively little. It is a question at once banal and nevertheless one difficult to respond to. One can attribute to the notion of a witness-country a double meaning: in the proper sense of the word, that of a witness (the Polish peasants around Treblinka or those who lived close to the ghettos), and in the sense of a collective entity in front of which the crime was committed. This collective entity, Poland, was largely conscious of its place: in the aftermath of the war everyone was so convinced of Poland's exceptional status as witness to the murder of the Jews that the first

Bulletin of the Central Commission of the Investigation of German Crimes in Poland was devoted principally to their extermination. (One reads in it primarily about Auschwitz, Treblinka, and Chelmno.[42])

By creating anti-fascist propaganda, Stalinism erased Poland's special identity as the witness-country. Such propaganda did the opposite: out of the very real martyrdom of the Polish population it created the Heroic Country. This dimension is very perceptible in the museological layout of the Auschwitz Museum, born in 1947 as "the museum of the martyrdom of Poland and other nations," thereby effacing the fact that Auschwitz was principally the cemetery for European Jews.[43] The anti-fascism of the postwar period presents numerous characteristics that, when it spoke of "six million Polish victims," smoothed over the most disturbing rough edges of the Jewish–Polish debate: questions about the Polish populace with respect to the isolation of the Jews, about how Jewish property was taken over by the Poles, and about anti-Semitism during the Occupation and afterward.

With the fall of the communist regime, the debates that began in the 1980s developed. Democracy contributed a great deal to fill the empty pages of the communist period, and not only about Jewish–Polish relations. Between 2000 and 2002 Poland went through its most intense public discussion of the Jewish past, as a result of the appearance of the book *Neighbors*[44] by the American academic Jan Gross, a professor at Princeton University who had emigrated from Poland in 1969. The work, which appeared in its Polish version in 2000, described the massacre of the Jews by their Polish neighbors on July 10, 1941, in the village of Jedwabne in the eastern part of Poland. It thereby suddenly posed the question of Polish co-responsibility for the Holocaust. The preceding public debates (about *Shoah*, about Błoński's text,[45] and about the Carmelite monastery at Auschwitz) had already underscored the Polish population's indifference, the hostility of the Church or of certain groups with respect to the Jews, when Gross's work arrived to demonstrate that within Polish society there existed murderous collective anti-Semitic impulses largely motivated by the lure of gain. This view brought together the pogrom at Jedwabne with the one at Kielce that took place on July 4, 1946. The image of a heroic, resisting Poland, a country "that never had either a Quisling or a Pétain" but was instead a veritable "clandestine state" with an army of many hundreds of thousands of combatants (the *Armia Krajowa*, or A.K.) was seriously sullied. The myth of a victimized, innocent nation provoked a national debate in which politicians, historians, churchmen, and journalists took part through the publication of dozens of books and hundreds of articles. On July 10, 2001, sixty years to the day after the massacre at Jedwabne, an official commemoration ceremony took place in the presence of numerous personalities from Poland and around the world, including Aleksander Kwasniewski, the President of the Polish Republic, who made a speech repenting for what had happened. The Polish Church made a similar move by celebrating a mass in Warsaw on May 28, 2001.

The emotions provoked by the discovery of the massacre at Jedwabne were such that the Institute of National Memory, a state institution charged with collecting the traces of crimes committed against the Polish nation by both the Nazi occupiers and the communist regime, "prodded" dozens of historians and other specialists to seek out other sources relating to this massacre in order to verify if Gross's assertions, based as they were on the testimony of a surviving Jew, were legitimate. At the end of 2002 the Institute of National Memory published two large volumes (more than 1,500 pages in all) that not only confirmed the facts established by Gross but also indicated that similar massacres had taken place in other locales in the eastern regions of Poland.[46] This gesture, to a large extent conveyed through the media, constituted a recognition by the state of this criminal chapter in the Jewish–Polish past; it was a gesture similar to the one made by France about the Vichy government and by Germany's official stance toward its Nazi past.

Before coming to a head in the public debate of 2000–2002, the Jewish past had been largely the province of historians and witnesses. Now a new generation of specialists in the social sciences has addressed the issue directly. Emblematic in this regard is the work of Barbara Engelking, who in 2003 created and directed the Polish Center for Holocaust Research in the Institute of Philosophy and Sociology at the Polish Academy of Sciences. Her books are haunted by Jewish memories of the Occupation[47] and the Warsaw Ghetto. In a work of more than 800 pages, she and Jacek Leociak, another scholar whom the ghetto will not leave in peace, seek to reconstitute the daily cultural, economic, and spiritual life of the ghetto.[48] These historians, sociologists, and literary figures, relieved of the prudent habitus of communist historiography, also address taboo subjects, at times much to the displeasure of "patriotic" historians.

Thus, on the basis of German documents in Polish archives, Jan Grabowski was able to raise the question of the *szmalcowniks*, the blackmailers who waited for Jews at the exit points from the ghettos,[49] while Barbara Engelking focused on denunciations, notably the denunciation of Jews in the Aryan zone.[50] I also wish to mention the work of Dariusz Libionka on the Catholic church and his work in press about the Polish state and the extermination of the Jews.[51] In this list so difficult to make exhaustive, one cannot also fail to mention the historical works on Jewish–Polish relations under the Soviet Occupation, in particular the publications of Andrzej Zbikowski[52] and Krzysztof Jasiewicz.[53]

Since 1989 dozens of texts written during the Occupation have emerged from dusty cartons at the Jewish Historical Institute in Warsaw and have been published along with memoirs of surviving Jews written sometime later; some are even translations from Hebrew. These are very different sorts of texts. I will mention the first and second volumes of the Ringelblum Archives,[54] the account by Janina Bauman, *Winter in the Morning* published in its Polish version in 1989, or that of Icchak Cukierman, deputy commander of the Jewish Fighting Organization in the Warsaw Ghetto.[55] Also the memoirs of Children of the Holocaust, an association of survivors who in the twilight of their lives feel the same way as the hidden children in France or the Holocaust Children in the United States: they wish to come together to express and transmit the trauma experienced by their generation.[56] The list is endless, and it is enough to go to the library of the Historical Institute in Warsaw to take note of the new bibliographical and documentary riches circulating in Poland.

What emerges from this brief examination of the itinerary Polish memory has followed over the parched territory of Judaism in Poland ("these frozen remnants of a great history," as the French historian Pierre Vidal-Naquet has called them) is that today there are many who vigorously scrutinize this history. Henceforth the debates will tend to move in two directions.

1. Concerning historical research on Jewish–Polish relations: The Jedwabne affair demonstrated to what extent the mechanisms of occultation (amnesia or distorting the truth, whichever you prefer) have been established and how witnesses, in particular Jewish witnesses (as victims), have played a central role. Curiously, the historian Jan Gross comes close to Lanzmann's stance concerning the irreplaceable role played by the act of witnessing. Research will thus forever look closely into the position of the witness in his or her *historical* reality even as it will necessarily expand to encompass the kilometers of still unexplored archival documents.

2. Concerning the witness *today*: There is the witness in the witness-country during the Occupation and there is the witness who lives with the trauma of witnessing and having done so for decades. The moral dimension of this question has been taken up by certain contemporary intellectuals. The anthropologist Joanna Tokarska-Bakir, for example, has vigorously criticized Polish historians in the past for having, conveniently, insufficiently grappled with the Holocaust in their research.[57] Or the writer Maria Janion, who asks of her fellow citizens, "The Poles were witnesses to an inexpressible crime but, as studies have shown, they did not *see* very much, for the most part, while it was taking place, and then later they did not concern themselves very much with the disappearance of ten percent of prewar Poland. How can one restore the memory of what took place here, right next to us?"[58]

In twenty years, the Jewish past has emerged from its state of neglect, thanks to the work of new generations of Poles and Jews. Even so, its recovery is far from complete. New questions are being raised continually.

Notes

1. See Celia S. Heller, *On the Edge of Destruction* (New York: Columbia University Press, 1977); Pawel Korzec, *Juifs en Pologne* (Paris: FNSP, 1980); Lucy Dawidowicz, *The Holocaust and the Historians* (Boston: Harvard University Press, 1981).

2. See J. Majchrowski, "Problem Zydowkiw programach glownych obozow polity-cznych" [The Jewish Problem in the Major Political Groups] in *Znak* (February–March 1983), pp. 383–394; J. Tomaszewski, "Polish Jewry in the 19th and 20th century," in *Polish Jewry: History and Culture* (Warsaw: Interpress, 1982).

3. See W. Bartoszewski, "Stosunki polsko-zydowskie w okupowanej Polsce" [Polish–Jewish Relations in Occupied Poland], in *Puls*, no. 24 (1984): 47–58.

4. Important meetings had taken place in Poland and Israel in 1984 and 1985 between historians from the two countries. The colloquium had given birth to an Institute for Polish–Jewish studies at Oxford, and an international journal *Polin* (Polish and Hebrew) whose first issue appeared in 1986.

5. *Znak* (February–March 1983); *Więź* (April 1983)

6. See the article "La Pologne au banc des accusés" [Poland the Dock], in *Libération* (April 25, 1985). In it, one reads notably, "The pitiless revelation of popular anti-Semitism in Poland just crashed headlong into the gesture of recent years. The dark legend of the Holocaust, woven from the monstrous reality reinvigorated by Lanzmann, just tele-scoped the golden legend of Solidarity, woven from this historical truth. Myth against myth, forgotten reality against the reality of today."

7. France is the only Western country in which a mobilized mass consensus stretch-ing from the extreme Left to the extreme Right—except the communists, naturally—has been produced around *Solidarnosc*. The CFDT and FO have seen in Solidarity a sister on the other side of the Iron Curtain; the extreme Left perceives in it a progressive form of self-management, and the Right takes comfort in its fight against communism. It is as if a historic collective remorse, not fully conscious, that is tied to France's abandonment of Poland [in 1939], was expressed in it: one must not let Danzig die a second time.

8. Colloquium of the École des Hautes Études en Sciences Sociales, *L'Allemagne nazie et le génocide juif* (Paris: Gallimard–Le Seuil, 1985), 7.

9. *Cahiers du Cinéma*, no. 374 (1985). See the translation in this volume.

10. *Rzeczywistosc*, no. 22 (1985).

11. *Polityka*, no. 31 (1985): 9.

12. Ibid.

13. Ibid.

14. *Polityka*, no. 46 (1985): 6.

15. Ibid.

16. *Tygodnik Mazowsze* (July 11, 1985).

17. *Polityka*, no. 49 (1985).

18. T. Szyma, "Shoah raz jeszce" [*Shoah*, one more time] in *Tygodnik Powszechny* (March 2, 1986).

19. *La Nouvelle Alternative* (April 1986).

20. J. Turowicz, "Shoah w oczach polskich" [*Shoah* in the eyes of Poles] in *Tygodnik Powszechny* (November 10, 1985).

21. See *Wyzwolenie*, no. 3 (1985): "Shoah: komu bije dzwon" [*Shoah*: For whom the bell tolls], *Ogniwo* (January 1986).

22. D. Warszawski, "Historia I falszerze" [History and its falsifiers], in *KOS* (May 19, 1985). This text was written before the film was screened in Poland.

23. A. Stanislawski, "Shoah a moze romantyzm rewolucyjny" [*Shoah*, or maybe rev-olutionary romanticism] in *Kurs*, no. 18 (1986).

24. Ibid.

25. M. Leski, "Grossa do 'Zydow polskich' Normana Daviesa" [Contribution to "Polish Jews" by Norman Davies] in *Arka*, no. 10 (1985): 102–108.

26. Discussion with Marek Edelman in *Biuletyn Dolnoslaski* (November–December 1985): 14–20.

27. See Pierre Vidal-Naquet, "Des musées et des hommes," in *Les Juifs, la Mémoire et le Présent* (Paris: Maspero, 1981), pp. 110–125.

28. See M. Borwicz, "1944–1947" in *Puls*, no. 24:61.

29. Ibid., 63.

30. These attitudes nevertheless remain weak compared with the silent certainty that it has expressed during the Carmel affair: visibly, at the highest levels of the ecclesiastical hierarchy, one neither wants to know what Auschwitz symbolizes for the Jews nor wants to concede in the face of mounting pressure the institution's sovereignty. The Church comforts itself in this way using the traditional perception of Polish anti-Semitism.

31. David Engel, "An Early Account of Polish Jewry under Nazi and Soviet Occupation Presented to the Polish Government-in-Exile, February 1940," in *Jewish Social Studies* 45, no. 1 (1983): 6.

32. Ibid., 10.

33. In his book *Social and Political History of the Jews in Poland, 1919–1939* (The Hague: Mouton, 1983), J. Marcus breaks with the usual "Jewish" historiography about this period.

34. See Jan T. Gross, *Polish Society under German Occupation* (Princeton, N.J.: Princeton University Press, 1979).

35. Emmanuel Ringelblum, *Stosunki polso-zydowkie podczas drugiej wojny swiatowej* (Warsaw, 1988) An English edition is available: Joseph Kermish and Shmuel Krakowski, eds., *Polish–Jewish Relations During the Second World War* (Evanston, Ill.: Northwestern University Press, 1992–Tr.).

36. See J. C. Szurek, "Sur rapports judéo-polonais: le point sur le recherche." In *Pardès*, no. 8 (1988): 36–39.

37. Jan Błonski, "Les pauvres Polonais regardent le ghetto," *Les Temps Modernes*, no. 516 (1989): 69–84.

38. *Cahiers du Cinéma*, no. 374:18.

39. Claude Lanzmann, "J'ai enquêté en Pologne," in Michel Deguy, ed., *Au sujet de "Shoah"* (Paris: Belin, 1990), pp. 211–217.

40. "The extermination of the Jews in Poland," he wrote, "was no secret: it was accomplished in full view and with the knowledge of everyone; it was an absolutely public matter. In the very heart of their cities, the Poles had first watched the installation of ghettos, they lived with the ghettos and for them it was the most natural, the least scandalous thing in the world. It was self-evident, something apart."

41. HarperCollins, 1992.

42. *Biuletyn Glownej Komisji Badania Zbrodni Hitlerowskich* 1 (1946).

43. Jean-Charles Szurek, "Le camp-musée d'Auschwitz," in the collective work *A l'Est, la mémoire retrouvée* (Paris: La Découverte, 1990), pp. 535–555.

44. Princeton, N.J.: Princeton University Press, 2001.

45. Jan Błonski, "The Poor Poles Look at the Ghetto," in *Tygodnik Powszechny* (January 11, 1987) and translated in *Polin*, no. 2 (1987).

46. Pawel Machcewicz and Krzystof Persak, eds., *Wokól Jedwabnego* [About Jedwabne] (Warsaw: Instytut Pamieci Narodowej, 2002).

47. Her first book, *Na lace popiolow, ocaleni z Holocaustu* [Under a heap of ashes, the survivors of the Holocaust], 1993, consisted of interviews with Polish Jews, including the pianist Władysław Szpilman, who remained in Poland.

48. Barbara Engelking and Jacek Leociak, *Getto warszawskie, przewodnik po nieistniejacym miescie* [The Warsaw Ghetto, guide to a city that no longer exists] (Warsaw: IfiS PAN, 2001), will appear in an English translation published by Yale University Press. One must also mention the literary analysis made by Jacek Leociak of texts (memoirs, newspapers, letters, etc.) written by Jewish survivors. *Tekst wobec Zagłady* [Texts confront the extermination] (Warsaw: FNP, 1997).

49. *Szantazowanie Żydow w Warszawie 1939–1943* [Blackmailing Jews in Warsaw 1939–1943] (Warsaw: IfiS PAN, 2004).

50. *Donosy do wladz niemieckich w Warszawie i okolicach* [Denunciations to German authorities in Warsaw and its environs] (Warsaw: IfiS PAN, 2003).

51. The works of Libionka include "The Catholic Church in Poland and the Holocaust 1939–1945," in C. Ritter, S. D. Smith, and I. Steinfeld, *The Holocaust and the Christian World* (London: Continuum Publishing, 2000); "Die Kirche in Polen und der Mord an den Juden im Licht der polnischen Publizistik und Historiographie nach 1945," in *Zeitschrift für Ostmitteleruopa-Forschung* 2 (2002), as well as his article that appeared in the first volume of *Wokol Jedwabniego*, "Duchowieństwo diecezji łomżyńskiej wobec antysemityzmu i zagłady żydów" [The clergy of the Lonza diocese confronting anti-Semitism and the extermination of the Jews].

52. Andrzej Zbikowski, "Pogromy i mordy ludności Żydowskiej w Łomżynskiem i na Białostocczyźnie latem 1941 roku w świetle relacji ocalałych Żydów i dokumentów sąowych" [Pogroms and murders of the Jewish population in the Lomza and Bialystok region in the light of accounts by Jewish survivors and judicial documents], in *Wokól Jedwabnego*, vol. 1, pp. 159–272. Also see his account, written with S. Szymanska, "Relacje ocalałych Żydów o losach ludności żydowskiej w Łomżyskiem i na Białostocczyźnie po 22 czerwca 1941 r" [Accounts by Jewish survivors about the fates of the Jewish population in the Lomza and Bialystok region after June 22, 1941], in *Wokól Jedwabnego*, vol. 2, pp. 179–374. Zbikowski has also edited a volume consisting of Jewish accounts devoted to the Shoah in the eastern region of Poland. *Archiwum ringelbluma, Relacje z Kresow* [Ringelblum Archives, Accounts from inside Poland], vol. 3 (Warsaw: Żydowski Instytut Historyczny, 2000).

53. *Pierwsi po diable, Elity sowieckie w okupowanej Polsce 1939–1941* [First after the devil; the Soviet elite in occupied Poland 1939–1941] (Warsaw: Rytm, 2001); and *Tygiel narodow, stosunki spoleczne i narodowosciowe w latach 1939–1953* [The melting pot of nations, social and ethnic relations in the former Eastern Borderlands of the Second Polish Republic, 1939–1953].

54. Vol. 1, *Listy o Zagladzie* [Letters about the Holocaust], ed. Ruta Sakowska (Warsaw: Żydowski Instytut Historyczny, 1997); and Volume II, *Dzieci—tajne nauczanie w getcie warszawskim* [The Children—Clandestine education in the Warsaw Ghetto], ed. Ruta Sakowska (Żydowski Instytut Historyczny, 2000).

55. Icchak Cukierman, *Nadmiar pamieci. Siedem owych lat. Wspomnienia 1939–1946* [An excess of memory. Those seven years. Memoirs 1939–1946] (Warsaw, 2000).

56. Wiktoria Śliwowska, ed., *Dzieci Holokaustu mowia* [Children of the Holocaust speak] (Warsaw: Association of the Children of the Holocaust in Poland, 1993).

57. Joanna Tokarska-Bakir, *Rzeczy mgliste* [Vague things] (Warsaw: Pogranicze Sejny, 2004).

58. Maria Janion, *Do Europy, tak ale z naszymi umarlymi* [Toward Europe, yes, but with our dead] (Warsaw: Sic, 2000).

Shoah

JAN KARSKI

Translated by Marek Nowak

At the beginning of last October I was invited to a private showing of the movie *Shoah*. The movie lasted more than nine hours. It has no actors and limits itself to interviews with victims of the Holocaust, its perpetrators, and eyewitnesses. Also shown are original German documents and reports. There are many contemporary photographs taken by Germans. Some of the interviews (with Germans) are filmed surreptitiously. In addition, the camps, crematoria, neighboring villages, and towns are shown as they appeared during the war and as they appear today. The movie's director is a Frenchman, Claude Lanzmann. He filmed in Poland, Czechoslovakia, Greece, Holland, Israel, Switzerland, Rumania, as well as the United States. He devoted a dozen years of his life to this work.

Shoah is unquestionably the greatest movie about the tragedy of the Jews that has appeared after the war. No one has managed to present the destruction of the Jews during World War II in such depth, with such blood-curdling brutality and lack of mercy for the viewer. At the same time, the interweaving of people, events, nature, and time is full of bewitching poetry. The soothing beauty of the trees grown over the places of slaughter, the country sod and fields covering the terrible secrets of the concentration camps; a procession exiting a church that served as a roundup point for deported Jews; the moving prayers in a synagogue of those who lived; and an old woman who survived and sings a Jewish song "from those times"—all this shocks us with dread or captivates by its beauty and innocence.

The Pope learned of *Shoah* and praised the movie and the conscientious-ness of its creator to an audience of French and Belgian war veterans. He also underscored the moral significance of the movie.

The subject of the movie is the torment and eventual extermination of de-fenseless Jews, including three million Poles practicing Judaism or of Jewish ancestry. Nothing more.

The movie does not portray the background of the war years, the con-quering of almost all of Europe by the Third Reich and the horrors carried out against the subjugated peoples. It does not speak about the suffering of the non-Jewish population of Poland, Russia, Greece, or Serbia. The rigorous construction of the movie does not allow for this.

Lanzmann's intention is to demonstrate to the viewer that the Jewish Holocaust was *unique* and *incomparable*. He is unquestionably right. To equate the extermination of the Jews with the suffering and losses of the non-Jewish population in Europe is, after all, although emotionally understandable, sim-ply spiritless. All nations had victims to a greater or lesser extent. But all Jews were victims. This Lanzmann does not forget for even a moment. Every viewer of this movie will understand this.

The uncomprosising restriction of the topic creates an impression that the Jews were abandoned by all mankind, that all mankind was insensitive to their fate. This is, however, untrue and disheartening, particularly for postwar and future generations of Jews. The Jews were abandoned by governments, by those who had the physical or spiritual power. They were not abandoned by mankind. After all, several hundred thousand Jews were saved in Europe. In Poland, tens of thousands survived. The penalty for harboring a Jew in Poland was death. In Western Europe, although the punishment was not as extreme, helping or harboring Jews exposed people to great dangers. Nevertheless mil-lions of peasants, workers, intellectuals, priests, nuns, endangering themselves and their relatives, provided aid to Jews in each country of Europe. How many of them perished? God only knows.

In Poland, a clandestine organization was created whose sole objective was to provide haven and aid to hiding Jews. Its head, Wladyslaw Bartoszewski, lives in Warsaw. Marek Edelman, one of the heroic leaders of the Warsaw Ghetto up-rising, lives in Lodz. Jan Nowak and Jerzy Lerski, two couriers of the Polish un-derground government, now living in the United States, carried messages and pleas from Jewish leaders in Poland to Western governments. Stefan Korbonski, the last chief of the Polish Underground State, and like Lerski awarded the "Righteous Among Nations," now lives in Washington D.C. Others live in other countries. They should at least be mentioned. The viewer should be made to re-alize, particularly the young generation or Jews and non-Jews, that such people existed, and this, it seems to me, is necessary regardless of the movie's construction. For some, it is necessary so that they do not lose faith in mankind and their place within mankind. For others, so that they understand what a lack of tolerance, racism, anti-Semitism, and hatred lead to and what love of neighbor can do. This is more important than any construction, particularly since this is such a great movie and will have such an impact on the viewer.

The movie's technique rests on interviews, some planned and some happenstance with individuals not known to Lanzmann. In this second group are the remarks of several Poles, residents of towns and villages adjacent to the camps. Some attest to sympathy and kindness of heart, most appal. For instance, some small-town peasant women, when asked what they think of the destruction of the Jews, answer that they live better than before. They took over homes left by the Jews which were grander than those in which they had lived before the war. A peasant woman from another group although not asked lectures Lanzmann that the fate that the Jews met was God's punishment for handing over the Savior to his death. She makes these statements just before a religious procession, with the church in the background. Apparently the teachings of the Second Vatican Council describing such views as sinful have not yet reached this parish.

An educated urban resident, without being asked, leaves a crowd to run before the movie camera in order to inform Lanzmann about what a friend had supposedly witnessed. A rabbi was explaining to the Jews gathered for deportation that their fate was due to the actions of their ancestors who, delivering Christ to His death, cried out that His blood would fall on them and their offspring. He did not say that the Jews and the rabbi were surrounded by SS men with revolvers and nightsticks in their hands.

An old farmer questioned if he is sorry that there are no more Jews answers with a smile, yes and no. When he was young he liked Jewish women. Now he is old and indifferent. Another Polish peasant from around Treblinka describes the transport of Jews from Western Europe, which he claims to have observed. At the last train stop prior to Treblinka, Pullman wagons pulled up. They were occupied by fat Jews and Jewish women with fancy hairdos. Inside the wagons were tables with bottles of perfumes. He saw suitcases with gold. At the stop one of the Jews left the wagon and walked up to the station buffet in order to buy something. The doors to the wagons were not guarded. He was allowed to get out—just before Treblinka. Dear God, how absurd!

The movie includes an interview with me. The circumstances surrounding the interview speak to the methods employed by Lanzmann and the planned parameters of *Shoah*. He visited me in 1977, providing me with materials attesting to his qualifications, previous movies, etc. He talked about his project. He had heard and read about me. He indicated it was my duty to agree to an interview. Initially I refused. I had walked away from my war experiences, and for more than thirty years I did not return to those memories. Finally I agreed, requesting written questions. I wanted to prepare. He refused. He did not want prepared answers. He would ask about those matters that belong in the movie. I would say what I remembered. I agreed, with the *caveat* that he not try to enmesh me in political discussions, assessments, or conclusions. He answered that that was not his intention.

The interview took place at my house in 1978. He filmed for two days, in total about eight hours. Lanzmann is a difficult person. Passionate. Completely devoted to his work. Uncompromising in his questioning and establishing of facts. A few times I broke down emotionally. Once he broke down. My wife, unable to bear it, left the house.

From the eight hours of filming, I saw about forty minutes of the interview on the screen, focusing on the suffering of the Jews in the Warsaw Ghetto as well as the desperate demands for assistance from the underground Jewish leaders aimed at the Western governments. I understood. The time devoted to my account and the construction of *Shoah* forced Lanzmann to omit the section of the interview that I felt was the most important part of my Jewish mission at the end of 1942.

As a courier of the Polish Underground State, who had personally witnessed the beginnings of the Final Solution, I was sent to alarm the Western World to the fate of European Jews under the Nazi occupation. The suffering of the Jews was described by others in the movie for more than seven hours. Many did it better than I. For me the central point of my interview was that, having made my way to the West, I described the tragedy and demands of the Jews to four members of the British War Cabinet, including Anthony Eden, President Roosevelt and three key members of the American government, the Apostolic Delegate in Washington, Jewish leaders in the United States, distinguished writers and political commentators such as Walter Lippmann, and George Sokolsky. None of these matters could be discussed by anyone else. After all, this would have demonstrated how the Allied governments, which alone were capable of providing assistance to the Jews, left the Jews to their own fate.

Including this material in the movie as well as general information about those who attempted to help the Jews would have presented the Holocaust in a historically more accurate perspective. The leaders of nations, powerful governments, either decided about the extermination or took part in the extermination or acted indifferently toward the extermination. People, ordinary people, millions of people sympathized with the Jews or provided assistance.

The movie *Shoah*, through its greatness of talent, determination, and fierce truth, but also by its self-limitation, has created the need for the next movie, equally great, equally truthful—a movie that will present a second reality of the Holocaust. Governments, social organizations, churches, people of talent and heart should find a form of cooperative effort in order to produce such a movie. Not in order to contradict that which *Shoah* shows but to complement it. After all, the Jewish Holocaust of the Second Warld War weighs on all of mankind like a curse.

Gendered Translations

Claude Lanzmann's *Shoah*

MARIANNE HIRSCH AND LEO SPITZER

> The film is made around my own obsessions.
>
> CLAUDE LANZMANN

> To live, as well as to die, a Jewish father needs to know that the future of his child is secure.
>
> SIGMUND FREUD

> The cinema is the medium that reaches far into Hades.
>
> KLAUS THEWELEIT

There are moments when gender does not impose itself as a category of analysis, when, displaced by other factors, it virtually disappears from view. The Holocaust is such a moment. While the experience and the representation of war generally places women and men in radically different positions—on the home- and battlefronts, for example—the Holocaust, at least for its victims, seems to be a moment that recognizes no gender differences, that erases gender as a category. Nazism would exterminate all Jews, regardless of gender, class, nationality, professional, or economic status. If Jews are vermin, as Hitler insisted, then distinctions among Jews normally applied in social interaction become irrelevant. In the elaborate "final solution" devised by the Nazis during the early 1940s, all victims were to be stripped of difference and rendered powerless. The Holocaust's victims were thus to be "degendered" by the process of persecution and extermination.

The opening scene of Claude Lanzmann's *Shoah* offers an ironic illustration of the representational divergences between gender and war, on the one hand, and gender and the Holocaust, on the other.[1] His nine-and-a-half-hour cinematic oral history of the Holocaust begins as Simon Srebnik, one of the only two survivors of the massive exterminations in the Polish village of Chelmno, reenacts for the camera an event that villagers there still remember to this day: his regular trip down the Narew River on a flat-bottomed rowboat when, at the prodding of his German guards, he sang Polish folk tunes and Prussian military songs in his beautiful tenor voice. In the mouth of the chained thirteen-year-old Jewish orphan boy, condemned to death, the immense gulf between the experience of Jewish males and the rewards and disappointments of a wartime masculinity emerges with pointed irony: "A mug of red wine, a slice of roast," he was taught to sing. "That's what the girls give their soldiers. When the soldiers march through town, the girls open their windows and their doors." [*Wenn die Soldaten durch die Stadt marschieren, öffnen die Mädchen die Fenster und die Türen.*][2]

Shoah's numerous witnesses attest to the erasure of gender as one of the prime instruments of Nazi dehumanization and extermination. As victims are shaved, stripped down or clad in identical striped uniforms, starved, screamed at, beaten, tormented; as they are reduced by the thousands to bodies (referred to not as "victims" or "corpses" but as *Figuren* and *Schmattes*, "figures," "junk"); as they are piled into wagons "like sardines," laid out in mass graves "like herrings"; as their flesh starts crumbling in the ground where they are dumped; as they fall out of gas vans and gas chambers "like potatoes"; as they become a "load," converted, within the space of hours, to ashes—gender, with humanity, gets erased. "It was not a world," the Polish courier Jan Karski insists as he describes his Dantesque journey through the Warsaw Ghetto at the end of *Shoah*: "There was not humanity. . . . Women with their babies, publicly feeding their babies, but they have no . . . no breast, just flat."[3]

Ironically, however, Claude Lanzmann's film itself *also* eradicates gender differences among the victims of the Final Solution. The almost obsessive thrust of *Shoah*, its primary goal, is to bring to memory and to record the workings of the Nazi machinery of destruction: to detail its operations and lethal course, from the ghettos, to the transports and trains, to the selection in the extermination camps, to mass murder in gas vans and gas chambers, to the burial and burning of the corpses. The film penetrates both the procedural and psychic dimension of this process: the secrecy that enabled it to work, the collusions of a world that stood by in silence and allowed it to happen. Lanzmann's primary witnesses for this daunting project—the persons he interviews and interrogates most fully—are those who were closest to the process and mechanics of extermination: some survivors of the special work details in the concentration camps, several German perpetrators, and a few Polish bystanders who lived and worked near the killing centers. Among the Jewish victims, those who were at once closest to the death machine and able to survive and to testify were, by selection, men. But *Shoah* elicits other voices as well. Lanzmann interviews some survivors of the Warsaw Ghetto, a few Auschwitz survivors from the Jewish community of Corfu, two survivors of the Riga Ghetto who appear in the film to sing a ghetto song, a woman who spent the war in hiding in Berlin, and one survivor of the Theresienstadt "family camp" in Auschwitz. Even among *these* witnesses, however, Lanzmann clearly privileges testimonies from men. Although the experience of Jewish women is described in the Jewish men's and the bystanders' and perpetrators' narratives— although they are talked about and represented by others—they themselves appear onscreen on only a few, and extremely brief, occasions. And even when they do appear, even when their voices are heard, the camera seems to shy away from sustained focus on their faces.

Some of the women who are seen and heard in the course of the film act as mediaries and interpreters from Polish, Hebrew, and Yiddish, carrying the words and the information of the narrators to Lanzmann, and the questions from Lanzmann, who is the only interviewer and the central presence in the film. A number of the Polish "bystander" witnesses are women as well, as is one of the German informants. The perpetrators and bystanders, inasmuch as they figure in the film, represent a range of groups, male and female, farmers and tradespeople. But among the Jewish survivors who speak and give their accounts in the film, the erasure of differences and, particularly, the almost complete absence of women are striking.

For Lanzmann, gender is irrelevant to the death machinery on which he focuses with such relentless energy: a machinery that is designed to render subject into object, to degender, to declass, to dehumanize, to exterminate, and to destroy the traces. But in focusing so resolutely on this machinery and privileging the detailed explanation of its operation, Lanzmann backgrounds the *subjective* experience of its victims—the differentiated individual realm within which, according to other survivor accounts, significant gender differences do emerge.[4] Indeed, women's Holocaust narratives and testimonies do bring out a gendered experience. In accounts collected by Lewin, Laska, Heinemann, Katz, and Ringelheim, women speak of the effects of their ceasing to menstruate and the fear that their fertility would never return; they speak of rape, sexual humiliation, sexual exchange, abuse, enforced abortions, and the necessity of killing their own and other women's babies. They speak of the extermination selection process in which maternity becomes a much greater liability than paternity. They describe most extensively and analyze most deeply the relationships and friendships that developed between women in concentration camps. Controversially, some even argue that women showed greater survival skills than men.[5]

These, however, are not the accounts we hear in *Shoah*.

This, then, is the paradox: From the perspective of the oppressor, the victim lacks subjectivity. If the critic scrutinizes that perspective, concentrating the focus on the machine that fulfills and implements the oppressor's deepest desires, he or she also risks an erasure of the subjective. Such an unintentional and ironic replication does emerge in *Shoah* when we interrogate gender as an inherent element of subjectivity. And yet, despite the erasure of women that Lanzmann performs through the focus and method of his inquiry, traces of gender difference are nonetheless reinscribed in his film. Perhaps unwittingly, they sustain and motivate much of the energy driving this monumental oral history. Our endeavor to uncover these traces, to excavate the feminine buried within the layered structure of the film's testimonies—a feminine cast in the archetypal roles of a Persephone, a Eurydice, a Medusa—is what we are calling "gendered translation."

Jewish women survivors do not themselves advance the central inquiry of *Shoah;* they do not further Lanzmann's investigation into the machine of death with information detailing its operations. They exist in the film for different purposes. The first Jewish woman to be seen onscreen is Hannah Zaïdel, the daughter of Motke Zaïdel, survivor of Vilna. She appears as a curious listener obsessed with her father's story: "I never stopped questioning him," she states in the film, "until I got at the scraps of truth he couldn't tell me. It came out haltingly. I had to tear the details out of him, and finally, when Mr. Lanzmann came, I heard the whole story for the second time."[6] But in the film it is Claude Lanzmann, not Hannah Zaïdel, who asks the questions. Indeed, as one of the few screened female listeners who is not also an interpreter, Hannah sits in a faded background, smoking a cigarette, when her father and his fellow survivors describe being forced to uncover mass graves and dig up bodies, including those of Zaïdel's mother and sisters, in order to burn them and eradicate their traces. Paula Biren appears next, a survivor of the Lodz ghetto who responds briefly, in the negative, to the only question she is asked ("You never returned to Poland since?"). Unlike most of the male witnesses who speak in the film on repeated occasions, Biren and the other Jewish women disappear after only one brief interview.[7]

While a great deal of energy is spent in the film to bring some of the men back to the scenes of extermination—to have them relive, intensely and relentlessly, the experience *in the present* so as to be able to remember and testify about *the past*—only one woman goes through this process. She is Inge Deutschkron, who returns to her native Berlin from Israel and declares, "This is no longer home." Her brief narrative recalls the day Jews were deported from the city while she herself remained behind in hiding, and relates how throughout the rest of the war she felt "utterly alone" and "terribly guilty" not to have departed on the transports with the rest. Her position—in hiding and removed from the central destiny of her people, a destiny Lanzmann interrogates through the *Sonderkommando* survivors and other men—emblematizes the position of women in the film as a whole. Unlike most of the male witnesses whose faces fill the screen for long periods of time, Inge Deutschkron is little more than a disembodied voice: her narrative is largely presented in voice-over as scenes of Berlin and departing trains occupy the space of the screen; her face and name appear only at the very end of her brief account.[8] And unlike most of the other male witnesses, she never returns in the film.

At a very important moment in *Shoah*, in the midst of Rudolf Vrba's and Filip Müller's narratives of the failed uprisings in Auschwitz, another Jewish female informant appears briefly. Her role in the film is also symptomatic. Ruth Elias initiates the narrative about the Theresienstadt "family camp" brought to Auschwitz by the Nazis for propaganda purposes—about the group that became a focus of resistance activities during the months of its cynical "reprieve," before almost all of its members were sent to the gas chambers. But Elias's story in the film is limited to the Theresienstadt group's transport to Auschwitz only, and to her disbelief at the news that she had arrived at an extermination camp. Details about the group's six-month stay in Auschwitz, about relations between its members, about the possibilities of resistance, about feelings generated by warnings of imminent gassing, about the exterminations themselves: these we receive not from Theresienstadt family camp member Elias, who quickly disappears from the film entirely without ever enlightening us about the means of her own escape from death, but from Rudolf Vrba and Filip Müller, who observed the Theresienstadt group as outsiders. This female witness, whose face, like Inge Deutschkron's, appears on screen only at the very end of her brief voice-over narration, is merely allowed to start the story, which is then taken over by the two men.[9]

Elias's role—to set the scene, provide the atmosphere, the affect, and not the facts or the details—allows us to understand one way in which *Shoah* uses women. We can gain additional insight from the last two Jewish women to be seen in the film, who immediately precede its final sequence recalling the Warsaw Ghetto uprising. Gertrud Schneider and her mother (who remains nameless in the film) come onscreen to sing a ghetto song, *Asoi muss seyn*— "Because that's how it must be."[10] Their broken voices are first heard in the background as we watch an unidentified barren landscape. Several measures into the song, the two women come into view, but only one, the daughter, carries the song. The mother becomes yet another of the film's emblems of gender distinction. She cannot sing the entire song; her voice breaks and she starts crying. But in crying and covering her face in lament, fingernails painted red, she acts out its words. This song is the only untranslated text in the film: its meaning for the non-Yiddish speaking viewer must be translated by the mother's gestures: "The best years, are finished / And gone—never to be recovered. / It's difficult to repair what has been destroyed. / . . . Because that's how it must be / That's how it must be, that's how it must be."[11] Besides expressing passivity and resignation, the film's staging of the *Asoi muss seyn* also demonstrates the double speechlessness of women: Gertrud Schneider sings but does not speak, and her nameless mother, overcome with the emotional weight of memory and the event captured by the camera, gestures but neither sings nor speaks. Such iconic moments, in which meaning is conveyed not through words but through images or music, structure the emotional texture of the film. They provide the background weave to the relentless factual fabric of Lanzmann's inquisitive project. And it is women who are most often relegated to that background.

The roles women act out in the film—hiding, passivity, lament, invisibility—are for the most part supported in the men's narratives about women. The image of the mother and child who jump from a train, resulting in the mother's being shot in the heart (its still-horrified male Polish peasant narrator repeating "in the heart"), serves to underscore emotionally the callousness of the oppressors and the hopelessness of escape. But other moments of female resistance introduce another element: the association of femininity with danger and death. Rudolf Vrba describes how secrecy became the key to the efficiency of the final solution. Panic, he explains, would have been a "hitch in the machinery," and panic was especially feared from women with small children. The film's male narrators recall how women unleashed several frightening scenes of destruction: how, at a transport stop, for instance, one woman threw her empty cup at a guard who refused to give her water, which led him to shoot senselessly and indiscriminately at the entire wagon. In Filip Müller's account, another woman, warned by a friend in the *Sonderkommandos* that she and her group would be gassed, tried to warn everyone but was not believed. In a gesture of anguish and desperation, she scratched her whole face and started to scream. She was tortured and the man who warned her was thrown into the oven alive. The story of her tormented rebellion releases some of the emotional pressure built up in the film in account after account of death and killing. Yet the pathos of Filip Müller's moving narrative is also rendered all the more powerfully poignant by her helplessness, and by the ultimate futility of her action.[12]

The male narratives, moreover, tend to reach a greater emotional power when encounters with women and memories of family and domesticity are evoked. Thus Michael Podchlebnik reports that he had asked to be killed after he unloaded his wife and children from a gas van in Chelmno. And, in what is one of the most frequently discussed scenes in the film, Abraham Bomba describes at length his job as a barber who had to cut the hair of women inside the undressing room of Treblinka's gas chamber: he testifies insistently that he felt nothing in carrying out his task, that in such situations it is impossible to have any feelings at all. But as he begins to tell how a friend of his, also a barber, met his own wife and sister in that room, his narrative breaks down, and he begins to cry and asks to be permitted to stop his account. When he resumes talking, at Lanzmann's insistence, his English turns into phrases mumbled in Yiddish. For Bomba, as for the others, encounters with women threaten whatever precarious emotional distance, whatever control and denial of feelings they had attempted to establish in order to survive.[13] Indeed, the interruption within the powerful scene with Bomba demonstrates that the evocation of these encounters on-screen endangers even the very continuity of the film's narrative flow.

In a film set on making distinctions in details (Were they Poles or Czechs? Were there 40,000 or 400,000? How many glasses of beer? How far? How long? How many minutes did it take? How many hours? How many bodies?), Lanzmann refuses to recognize or acknowledge differences in role or experience among the Jewish victims, irrespective of whether these relate to gender, age, or other social demarcations. *Eine Masse* (one pile)—the phrase uttered by Richard Glazar in his descriptions of the crowd of naked victims waiting to be gassed, and of the piles of belongings that had to be disposed of, like their owners, with speed and efficiency—describes not only the Jews as they were treated by the Nazis, but, ironically, also the Jews as they are represented in the film. For Lanzmann, distinctions among Jewish victims are ultimately either irrelevant or outright disturbing. When, for example, Polish peasants point to different treatment of Jews on the basis of class by describing how some Central European Jews arrived in passenger instead of freight or cattle trains, Lanzmann insists that such class discriminations were not very frequent. He includes a narrative about Jews who tried to trade diamonds for water to show that, of course, it did not matter whether you had diamonds: the guards took the diamonds and did not bring water. And when the German SS *Unterstürm-führer*, Franz Suchomel, describes the experiences of the Treblinka "funnel," Lanzmann seems uncomfortable with the gender distinctions that emerge. The men were gassed first, Suchomel explains, and the women had to wait for extended periods of time in the funnel outside the gas chambers. Describing the fear of death and the physical evacuation it often provoked in the victims, Suchomel connects these reactions to those of his own mother on her deathbed. But when he insists that the men were beaten and the women were not, Lanzmann refuses this distinguishing "humanity" on the part of the guards and presses Suchomel to admit that, probably, the women were beaten as well.[14]

Shoah's equalization of victims, its reluctance to explore differences among them, extends to the realm of morality as well. Many of Lanzmann's informants, for example, actually belonged to that area that Primo Levi identified as the moral "gray zone"—a zone inhabited by Jews who ultimately survived because they participated as Kapos or in the work details of the death machines.[15] Lanzmann does not contemplate the implications of this participation. Nor does he encourage or include stories that would exalt his informants or make them heroic. Thus we never find out how Rudolf Vrba escaped from Auschwitz, merely that he did so. We never hear about Richard Glazar's role in the Treblinka uprising, merely that such an uprising was planned. If important differences emerge among persons whom we get to know within the film, these are due primarily to individual variations in storytelling talent, to differences in insight and analytical skill, to the amount of prodding and manipulation required to jolt memories and elicit recollections.

Lanzmann, in effect, allows differences in testimony to emerge and develop but downplays differences in experience. The story of the victims, as revealed in *Shoah, is one story*. Might Lanzmann fear that any detailed exploration of distinctions would replay and recall the divide-and-conquer tactic by which Nazis persuaded Jewish councils and individuals to help the work of the death machine? Might any focus on real differences unduly echo the *illusion of difference* encouraged by the Nazis that led some Jews to believe that if *they* collaborated, *they* might be saved, that the death of some might save the lives of others?[16] Might distinctions appear trivial within the "giant crime," the unparalleled devastation of the Holocaust?[17] Whatever the explanation, it is clear that Lanzmann's general discomfort and uneasiness concerning discussions of distinctions—his resolute unwillingness to contemplate and explore differences among the victims in *Shoah*—is most vehement when it comes to gender.

Women's presences do more than to punctuate *Shoah* with emotional power and pathos. At the end of the film, Simha Rottem, one of two Warsaw Ghetto survivors interviewed by Lanzmann in Israel, recalls walking through the abandoned ghetto after his emergence from the underground sewers. His lengthy narrative concludes with his evocation of a disembodied, haunting, and dangerous female voice. "I suddenly heard a woman calling from the ruins," he recalls.

> It was darkest night, no lights, you saw nothing. All the houses were in ruins, and I heard only one voice. I thought some evil spell had been cast on me, a woman's voice talking from the rubble. I circled the ruins. I didn't look at my watch, but I must have spent half an hour exploring, trying to find the woman whose voice guided me, but unfortunately I didn't find her. . . . Except for that woman's voice and a man I met as I came out of the sewers, I was alone throughout my tour of the ghetto. I didn't meet a living soul. At one point I recall feeling a kind of peace, of serenity. I said to myself: "I'm the last Jew. I'll wait for morning, and for the Germans."[18]

This image of the "last Jew" spoken by Rottem at the very end of the film echoes the final words of *Shoah*'s first part,[19] uttered by Simon Srebnik:

> But I dreamed too that if I survive, I'll be the only one left in the world, not another soul. Just me. One. Only me left in the world if I get out of here.[20]

The mysterious female voice heard by Simha Rottem (which in Hebrew he describes as emanating from a "fata morgana") and the feelings of abandonment that Rottem shares with Srebnik summarize *Shoah*'s representations of femininity—the danger of women, their helplessness and passivity, their emotional power, and their disembodied haunting presence. But the conclusions Rottem and Srebnik draw from their own sense of desertion allow us to see yet another dimension of femininity in the film: its connection to death without hope of rebirth, to destruction without a parallel generativity. Rottem, like Srebnik, is the "last Jew alive." His failure to locate and to identify the distant female voice—a woman in need of help, or an evil spell luring him toward destruction—echoes the finality of the final solution, a process of extermination designed to erase all trace of Jewish existence, past, present, and future. As *Shoah*'s witnesses make devastatingly clear, in the Holocaust mothers cannot protect or nourish their children, they cannot keep them alive, and they cannot produce more. Within this context of hopelessness, Rottem and Srebnik see themselves each as the last Jew, forever cut off from his future, the terminus of Judaism. And Lanzmann places both their voices at climactic moments in the film—at the very end of each of its two parts—reinforcing, with devastating and conclusive effect, the impact of total death built up during *Shoah*'s nine and a half hours.

It would appear, then, that despite its effort to scrutinize the workings and details surrounding the Nazi machinery of death and extermination, this film cannot fathom the particular conjunction between femininity and the absence of generativity. Its inability to do so is underscored in two significant scenes of male suicide, which dominate the second part of *Shoah*. The first, the untimely suicide of Freddy Hirsch, considered by many as "the moral leader" of the Theresienstadt family camp in Auschwitz, is recalled with great sympathy by Rudolf Vrba. When it became certain that his group would be gassed the next morning, Hirsch was asked by the underground resisters to lead them in an uprising. "If we make the uprising," Hirsch inquired, "what is going to happen to the children? Who is going to take care of them?" Vrba, his contact, responded that the children would probably die in any case, "that there is no way out for them." This direct and undoubtedly truthful assessment proved to be paralyzing for Hirsch. According to Vrba: "He [Hirsch] explains to me that he understands the situation, that it is extremely difficult for him to make any decisions because of the children, and that he cannot see how he can just leave those children to their fate. He was sort of their father. I mean he was only thirty at the time, but the relationship between him and those children was very strong." An hour after proposing the uprising to Hirsch, Vrba found his dying of an overdose of barbiturates. The uprising, consequently, never took place.[21]

Hirsch's suicide, a direct result of his perceived failed paternity, is echoed at the end of the film by an uncannily similar description of what caused the suicide of Adam Czerniakow, the leader of the Warsaw Ghetto Jewish council. In the film, Raul Hilberg summarizes relevant passages from the final pages of the diary Czerniakow left behind. According to Hilberg, Czerniakow "is terribly worried that the orphans will be deported [from the Warsaw Ghetto] and repeatedly brings up the orphans. . . . Now if he cannot be the caretaker of the orphans, then he has lost his war, he has lost his struggle. *Why the orphans?*

They are the most helpless element in the community. They are the little children, its future, who have lost their parents. . . . If he cannot take care of the children, what else can he do?" Hilberg, in apparent identification with Czerniakow's assessment, adds, "Some people report that he wrote a note after he closed the book on the diary in which he said, 'They want me to kill the children with my own hands.' "[22]

The suicides of Hirsch and Czerniakow, placed as prominently in the film as they are and echoing each other in the similarity of their presumed motivations, can be useful in explaining the film's relation to the category of gender. Hirsch and Czerniakow take the masculine role of responsible paternity extremely seriously. Both see in the children the possibility of a future, and cut off from that future, impeded from exercising their own power to ensure continuity into that future, they cannot go on.[23] Hirsch and Czerniakow act out the masculine response to the realization that there is no future left, a realization repeated in the film's last words by Simha Rottem. They can neither face nor suppress that insight and are unable to remain with the children to offer them adult support and solace in their final moments.[24] In privileging these incidents and their masculine perspectives, the film itself resonates their evasion.[25] In contrast, Shoah's much briefer recollections of female suicide—of women who slash their own wrists and those of their children, of women who poison themselves and their daughters and sons—offer a poignant alternative response. Although we learn neither the name nor story of these women, their suicide/killings reveal equally despondent but less self-centered motivations than those of Hirsch and Czerniakow. For these women, death is an act of final resistance: escape for themselves and their offspring from prolonged suffering at the hands of their oppressors. It is a chosen end that reveals the women's more local and modest confrontation with death as opposed to the global ambition and ultimate denial of Hirsch and Czerniakow.

In his analysis of different cultures' responses to death, the anthropologist Maurice Bloch demonstrates a deep connection between death and femininity, a connection that, he argues, is cross-culturally present. But most cultures, Bloch explains, go further. Women not only manage rituals connected with death, thereby representing death, but they also occupy the space of regeneration, rebirth, and continuity, signifying the conquest of death.[26] In Greek and Roman mythology, certainly, Persephone, the goddess of the underworld, is also a symbol of spring, renewal, and generativity—represented both as the daughter of Demeter, goddess of the grain, and the mother of Demoophon. In the exploration of the genocidal machinery of destruction that is the subject of Shoah, that second position, the feminine connection to generativity, is eradicated, which seems to make the first, connection to destruction, doubly terrifying. Within the context of this film, women come to represent death without regeneration. Could it be, therefore, that women figure the Nazi destruction of the Jews so unbearably that they must virtually be excised from representation altogether?

"Is it possible to literally *speak from inside the Holocaust*—to bear witness from the very *burning* of the witness?" Shoshana Felman asks in her essay "The Return of the Voice: Claude Lanzmann's *Shoah*." Exploring the act of testifying about the the event-without-a-witness, Felman elaborates: "In what ways, by what creative means (and at what price) would it become possible *for us* to witness the event-without-a-witness? A question which translates into the following terms of the film: Is it possible to witness *Shoah* (the Holocaust and/or the film) from inside?"[27]

As Felman insists, *Shoah* is a film about the act of witnessing and about the process of survival. Since *Shoah* uses no documentary footage from the period, the Jewish witnesses we see onscreen are all Holocaust survivors, and since Lanzmann interrogates primarily those who have been in the deepest pits of the death machine, who have been farthest within the crypts of extermination, they are survivors who have literally been *inside* Hades. Not only have they been inside the camps and the ghettos, inside the gas chambers and the crematoriums, but some have also been left for dead, shot by bullets that failed to reach their vital organs. Against all odds, and certainly against the Nazi design for the final solution, they have literally come out again to testify. Thus Filip Müller, the *Sonderkommando* crematorium worker who wanted to die, was sent out of the gas chamber by the women of his village so that he might bear witness. In the words of Richard Glazar, "It was normal that for everyone behind whom the gate of Treblinka closed, there was death, had to be death, for no one was supposed to be left to bear witness. I already knew that, three hours after arriving at Treblinka"[28] This paradox, presented by Felman as the paradox of "witnessing about the event without witness," emerges in this film as a process marked by gender distinction.

Only men are in the position of descending into this underworld, the place that the modern imagination has most closely associated with a vision of Hades, and of coming out again to testify. And the power of their testimonies is heightened by the women they meet and are forced to leave behind. In this sense they are like Orpheus, the witness: the one who has come out of Hades alive, and whose song is made hauntingly beautiful by an encounter no other living human has been able to experience and to speak about. Like Orpheus, *Shoah*'s Jewish male witnesses have all survived intimate confrontations with death. If we read *Shoah* as an Orphic text in the terms of Klaus Theweleit's *Buch der Könige*, we can further illuminate the gendering of testimony and of survival that motivates the distinctive creative energies driving this monumental cinematic document.[29]

The essential elements of Theweleit's elaborate model of "Orphic creation" are acted out within *Shoah*: Orpheus's descent and reemergence from Hades after his encounter with Eurydice, the dead woman who herself cannot come out and speak, the power and beauty of his song, and the interdiction against looking at the dead woman's face. In Theweleit's terms, Orphic creation—the birth of human art forms, social institutions, and technological inventions—results from descent *and emergence*, a possibility denied to Eurydice. It is thus an artificial "birth" produced by men: by male couples able to bypass the generativity of women. In this process, women play the role of "media," of intermediaries—voices and translators—not of primary creators or witnesses. This type of masculine collaboration and historical creation, dependent on the intermediary role of women, is reflected in *Shoah*, where the masculine anxiety about the curtailment of female reproduction, about the cessation of Jewish transmission through the female line, gives rise to an alternate form of reproduction: to creation in which Lanzmann and Raul Hilberg, Lanzmann and each of his articulate male witnesses, together, "give birth" to the story that was never supposed to have come to light, never to have been heard. We see the pleasure of this collaborative relationship in the scene where Lanzmann and Hilberg together reconstruct, by means of Nazi train schedules and records, "*Fahrplanordnung 587,*" the route of a particular transport train from its origin to Auschwitz.[30] We see it also in the obvious rapport and apparent common cause—in the pleasurable ease of exchange characterizing the conversations between Lanzmann and Richard Glazar, Filip Müller, and Rudolf Vrba. In a modern manifestation of Orphic creation, together with these "Orphic" male survivors of the journey to Hell, Lanzmann circumvents women and mothers and initiates a new form of transmission for modern Jewish history.

As in Theweleit's Orphic model, *Shoah*'s women, whose faces can virtually not be seen, become the midwives of male creation, the mediators who deliver the stories' words from one male to another. Indeed, the film relies on a process of "gendered translation" to make its inquiry comprehensible. As memory enters speech in the witnesses, female translators are the midwives of a multilingual process of signification, repeating, through mimicry, the act of remembering itself. Listening to questions and answers, they carry words back and forth, transform and reformulate them, often significantly, and render them understandable and acceptable. Through their tedious and repetitive work, they become essential supplements to the film's project of exploration. Not only do they act out its search for an intelligible language with which to convey the unspeakable, but they are the shadowy intermediary voices between language and silence, between what is articulated and what must remain unspeakable.

Shoah's primary interlocutors, then, are truly Orphic voices, literally talking heads, whose song is as transgressive, as endangering, as the song of the poet whose body was torn asunder by angry Maenads. All have literally *survived*—lived *too* long, lived *beyond* the limits of their lives. Ultimately, of course, it is the film itself that *is* Orpheus, and we as viewers are implicated in its creative agenda, also cast as witnesses in an endless chain of bearing witness, also impeded, if not forbidden, to *look* at the faces of dead women.

In fact, the determination and consistency with which women's faces are avoided in the film evoke the Medusa, another female underworld figure, more threatening than Eurydice. If gazing at Eurydice will definitively kill *her*, gazing at Medusa will kill the one who looks. Medusa is the absolute other, the figure for the encounter with total death. According to Jean-Pierre Vernant's study, *La mort dans les yeux*, she combines "faciality" with monstrousness: what threatens to kill, what turns to stone, is the act of *looking* at her face.[31] Thus in the *Odyssey* Medusa's face is the guardian of the realm of death, whose radical otherness she maintains against all the living. She is also a figure associated with war and, in that context, she signifies the absence of generativity. Medusa gives birth (unnaturally, from the neck) only at the moment when she is decapitated by Perseus. To look at Medusa is to enter a world where all boundaries are erased: to look is also to be looked at; her eyes are mirrors in which her monstrousness is reflected back to the viewer. She calls into question the very act of looking: to look is to be possessed, to lose oneself, to find oneself pulled into the absolute alterity of death. In that sense, Medusa is the figure most endangering for cinema, especially for the cinematic evocation and representation of death. If women's faces are indeed associated not only with Eurydice but also with Medusa, their absence from the screen of *Shoah* undergirds the film's mythic structure.

And yet Inge Deutschkron, Ruth Elias, Gertrud Schneider, and her mother do offer their own examples of survival, curtailed as they are by Lanzmann's mythic vision. Together with the translators, they disrupt the film's relentless pursuit with traces of alternate stories. Their presence, minimal as it is, serves as a reminder of the *price* this film pays for its remarkable ability to make possible the testimony from the *inside*. And the *inside* here is not only the underworld of the death machinery, it is also the hell created by the encounter between past and present, an encounter that makes the past present with unexpected and unbearable force. What would it have meant to include women in that encounter, to confront masculine and feminine modes of survival and remembrance? *Shoah* does not permit us to answer this question.[32]

Lanzmann insists that his film is not a documentary but a performance. He hires the trains, asks the engineer to drive them, takes Srebnik back to Chelmno, places Bomba in the barbershop. Like an analyst, he brings each of them to the point of reexperiencing their most profound encounter with the Nazi death machinery. Women are left out of these remarkable performances. While Lanzmann's film—in bearing witness to the event-without-a-witness and erasing the distance between past and present—has the mythic and artistic force of Orphic creation, it also reveals the politics of this mythology by replicating the sacrifice of Eurydice and the slaying of Medusa.

Notes

1. All references are to *Shoah* (1985), written and directed by Claude Lanzmann, distributed by New Yorker Films, and to *Shoah: An Oral History of the Holocaust*, the complete text of the film by Claude Lanzmann, preface by Simone de Beauvoir (New York: Pantheon, 1985). The authors wish to thank the participants of the humanities institute Gender and War: Roles and Representations at Dartmouth College as well as the members of the Dartmouth faculty seminar Domination, Subordination, and Consciousness for insightful comments on earlier versions of this paper. We are also grateful to Jane Caplan, Michael Ermarth, Claudia Koonz, Miranda Pollard, Paula Schwartz, Linda Williams, and Marilyn Young for their suggestions.

2. Lanzmann, *Shoah*, p. 6.

3. Ibid., pp. 172–174.

4. Among the many accounts, see for example: Rudolf Vrba and Alan Bestic, *44070: The Conspiracy of the Twentieth Century* (Bellingham, Wash.: Star and Cross, 1989); Ruth Schwertfege, *Women of Theresienstadt: Voices from a Concentration Camp* (Oxford: Berg, 1989); Khoda G. Lewin, ed., *Witnesses to the Holocaust* (Boston: Twayne, 1990); Vera Laska, ed., *Women in the Resistance and in the Holocaust: The Voices of Eyewitnesses* (Westport, Conn: Greenwood Press, 1983); Marlene E. Heinemann, *Gender and Destiny: Women Writers and the Holocaust* (New York: Greenwood Press, 1986); Fania Fénelon (with Marcelle Routier), *Playing for Time* (New York: Atheneum, 1977); Julie Heifetz, *Too Young to Remember* (Detroit: Wayne State University Press, 1989).

5. See Esther Katz and Joan Miriam Ringelheim, eds., *Proceedings of the Conference, Women Surviving: The Holocaust* (New York: Institute for Research in History, 1983); Joan Miriam Ringelheim, "The Unethical and the Unspeakable: Women and the Holocaust," *Simon Wiesenthal Annual* 1 (1984): 69–87, and "Women and the Holocaust: A Reconsideration of Research," *Signs: Journal of Women in Culture and Society* 10 (Summer 1985): 741–761. Also see Sybil Milton, "Women and the Holocaust: The Case of German and German-Jewish Women," in Renate Bridenthal, Atina Grossman, and Marion Kaplan, eds., *When Biology Became Destiny: Women in Weimar and Nazi Germany* (New York: Monthly Review Press, 1984), pp. 297–333; Schwertfeger, *Women of Theresienstadt*; Lewin, *Witnesses to the Holocaust*; Laska, *Women in the Resistance and in the Holocaust*.

6. Lanzmann, *Shoah*, p. 8.

7. Ibid., p. 16.

8. Ibid., pp. 50–51. For Deutschkron's memoir of her survival in Berlin during the war, see Inge Deutschkron, *Ich trug den gelben Stern* (Munich: Deutscher Taschenbuch Verlag, 1985). It is interesting to compare Lanzmann's evocation of disembodied female voices with Kaja Silverman's analysis of embodied female voices in classic Hollywood cinema in *The Acoustic Mirror: The Female Voice in Psychoanalysis and Cinema* (Bloomington: Indiana University Press, 1988). Dissociating body from voice in Hollywood film increases authority; it is a tactic generally reserved for men, a tactic that masks the precariousness of male subjectivity. Folding the voice inside the image, as is done for women, diminishes authority; women, Silverman suggests, need to be freed from their claustral confinement in their bodies. Lanzmann's approach is the opposite: the male voices are both embodied and authoritative, while the female voices carry little substantive information.

9. Lanzmann, *Shoah*, pp. 154–166. For Vrba's more detailed account of the first Theresienstadt group in Auschwitz, see Vrba and Bestic, *44070*, pp. 180–196.

10. Lanzmann, *Shoah*, pp. 194–195.

11. Ibid., p. 195.

12. Ibid., pp. 29–30, 123, 126.

13. Ibid., pp. 11, 116–117.

14. Ibid., pp. 35–36, 40, 111. It is interesting to compare this sequence of the film with Saul Friedländer's account of a conversation with Lanzmann as the film was being shot: " 'Tell me, sir,' Claude asks the officer from Treblinka, 'which burn faster, men's bodies or women's?' and the SS officer calmly begins to expatiate." See *When Memory Comes*, trans. Helen R. Lane (New York: Farrar, Straus & Giroux, 1979), pp. 116–118. Does Friedländer misremember the conversation, or did this question Lanzmann's remain on the cutting-room floor?

15. Primo Levi, *The Drowned and the Saved*, trans. Raymond Rosenthal (New York: Summit Books, 1989).

16. See Zygmund Bauman, *Modernity and the Holocaust* (Ithaca, N.Y.: Cornell University Press, 1989), esp. chap. 5, "Soliciting the Co-operation of Victims."

17. See Terence des Pres, *The Survivor* (New York: Oxford University Press, 1976).

18. Lanzmann, *Shoah*, pp. 199–200.

19. When projected in theaters, the film is normally shown in two parts, each with an intermission.

20. Lanzmann, *Shoah*, p. 103.

21. Ibid., pp. 161–162. For a fuller account of the resistance within Auschwitz and of Freddy Hirsch's suicide, see Vrba and Bestic, *44070*, pp. 167–196.

22. Lanzmann, *Shoah*, pp. 188–190.

23. Inadvertently, Simon Srebnik echoes their realization when he subtly changes the refrain of the military song he had been taught by the Nazi soldiers. Instead of singing, *Ei warum, Ei darum / Ei bloss wegen dem / Tschindarassa-bumdarassa -sa* ("Oh why, oh because / Only because of the / Tschindarassa-*bumdarassa -sa*), he sings, *Warum-darum / Warum-darum / Wegen der Kinderrasse, Kinderhasser, Bum*" ("Why-because, why-because / Because of the race of children, the child-haters, Bum"). With his flat *warum-darum*, Srebnik echoes the tone and message of the *Asoi muss seyn*, and with his shift from the sounds that mimic the sexual encounter between the girls and the soldiers to his interpretation of those sounds—the intercourse between the "child-haters," whose procreation eradicates the "race of children"—Srebnik, himself a child, underscores the feelings of being the last Jew alive. See Anne-Lise Stern, "Ei Warum, Ei Darum: O pourquoi," in E. Didier, A.-M. Houdebine, and J.-J. Moscovitz, eds., *Shoah, le film: Des psychanalystes parlent* (Paris: Jacques Grancher, 1990).

24. For a contrasting male response, see Betty Jean Lifton, *The King of Children: A Biography of Janucz Korczak* (New York: Farrar, Straus & Giroux, 1988).

25. Saul Friedländer mentions another account filmed by Lanzmann but curiously not included in the film, the story of the two hundred children of Bialystok who were deported to Theresienstadt, kept there for two months, used in negotiations that fell through, and eventually killed. See *When Memory Comes*, p. 117.

26. Maurice Bloch, Introduction, in Maurice Bloch and Jonathan Parry, eds., *Death and the Regeneration of Life* (New York: Cambridge University Press, 1982).

27. Shoshana Felman, "The Return of the Voice: Claude Lanzmann's *Shoah*," in Shoshana Felman and Dori Laub, *Testimony: Crises of Witnessing in Literature, Psychoanalysis, and History* (New York: Routledge, 1991), p. 227. See also Felman's "A l'age du témoignage: *Shoah* de Claude Lanzmann," in Michel Deguy, ed., *Au sujet de "Shoah"* (Paris: Belin, 1989), p. 81.

28. Lanzmann, *Shoah*, p. 50.

29. Klaus Theweleit, *Buch der Könige: Orpheus und Euridike* (Frankfurt: Stroemfeld/Roter Stern, 1988). For an English translation and condensation of his argument, see "The Politics of Orpheus between Women, Hades, Political Power and the Media: Some Thoughts on the Configuration of the European Artist, Starting with the Figure of Gottfried Benn, or: What Happened to Eurydice?" *New German Critique* 36 (Fall 1985): 133–156.

30. Lanzmann, *Shoah*, pp. 138–145. Lanzmann has credited Hilberg's massive study *The Destruction of the European Jews* with inspiring his own project. On male collaboration, see also Wayne Koestenbaum, *Double Talk* (New York: Routledge, 1989). See Klaus Theweleit's essay "The Bomb's Womb and the Genders of War: (War Goes on Preventing Women from Becoming the Mothers of Invention)," in Miriam Cooke and Angela Woolacott, eds., *Gendering War Talk* (Princeton, N.J.: Princeton University Press, 1993), pp. 283–315, further suggestions about the attractions of masculine collaboration and the concomitant exclusion of women.

31. Jean-Pierre Vernant, *La mort dans les yeux: Figures de l'autre en Grèce ancienne* (Paris: Hachette, 1985).

32. See Klaus Theweleit, "The Bomb's Womb," for a suggestive discussion of gendered models of memory.

Lanzmann's *Shoah*

"Here There Is No Why"

DOMINICK LaCAPRA

Un pur chef-d'oeuvre. With these words Simone de Beauvoir concludes her preface to the French edition of the text of the film *Shoah* (1985) by Claude Lanzmann.[1] Any discussion of the film must begin with an affirmation of its importance and of Lanzmann's achievement in making it. It is a chef-d'oeuvre. But no chef-d'oeuvre is pure. Its status is both confirmed and tested to the extent that it can withstand the closest scrutiny and the most sustained criticism. Indeed a temptation in discussing Lanzmann's remarkable film is to transfer to it the tendency to sacralize and surround with a taboo the Shoah itself. Or, less controversially, there may at least be an understandable inclination to ritualize the film and to regard its viewing as a ceremonial event with respect to which criticism pales or even seems irreverent. Without denying other possible readings or receptions of the film, I shall try to address critically the nature of Lanzmann's self-understanding as filmmaker and the way it informs at least some aspects of *Shoah*. This approach in no way exhausts the nature of the film or even provides a dominant manner of viewing it, but it does allow one to see things in it that are often ignored or obscured in other interpretations.

Although I shall attribute much importance to what Lanzmann says about his film, I shall resist one of his major inclinations in discussing it. Lanzmann insists that his film is not a documentary, that it is not primarily historical, and that it should not be viewed as first and foremost about the Shoah itself. In one limited sense, he is right. *Shoah* is not strictly a documentary film in that scenes in it are carefully constructed. The role of mise-en-scène in the film is indeed crucial. For example, one of the most salient scenes, to which I shall later return, is staged in a particular manner. It involves Abraham Bomba discussing his role as a barber in Treblinka as he cuts someone's hair on screen. The viewer is, I think, shocked in learning that the barber shop was rented and that the men in it are simply extras who do not understand the language (English) in which the exchange between Lanzmann and Bomba is conducted. Moreover, the manner in which the historical dimensions of *Shoah* are in certain respects open to question shall be one of my principal concerns. The viewer expects *Shoah* to be historical and even to be a documentary—an expectation invited by the narrative prologue that introduces the film by discussing in fact-laden terms the death camp at Chelmno. Hence the subtitle of the 1985 English edition of the work conforms to plausible viewer or reader expectations: *An Oral History of the Holocaust*. One is, I think, taken aback when Lanzmann insists, "what interests me is the film. One has been able to discuss Nazism for forty years. One doesn't need the film for that."[2] Or again: "*Shoah* is not a documentary. . . . The film is not at all representational."[3] Most provocatively, Lanzmann has also said that *Shoah* is "a fiction of the real."[4] In his self-understanding and commentary, Lanzmann gives priority to film, art, and personal vision in making *Shoah*. His primary concern is his personal vision of his film as a work of art. Here two central questions are what one means by "a fiction of the real" and where one sets limits or establishes priorities insofar as they must be set or established.

One need not always agree with Lanzmann's interpretations concerning the nature of his film, and one may even see his own role in it as at times exceeding his self-understanding. In fact, one of my goals is to disengage the film from his view of it to make other readings more possible. Yet his reading or interpretation is compelling and casts a particular light on the film. Indeed the degree to which his views are taken to inform the film may perhaps be indicated by the prevalent critical practice of using them to initiate, substantiate, or illustrate the critic's own conception of the film without subjecting them to critical scrutiny. Lanzmann's views resonate, moreover, with important postmodern and poststructural tendencies in reading and interpretation, as is evidenced, for example, in Shoshana Felman's influential article on *Shoah*— an article Lanzmann himself obviously saw as crucial since he himself was co-translator of it into French for the important volume *Au sujet de "Shoah": Le Film de Claude Lanzmann*.[5] In certain respects, these tendencies connect as well with a long tradition in French thought that emphasizes tragic, self-rendingly ecstatic experience—a complex tradition often drawing from Nietzsche and Heidegger and passing through Georges Bataille and Maurice

Blanchot to reach recent thinkers such as Michel Foucault, Gilles Deleuze, Jacques Lacan, and Jacques Derrida. This tradition has also played a pivotal role in poststructural and postmodern approaches in general.

Lanzmann's art poses provocative questions to history. To some extent, I shall reverse the procedure and, from a certain perspective, have history pose questions to art. I would suggest that the very limits of art's autonomy are tested on not only historical but ethical grounds insofar as art addresses limit-cases that still present live, emotion-laden, at times intractable issues. In this sense, not everything is possible in art when one asserts its autonomy or even when one postulates a more disturbing sense of its enigmatic and abyssal nature as a "writing of disaster" in the face of the impossible and unspeakable.[6] Still, *Shoah* is probably best viewed as neither representational nor autonomous art but as a disturbingly mixed generic performance that traces and tracks the traumatic effects of limit-experiences, particularly in the lives (or afterlives) of victims. It is a film of endless lamentation or grieving that is tensely suspended between the acting out of a traumatic past and the difficult effort to work through it. In Lanzmann's influential self-understanding, which at the very least informs important aspects of the film, acting out or reliving the past tends to outweigh attempts to work through it. To some extent, the historical shortfalls of the film may be related to this self-understanding and its role in the film. A more thorough memory of the past might conceivably further efforts to work through it. Moreover, there may be a sense in which the greatest challenges to art include—but of course are not reducible to—the attempt at historically valid reconstruction and understanding, particularly with respect to limit-events of the magnitude of the Holocaust.

Here one may turn for initial guidance to Pierre Vidal-Naquet. At first Vidal-Naquet seems to make contradictory statements that are perhaps symptomatic of his divided reaction to the film. On the one hand, he asserts in no uncertain terms, "the only great French historical work on the theme of Hitler's genocide is the film by Claude Lanzmann, *Shoah*."[7] On the other hand, he states, "if it is true that historical research demands 'rectification without end,' fiction, especially when it is deliberate, and true history nonetheless form two extremes which never meet (HC, p. 30). The mediation between these contradictory statements is provided by the issue of the way history and art pose questions to each other without ever becoming identical. "How," asks Vidal-Naquet, "does this film question the historian?" (HC, p. 31). His first answer is that the film is not chronological or concerned with causes and effects. Vidal-Naquet asks,

> In effect, how can one avoid moving backward from the gas chambers to the *Einsatzgruppen* and, step by step, to the laws of exclusion, to German anti-Semitism, to that which distinguishes and opposes Hitler's anti-Semitism and that of Wilhelm II, and so on *ad infinitum*? Raul Hilberg, for instance, proceeded in such a way in his admirable volume. [HC, pp. 31–32]

As we shall see, however, Lanzmann in his extrafilmic commentary is himself not altogether consistent on these points, for he stresses the radically disjunctive nature and uniqueness of the Holocaust on the one hand and presents it as the culmination of Western history, especially with respect to anti-Semitism, on the other.

For Vidal-Naquet, "the second question Lanzmann's film asks the historian is perhaps even more fundamental. His attempt contains an element of folly: to have made a work of history at a juncture where memory alone, a present-day memory, is called upon to bear witness" (HC, p. 32). Here Vidal-Naquet refers to Lanzmann's insistent exclusion of archival material, especially documentary footage, from the Nazi period and the Holocaust and his insistence on discovering the past in and through the present alone—through testimonies or acts of witnessing. Yet there is an important sense in which Lanzmann relies on an anti-memory or on the silences and indirections of memory in arriving at what I take to be the object of his quest: the incarnation, actual reliving, or compulsive acting out of the past—particularly its traumatic suffering—in the present.

Vidal-Naquet draws on Thucydides in eliciting three characteristics of history but without making their bearing on Lanzmann's *Shoah* explicit. First, "a history of the present is indeed possible." Second, "any history, including that of the present, presupposes a distancing of the historian from the events." And "finally and perhaps essentially, any history is comparative, even when it believes it is not" (HC, p. 26). Here one may note that Lanzmann often seems to remove any distance between the present and the past and that he adamantly rejects comparisons as invariably normalizing attempts to deny the absolute uniqueness and disjunctiveness of the Shoah. Moreover, what is even meant by *history*, including a history of the present, with respect to Lanzmann's understanding of *Shoah*—indeed his very understanding of understanding—is open to question.

A key document in respect to the foregoing is Lanzmann's one-page manifesto, "Hier ist kein Warum." It is written in an apodictic, almost prophetic mode. Like much of Lanzmann's writing and commentary, it trades in absolutes. It begins with the hyperbolic statement, "All one has to do is perhaps formulate the question in the simplest form, to ask: 'Why were the Jews killed?' The question immediately reveals its obscenity. There is indeed an absolute obscenity in the project of understanding."[8] "Absolute obscenity": Lanzmann's use of such a phrase and the entire cast of this—and of comparable—statements raise a question: To what extent do references to art, fiction, personal obsession or vision, and even ethics serve in good part as a screen for the role of displaced, disguised, and often denied religious elements in Lanzmann's approach? I would suggest that Lanzmann returns to what he explicitly denies, represses, or suppresses: a tendency to sacralize the Holocaust and to surround it with taboos. He especially affirms a *Bilderverbot*, or prohibition on images, with respect to representation, notably representation relying on archival documentation or footage, and he also insists on what might be

194 DOMINICK LaCAPRA

called a *Warumverbot,* or a prohibition on the question *why.* The most pronounced manifestation of a displaced secular religiosity may well be in Lanzmann's tendency to grant the highest, perhaps the sole legitimate status to the witness who not only provides testimony but who self-rendingly relives the traumatic suffering of the past—a status with which Lanzmann as filmmaker would like to identify. A further question that agitates my own inquiry is whether this "tragic" identification, or rather uncontrolled transferential relation, has something problematic about it both in its attempt to provoke repetition of trauma in the other and in its desire to relive that suffering in the shattered self.

For Lanzmann, on the contrary, his "blindness" to the *why* question is identical to his insight and constitutes "the vital condition of creation." Without mitigating its shock effect, he elaborates his absolute, unmediated paradox in this way:

> Blindness should be understood here as the purest mode of looking, the only way not to turn away from a reality that is literally blinding: clairvoyance itself. To direct a frontal look at horror requires that one renounce distractions and escape-hatches, first the primary among them, the most falsely central, the question why, with the indefinite retinue of academic frivolities and dirty tricks *[canailleries]* that it ceaselessly induces. [HKW, p. 279]

It may again seem paradoxical that Lanzmann refers to "a frontal look at horror" insofar as he rejects direct representation, notably in the familiar but still disconcerting form of archival film and photographs. But here the paradox may be dissipated, or at least transformed, when one understands the frontal look in terms of the actual reliving or acting out of a traumatic past.

Still, Lanzmann proceeds to make a series of statements whose shock may not be dissipated but only increased through exegesis. He concludes his manifesto thus:

> *Hier ist kein Warum* ("Here there is no why"): Primo Levi tells us that the rule of Auschwitz was thus taught from his arrival in the camp by an SS guard. "There is no why": this law is also valid for whoever assumes the charge of such a transmission. Because the act of transmitting alone is important and no intelligibility, that is, no true knowledge, preexists the transmission. It is the transmission that is knowledge itself. Radicality cannot be divided: no why, but also no response to the refusal of why under the penalty of instantly reinscribing oneself in the aforementioned obscenity. [HKW, p. 279]

What is the process of "transmission" that Lanzmann contrasts with the *why* question and equates with knowledge? A first answer is that it is testimony or witnessing—that of the primary witness, particularly the survivor or victim, and that of the secondary witness empathetically attentive to the voice, silences, and gestures of the primary witness. We shall return to this answer, which in turn raises many questions, notably: Granting the crucial importance of witnessing and testimony, can one simply equate them with knowledge? Do they radically exclude all other modes of representation and understanding? What is the relationship between the primary and the secondary witness? Is it—or ought it be—one of full identification or total empathy? The force of these questions is increased when one realizes that by *transmission* Lanzmann means not only testimony but also—and more insistently—incarnation, actual reliving, or what would in psychoanalytic terminology be called acting-out.

Before returning to these questions and documenting further my assertions about Lanzmann's self-understanding, I shall pause over Lanzmann's use of Levi and then make some preliminary theoretical remarks about the problems of representation and understanding—the attempts to pose and address the *why* question. What is surprising is that Lanzmann takes up in his own voice, without adequate qualification and exegesis, the statement of an SS guard to Levi. He postulates this statement as constituting a valid law for one charged with transmission of . . . what precisely remains unclear: the testimony of witnesses, traumatic suffering, the horror of the Shoah, the unspeakable or impossible itself? Here one may refer to the context of the statement Lanzmann quotes in Levi's *Survival in Auschwitz:*

> In fact, the whole process of introduction to what was for us a new order took place in a grotesque and sarcastic manner. . . . Driven by thirst, I eyed a fine icicle outside the window, within hand's reach. I opened the window and broke off the icicle but at once a large, heavy guard prowling outside brutally snatched it away from me. *"Warum?"* I asked him in my poor German. *"Hier ist kein warum"* (there is no why here), he replied, pushing me inside with a shove.
>
> This explanation is repugnant but simple . . . not for hidden reasons, but because the camp has been created for that purpose. If one wants to live one must learn this quickly and well: "No Sacred Face will help thee here! it's not / A Serchio bathing-party."[9]

Levi does not present the guard's "explanation" as a mere lesson in survival; he qualifies it as repugnant but simple while situating it as a "grotesque and sarcastic" aspect of the concentration camp context. Does it change its basic character in Lanzmann's use of it? Is its postulation as a general law valid only if one accepts the concentration camp and its "new order" as a model for the world as a whole? Is the danger in this acceptance the possibility that one's outlook or "law" may become a self-fulfilling prophecy?

A great deal—everything perhaps—depends not on whether one poses the *why* question but on how and why one poses it. Nor can one escape the dilemmas and opportunities of critical self-reflection. Levi himself wanted an answer, however partial and inadequate. He did not take up the words of the SS guard in his own voice, and he attempted in his own work to address the *why* question with humility and in the belief that even partial understanding might prove of some use in the attempt to resist tendencies that led to, or were manifest in, the Nazi genocide. This belief may be naive or at least based on a kind of faith. But the question is whether Lanzmann's view is preferable. Here one may attempt to elaborate a set of difficult distinctions—distinctions indicating orientations toward which Lanzmann has significantly different reactions.

One may distinguish among at least three ways of approaching the *why* question. The first involves the expectation of a totally satisfying answer on the level of representation and understanding. A prominent variant of this first approach has been the object of deconstructive criticism and is generally the butt of poststructural and postmodern attacks. It is the attempt at totalization. Jean-François Lyotard detects totalization in master narratives and total theories of liberation. For Derrida, it is embodied in the metaphysical idea of representation as the reproduction or mimetic re-creation of a putative full presence. A basic point in these critiques is that there is no full presence that may be re-presented. Instead there is a mutual marking of past, present, and future, and the past itself is an object of reconstruction on the basis of traces and traces of traces. Interestingly, Lanzmann will himself describe his effort in terms of working with traces of traces in a present that is marked by its relation to the past and future, although one may contest some of the denials and inferences he draws from his description.

> When I say that I constructed the film with what I had, it means that the film is not a product of the Holocaust, that it is not a historical film: it's a sort of originary event since I made it in the present. I was obligated to construct it with traces of traces, with what was strong in what I had made. [LP, pp. 303–304]

But, as we shall see, Lanzmann will also—and even more insistently—employ language that would seem to involve him in a quest for full presence in the attempt to erase or fully instantiate traces by incarnating and reliving a past not marked by distance from the present.

One may detect a quest for full presence in a number of tendencies still current in contemporary thought. On a religious level, there is the idea of full incarnation of divinity in the world—an idea that may of course be seen as idolatrous. The *Bilderverbot* would apply most clearly to representations of divinity or of objects construed as immanently sacred or as incarnations of divinity. On an epistemological level, there is positivism in the idea that an objectifying notational system can ideally represent, transparently render, or capture the essence of an object. On a psychological level, there is what might be seen as the reversal of positivism in the reliving or reincarnation of a past that is experienced as fully present. I shall stress the last sense, since it is so important in Lanzmann's self-understanding. Positivism and objectivism, which Lanzmann clearly rejects, deny or repress a transferential relation to the object whereby crucial aspects of it are repeated in the discourse or experience of the observer. In acting-out, on the contrary, one reincarnates or relives the past in an unmediated transferential process that subjects one to possession by haunting objects and to compulsively repeated incursions of traumatic residues (hallucinations, flashbacks, nightmares). Here the quest for full presence becomes phantasmatic and entirely uncontrolled.

Another variant of fully satisfying representation and understanding is insistently rejected by Lanzmann. This is the harmonizing, normalizing account—narrative or theory—in which the past is seen to lead continuously up to a present or in which the present is derived from a past or from some general theory. Here knowledge would preexist its transmission because one would have a schema, developmental process, or general theory of causation that would explain the event before its "transmission" or even its investigation. An analogous procedure would be the kind of account (or presentation) that would give the reader or viewer a pleasure of the sort that would deny or repress the very existence of the trauma that called the account into being. Certain uses of archival footage or direct representations of the Holocaust, for example re-creations of scenes of mass death, might fall prey to this harmonizing, normalizing approach, although they might also traumatize the viewer.

Lanzmann indicts conventional historiography precisely because of its normalizing, harmonizing, idealizing proclivities. For example, he states:

> The worst crime, simultaneously moral and artistic, that can be committed when it is a question of realizing a work dedicated to the Holocaust is to consider the latter as *past*. The Holocaust is either legend or present. It is in no case of the order of memory. A film consecrated to the Holocaust can only be a countermyth, that is, an inquiry into the present of the Holocaust or at the very least into a past whose scars are still so freshly and vividly inscribed in places and consciences that it gives itself to be seen in a hallucinatory intemporality.[10]

Here Lanzmann indicts full objectification of the Holocaust, which would relegate it to an inert past or assume that it has been thoroughly historicized and normalized. With implicit reference to a phrase of Pierre Nora, he also brings out how the sites that are so important in his film are "non-lieux de la mémoire" in that they are traumatic sites that challenge or undermine the work of memory. And aspects of his comment, notably the reference to a "hallucinatory intemporality," raise the general issue of acting-out or reliving the past.

Lanzmann's rejection of chronology is comparably insistent. "The six million assassinated Jews did not die in their own good time, and that's why any work that today wants to do justice to the Holocaust must take as its first principle to break with chronology" (HH, p. 316). Lanzmann would seem to be referring not to simple chronology, but to the narrative integration of chronology in a developmental story having a satisfying beginning, middle, and end— a story dedicated to filling in gaps, reaching some sort of closure, providing the reader or viewer with pleasure, and perforce denying or remaining untroubled by trauma.

One may note that in *Shoah* the former *Sonderkommando* member Filip Müller has a traditional narrative style that to some extent conveys his disconcerting story in a conciliatory, modulated form. He seems to have recounted his tale many times before and is able to proceed with the virtuosity of a seasoned narrator, almost becoming a bard of ultimate disaster. Lanzmann does nothing to disturb Müller's narrative and is a patient, attentive, and responsive listener. Müller's narration breaks down only when he himself comes to a breaking point as he tells of the way in which his compatriots on the verge of death in the "'undressing room'" began to sing the Czech national anthem and *Hatikvah*. With tears in his eyes, he says, "that was happening to my countrymen, and I realized that my life had become meaningless. Why go on living? For what? So I went into the gas chamber with them, resolved to die. With them" (*S*, pp. 151–152). Müller leaves the gas chamber only when one of the women about to die tells him his act is senseless: "'You must get out of here alive, you must bear witness to our suffering, and to the injustice done to us'" (*S*, p. 152). Lanzmann, as we shall see, makes comments concerning his own desire to die with victims that indicate how close he feels to Müller.

In art, the term for works that bring unearned, premature pleasure is *kitsch*—the harmonizing and sentimentalizing rendition of disconcerting, potentially traumatizing subjects. A good example of kitsch is George Segal's 1984 sculpture *The Holocaust*, which is on display in Lincoln Park, San Francisco. In it there are simulacra of dead bodies strewn casually on the ground in a contemplative scene that somehow soothes the onlooker. Another example is the 1979 American miniseries *Holocaust*, which, as Lanzmann notes, "shows the Jews entering gas chambers holding one another by the shoulder, stoic, like Romans. It's Socrates drinking the hemlock. These are idealist images that permit every sort of consoling identification. Well, *Shoah* is anything but consoling." As Lanzmann observes, harmonizing efforts in general—and the 1979 miniseries in particular—fail to recognize that in all transmissions of the traumatic, there is always a part "that is not transmissible" (LP, p. 295).[11]

This last statement introduces a second approach to the *why* question that certain of Lanzmann's comments seem to support and that provides one way to view or "read" *Shoah*. This approach requires the active recognition that any account—representation, narrative, understanding, explanation, form of knowledge—is *constitutively* limited, notably when it addresses certain phenomena. In historiography this recognition would require the elaboration of different ways of representing, narrating, and understanding the Holocaust that do not fall prey to harmonization, idealization, kitsch, and premature pleasure in narration. Saul Friedlander has suggested two requirements of this kind of historiography: the interruption of the narrative of the historian by the voices of victims—precisely the kinds of testimony that form the basis of Lanzmann's film—and the further disruption of narration (or any continuous, harmonizing account) by the critical and self-critically reflective commentary of the historian. As Friedlander formulates the latter point:

> Whether . . . commentary is built into the narrative structure of a history or developed as a separate, superimposed text is a matter of choice, but the voice of the commentator must be clearly heard. The commentary should disrupt the facile linear progression of the narration, introduce alternative interpretations, question any partial conclusion, withstand the need for closure. Because of the necessity of some form of narrative sequence in the writing of history, such commentary may introduce splintered or constantly recurring refractions of a traumatic past by using any number of different vantage points.[12]

I would suggest that one function of these interruptions or disruptions is to introduce into one's account a muted dosage or form of trauma that—at some degree of distance allowing for critical thought and working-through—reactivates, but does not simply reincarnate or make live again, the traumas of the past. I would also observe that Friedlander's view is not an invitation to narcissim or endless self-reflexivity but an insistence on inquiry into procedures of representation and understanding, particularly with respect to limit-cases that most forcefully bring out the constitutively limited nature of inquiry. Indeed the avoidance of such critical self-reflection may invite narcissism and even involuted, aestheticizing self-reflexivity.

Lanzmann himself seems close to this second position on the *why* question when he writes:

> One must know and see, and one must see and know. Indissolubly. If you go to Auschwitz without knowing anything about Auschwitz and the history of this camp, you will not see anything, you will understand nothing. Similarly, if you know without having been, you will not understand anything either. There must therefore be a conjunction of the two. This is why the problem of places or sites is capital. It is not an idealist film that I made, not a film with grand metaphysical and theological reflections on why all this happened to the Jews, why one killed them. It's a film on the ground level, a film of topography, of geography. [LP, p. 294]

At times, moreover, Lanzmann sees that his rejection of direct representation cannot itself be total and that there are no pure traces of traces. The archival documentary footage he excludes makes its presence felt, and his method of confining himself to present words and sites derives its effect from its relation to what is omitted. Indeed the scenes of the present state of camp and ghetto sites will themselves be haunted by afterimages of films and photographs that almost everyone of a certain age has seen, including Lanzmann's witnesses. He notes, for example:

> It happens at times that I meet people who are convinced that they saw documents in the film: they hallucinated them. The film makes the imagination work. Someone wrote me, quite magnificently: "It is the first time that I heard the cry of an infant in a gas chamber." Here one has all the power of evocation and of the word. [LP, p. 297]

A question, however, is what will happen for a later generation that may not be familiar with the images Lanzmann intentionally excludes. Will they, for example, see his beautiful pastoral landscapes at face value or simply as nostalgic, often chiaroscuro aestheticizations of ruins from a forgotten past rather than as a bitterly ironic commentary on the past they conceal and, for those with certain afterimages and knowledge, simultaneously reveal? Moreover, is it possible that archival documents, images, and footage would not have a merely banalizing effect but might serve to provide reality tests for an imagination that can otherwise run rampant to the point of obsession and hallucination? Indeed might they even increase the challenge confronted by the artistic imagination in rendering the impossible?

Here one may also quote one of Lanzmann's own most haunting and memorable statements about his film—a statement on the brink between a conception of understanding and representation as constitutively limited and one that goes beyond this recognition to a third position: the absolute refusal of the *why* question.

> I began precisely with the impossibility of recounting this story. I put this impossibility at the beginning. What there is at the beginning of this film is on the one hand the disappearance of traces: there is no longer anything. There is nothing *[le néant]*, and I had to make a film starting with this nothing. On the other hand, there was the impossibility of telling this story for survivors themselves, the impossibility of speaking, the difficulty—which is seen throughout the film—of giving birth to the thing, and the impossibility of naming it: its unnamable character. This is why I had such difficulty in finding a title. [LP, p. 295]

I would succinctly interject that an account addressing the *why* question is constitutively limited by at least two sets of factors or forces: trauma and performativity, particularly performativity involving normative issues. I have already repeatedly invoked trauma, and it is indeed crucial for understanding Lanzmann's approach to understanding. Trauma is precisely the gap—the open wound—in the past that resists being entirely filled in, healed, or harmonized in the present. In a sense it is a nothing that remains unnamable. As Cathy Caruth has written:

> [In] "Post-Traumatic Stress Disorder" (PTSD) . . . the overwhelming events of the past repeatedly possess, in intrusive images and thoughts, the one who has lived through them. This singular *possession by the past* . . . extends beyond the bounds of a marginal pathology and has become a central characteristic of the survivor experience of our time. Yet what is particularly striking in this singular experience is that its insistent reenactments of the past do not simply serve as testimony to an event, but may also, paradoxically enough, bear witness to a past that was never fully experienced as it occurred. Trauma, that is, does not simply serve as record of the past but precisely registers the force of an experience that is not yet fully owned.[13]

One may maintain that anyone severely traumatized cannot fully transcend trauma but must to some extent act it out or relive it. Moreover, one may insist that any attentive secondary witness to, or acceptable account of, traumatic experiences must in some significant way be marked by trauma or allow trauma to register in its own procedures. This is a crucial reason why certain conventional, harmonizing histories or works of art may indeed be unacceptable. But one may differ in how one believes trauma should be addressed in life, in history, and in art. Freud argued that the perhaps inevitable tendency to act out the past by reliving it compulsively should be countered by the effort to work it through in a manner that would, to some viable extent, convert the past into memory and provide a measure of responsible control over one's behavior with respect to it and to the current demands of life. For example, the isolation and despair of melancholy and depression, bound up with the compulsively repeated reliving of trauma, may be engaged and to some extent countered by mourning in which there is a reinvestment in life, as some critical distance is achieved on the past and the lost other is no longer an object of unmediated identification.[14] It would be presumptuous—indeed worse than *canaillerie*—to pass judgment on the lives of Holocaust victims. But one may argue that, at least with respect to secondary witnesses in art and in historiography, there should be interrelated but differentiated attempts to supplement acting-out with modes of working-through.

The problem of working-through brings up the question of the nature of performativity that goes beyond any restricted idea of representation or understanding. Performativity may be identified with acting-out or reliving the past. But this is a truncated view, however prevalent it may be in post-Freudian analysis or criticism. Performativity in a larger sense may be argued to require the conjunction of necessary acting-out in the face of trauma with attempts to work through problems in a desirable manner—attempts that engage social and political problems and provide a measure of responsible control in action. The question is whether Lanzmann in his more absolutist gestures tends to confine performativity to acting-out and tends even to give way to a displaced, secular religiosity in which authenticity becomes tantamount to a movement beyond secondary witnessing to a full identification with the victim. This full identification would allow one not only to act out trauma vicariously in the self as surrogate victim but to cause one to insist on having the victim relive traumatizing events, thus concealing one's own intrusiveness in asking questions that prod the victim to the point of breakdown.

Before returning to what I have termed Lanzmann's absolutist turn—his movement from an idea of the constitutively limited nature of an account to his absolute refusal of the *why* question and of understanding—I shall briefly turn to Shoshana Felman's important essay. Felman's is an extended—and perhaps the most famous and influential—treatment of *Shoah*, and it is truly exceptional in that it has met with Lanzmann's favorable reception. Indeed it might almost be seen as the authorized reading of *Shoah*. One might say that there is a kind of convergence if not identity between Felman and a certain Lanzmann—the Lanzmann of the absolute refusal of the *why* question. In Felman's essay, *Shoah* becomes a fiction of the Lacanian Real rather than of the historically real, and the result is an absolutization of trauma and of the limits of representation and understanding. Trauma becomes a universal hole in Being or an unnamable Thing, and history is marginalized in the interest of History as trauma indiscriminately writ large. More precisely, there is, in Felman's approach to *Shoah*, a distinctive combination of Paul de Man and Lacan, and there is also an unmediated transition from the status of the witness to that of the shattered, traumatized victim, not only in the object of discussion but in the subject-position of the narrator or writer. There is also a routinization of hyperbole or excess, and uncontrolled transference and acting-out—often justified through a restricted theory of performativity or enactment—seem to be the horizon of psychoanalysis and of Felman's own discourse. A symptomatic indication of the routinization of excess and the absolutization of trauma is the repeated use by Felman of the phrase *paradoxically enough* (or the word *paradoxically*)—a use that attests to the force of the repetition compulsion but may also flatten paradox, evacuate its generative possibilities, and generalize the double bind as the well-nigh ubiquitous stumbling block in language and life.

Felman's discussion of *Shoah* is distinctive in that it is one significant place in her contributions to the book *Testimony* in which de Man is not present either in his own voice or as ventriloquized by others (such as Melville, Camus, or even Levi) whose words she turns to in order to fill in de Man's silences concerning the Holocaust and his relation to it. Indeed de Man hallucinatingly haunts *Testimony,* and Felman's analysis tends to be apologetic with respect to him and his "silence" concerning his early World War II journalism.[15] Through conflation with Levi, de Man even emerges as a traumatized victim who can only, in admirable silence, bear witness to the collapse of witnessing. Felman's general arguments about silence, indirection, and the "paradoxical" witnessing of the breakdown of witnessing tend to be compromised by the specific purposes to which they are put with respect to de Man. Still, her turn to Lanzmann enables her to work through—or at least leave behind—her uncritical transferential relation to de Man. The disconcertingly moving consequence seems, however, to be a comparable relation to Lanzmann.

Felman's approach to *Shoah* is one of celebratory participation based on empathy or positive transference undisturbed by critical judgment. Her discourse resonates with a certain dimension of the film that is most pronounced in Lanzmann's *Warumverbot*. Her discursive strategy is to repeat themes or motifs of the film in a fragmented, often arresting series of comments whose dominant chord is the idea that *Shoah,* "paradoxically enough," bears witness to the breakdown and impossibility of witnessing in a world in which trauma is tantamount to History and true writing is necessarily a writing of disaster. "To understand *Shoah* is not to *know* the Holocaust, but to gain new insights into what *not knowing* means, to grasp the ways in which *erasure* is itself part of the functioning of our *history*" (RV, p. 253).

Felman emphasizes the limits of understanding and knowledge and the importance of recognizing what escapes cognition and mastery. Yet, from her perspective, this emphasis becomes so prepossessing and pervasive that witnessing the impossibility of witnessing becomes an all-consuming process; trauma is so overwhelming that distinctions threaten to collapse and the world emerges as a *univers concentrationnaire*. The reliance on the rhetorical question (or the related use of emphasis) spreads throughout the text, and theory seems to consume itself and to confuse life with both self-reflexive art and self-dramatizing criticism.[16] Thus:

> *Shoah* addresses the spectator with a challenge. When we are made to witness this re-enactment of the murder of the witness, this second Holocaust that appears spontaneously before the camera and on the screen, can we in our turn become *contemporaneous* with the meaning and with the significance of that enactment? Can we become contemporaneous with the shock, with the displacement, with the disorientation process that is triggered by such testimonial reenactment? Can we, in other words, assume in earnest, not the finite task of making sense out of the Holocaust, but the infinite task of encountering *Shoah?* [RV, p. 268]

Here the "infinite task" of "encountering" a film seems bizarrely to displace the "finite task" of "making sense out of the Holocaust." One might instead insist on the priority of making sense—and actively recognizing the limits of sense making—with respect to the Holocaust and situate a film, however important, as an element in that attempt. For Felman, to become contemporaneous with the shock, displacement, and disorientation triggered by testimonial reenactment at times seems tantamount to reliving or acting out the past through self-rending identification with the victim—a process that attests to the futility of total mastery and the inescapability of compulsive mechanisms. Yet, in its unmediated form, this process not only has self-dramatizing implications but also forecloses the possibility of working through problems in however limited and differential a manner for victim and secondary witness alike.[17] The "second Holocaust" to which Felman refers is the scene in *Shoah* outside the church in a Polish village near Chelmno where Simon Srebnik, one of the two survivors of the death camp in which 400,000 were killed, is indeed subjected to a process of revictimization.

Shoah is a film very long on *hows* and *how preciselys* and very short on *whys*. In this scene, Lanzmann poses his only *why* question. He asks Polish peasants, outside the very church where Jews were incarcerated on their way to Chelmno, why the Jews were killed. He receives versions of the age-old blood-guilt story. First, a Mr. Kantorowski, organ player and singer in the church (a role with an ironic relation to Srebnik's as boy singer during the Holocaust), steps forth and enacts a doubly displaced blaming of the victim. He states that his friend told him about a story presumably recounted by a rabbi:

> The Jews there were gathered in a square. The rabbi asked an SS man: "Can I talk to them?" The SS man said yes. So the rabbi said that around two thousand years ago the Jews condemned the innocent Christ to death. And when they did that, they cried out: "Let his blood fall on our heads and on our sons' heads." Then the rabbi told them: "Perhaps the time has come for that, so let us do nothing, let us go, let us do as we're asked."

Lanzmann asks the translator, "He thinks the Jews expiated the death of Christ?" The translator answers, "He doesn't think so, or even that Christ sought revenge. . . . The rabbi said it. It was God's will, that's all!" (*S*, p. 89). But then, as if to contradict the translator and to express the collective *mentalité* of the crowd, a woman erupts in her own voice: "So Pilate washed his hands and said: 'Christ is innocent,' and he sent Barrabas. But the Jews cried out: 'Let his blood fall on our heads!' That's all; now you know!" (*S*, p. 90). Here one indeed does seem to have an uncanny acting-out of the return of the seemingly repressed.

Lanzmann at times appears to think that any *why* question must elicit a response similar to that of the Polish peasants—a view that indiscriminately conflates all modes of inquiry and approximates historical understanding to myth and prejudice. Felman herself not only tends to share this view but offers a marked overinterpretation of the scene in front of the church.

> What *speaks through him* [Mr. Kantorowski] (in such a way as to account for his role during the Holocaust) is, on the one hand, the (historic) silence of the church and, on the other hand, the silence of all given frames of explanation, the nonspeech of all preconceived interpretative schemes, which dispose of the event—and of the bodies—by

reference to some other frame. The collapse of the materiality of history and of the seduction of a fable, the reduction of a threatening and
incomprehensible event to a reassuring mythic, totalizing unity of
explanation, is in effect what all interpretive schemes tend to do.
Mr. Kantorowski's satisfied and vacuous interpretation stands, however, for the failure of all ready-made cultural discourses both to account for—and to bear witness to—the Holocaust. . . .

What the church scene dramatizes is the only possible encounter
with the Holocaust, in the only possible form of a *missed encounter.*
[RV, pp. 266, 267–268]

The "(historic) silence of the church" is closely associated with Lanzmann's
belief, developed in a more qualified form by Felman, that Nazi anti-Semitism
and genocide, while unique and radically disjunctive, were nonetheless continuous with traditional Christian anti-Semitism—a belief that may itself rely
overmuch on a preconceived interpretive scheme insufficiently sensitive to
the specificity of historical developments. But the more general point is that
Felman confines options to the "preconceived interpretative schemes," "reassuring . . . , totalizing unity of explanation," or "ready-made cultural discourses" on the one hand and the "threatening and incomprehensible event"
or "missed encounter" on the other. The only discourse able to address the latter is indirect or paradoxical discourse that makes "*the silence speak* from
within and from around the false witness" (RV, p. 266). The point, I would
suggest, is not that indirect discourse and the paradox are unimportant but
that restriction of all valid discourse to them depends on an excessively truncated understanding of understanding that dismissively conflates history and
myth (or confines History to a theoretically conceived, abstract "materiality"); moreover, such a restriction tends to exclude the possibility of constitutively limited historical discourse that addresses the difficult issue of how to
work through problems without discounting the significance of trauma and
the intricate relation of the direct and the indirect in addressing it.

Felman would seem to restrict herself to indirection and acting-out, and
her own prose testifies or bears witness to an interminable repetition compulsion, as she makes and remakes her argument with obsessive intensity, turning
and returning to scenes in *Shoah* that are read in its light. Felman's approach
effectively brings out the film's compulsive power over the empathetic viewer
in a manner that may not be fully conveyed in a more critical analysis. I
would therefore urge the reader to examine Felman's essay closely and use it
as a counterpoint to my own approach. But one may ask whether the very
length of her essay testifies to a melancholic mode of repetition that has a
mimetic or emulatory relation to the length and movements of Lanzmann's
film.

In the case of *Shoah*, the issue of length is nonetheless more problematic.
On the one hand, one might argue that the very subject of the film (in significant contrast to the film as the subject of Felman's essay) is so vast and

important that any length is small and inadequate—indeed that the very length, seeming repetitiveness, and empty stretches or silences of the film are necessary to transmit to the viewer a muted trauma required for empathetic "understanding." On the other hand, one might contend that the nine and one half hours of *Shoah* indicate the role of a mode of acting-out and that the repetitions of the film, while often bringing subtle modulations, also attest to the working of a melancholic repetition compulsion in which trauma may at times be enacted or transmitted with insufficient attention to attempts—including survivors' attempts—to work through problems.[18] Both the first and the second parts of the film seem to end—or terminate without ending—in the same place: the first with the melancholic despair of Srebnik, who thought he would be the last person, and the rolling by of a type of truck reminiscent of one earlier used to gas Jews; the second with the desperation of a surviving leader of the Warsaw Ghetto uprising (Simha Rottem), who thought he would be the last Jew, and the rolling by of a train. Certainly and significantly, these scenes resist closure and attest to a past that will not—and should not—pass away, a past that must remain an open wound in the present, but they do so with a dominant tonality of unrelieved melancholy and desperation. These "endings" almost seem to set the stage for Lanzmann's next film, *Tsahal* (1994), where Israel does in one sense seem to be the land of rebirth if not of redemption, and the opportunity for Jews to be agents stands in stark contrast to their role in the diaspora as victims. Moreover, the army seems to be the problematic but nonetheless celebrated, even sacred, exemplar of agency, and the tank or airplane is the machine that contrasts with yet somehow recalls the truck or the train in *Shoah*. This reading of *Tsahal* and its relation to *Shoah* is too simplistic but does suggest itself strongly on one level. One should note that in *Tsahal* the Holocaust remains a crucial reference point and a haunting motif, and in the land of rebirth one still lives in constant fear and with the taste of death. There is nonetheless a marked contrast between the position of Jews in the two films, and in *Shoah* there is a limited construction of the role of Jewish agency and resistance in the Holocaust itself.

Rudolf Vrba, a resister who escaped from Auschwitz, testifies most notably to the elimination of the deceived Jews in the Czech family camp and the suicide of Freddy Hirsch, their leader, who felt a special responsibility for the children and thus could not bring himself to lead a revolt.[19] These events are inserted into an editorially orchestrated sequence involving Vrba, Müller, and Richard Glazar—a sequence that includes as subdued motifs the explosion of one of the Auschwitz crematoria and preparations for revolt at Treblinka. (It is during this sequence that Müller breaks down.) The Warsaw Ghetto uprising is presented with little sense of its genuinely heroic dimension—a dimension perhaps overly monumentalized in Nathan Rapoport's famous sculpture that serves primarily as ironic counterpoint in *Shoah*. The dominant view of the uprising is through the eyes of two surviving leaders in Israel who dwell on its devastation and hopelessness. The second in command of the Jewish Combat Organization, Itzhak Zuckermann ("Antek"), speaks off screen as a ghostly voice-over to a ravaged face and body. He says, "I began drinking after the war. It was very difficult. Claude, you asked for my impression. If you could lick my heart, it would poison you" (*S*, p. 182). The longer testimony of Simha Rottem ("Kajik") is more composed but consonant with Zuckerman's words.

Let us return to Lanzmann's absolute refusal of the *why* question and examine more closely how it informs dimensions of his self-understanding—and his desire—as filmmaker. Lanzmann is frank about the role of his obsessions in making *Shoah*:

> One also always asked me: "What was your concept?" This was the most absurd question. *I had no concept.* I knew there would be no archives; I had some personal obsessions. . . . I have always asked the same questions. The circularity of the film is linked to the obsessional character of my questions, of my own obsessions. [LP, pp. 294, 300]

It is perhaps not irrelevant that these obsessions were those of a secular intellectual who was not raised as a practicing Jew but who assumed a certain Jewish identity in significant measure through the making of his trilogy of films (*Why Israel*, 1973; *Shoah*, 1985; and *Tsahal*, 1994). And in making *Shoah*, Lanzmann had the sense that "there was an absolute gap between the bookish knowledge I had acquired and what these people told me" (LP, p. 294).

One thing Lanzmann apparently learned in making the film was the absolute uniqueness and purely disjunctive nature of the Holocaust, and it was precisely this that invalidated historical understanding in trying to account for it. "Between the conditions that permitted the extermination and the extermination itself—the *fact* of extermination—there is a break in continuity, there is a hiatus, there is a leap, there is an abyss" (HH, pp. 314–315). Thus "there is for me an absolute specificity of anti-Semitism." Moreover, "the destiny and the history of the Jewish people cannot be compared to that of any other people" (HH, p. 310). Similarly, "Auschwitz and Treblinka cannot be compared to anything, will never be compared to anything" (HH, p. 307). And it is precisely "this certain absolute of horror that is not transmissible" (HH, pp. 309–310). Yet Lanzmann contradicts himself insofar as he believes that the Holocaust is "the monstrous but legitimate product of the entire history of the Western world" (HH, p. 307). He mitigates the contradiction in asserting, "*The Holocaust is unique but not aberrant. It is not the work of a group of irresponsible, atypical criminals but must be regarded, on the contrary, as the expression of the most fundamental tendencies of Western civilization*" (HH, pp. 311–312). But the mere qualification that the Holocaust is not aberrant does not eliminate the contradiction between asserting that it is absolutely unique and disjunctive and asserting that it is the "product of the entire history of the Western world" or "the expression of the most fundamental tendencies of Western civilization." Lanzmann never clarifies the specific sense in which he thinks the Holocaust is the product of the entire history or of the most fundamental tendencies of the West. He does not, for example, in the manner of Philippe Lacoue-Labarthe, rely on Heidegger's notion of the destiny of Being that assumes the modern form of a technological *Gestell*.[20] He probably relies most, here, as elsewhere, on Raul Hilberg's notion of the development of Christian anti-Semitism into Nazi anti-Semitism, although certain subtleties of Hilberg's analysis are lost in the absolutism and starkness of Lanzmann's formulations. Here one may quote one of Hilberg's statements from *Shoah*.

> They [the Nazis] had to become inventive with the "final solution." That was their great invention, and that is what made this entire process different from all others that had preceded that event. In this respect, what transpired when the "final solution" was adopted—or, to be more precise, bureaucracy moved into it—was a turning point in history. Even here I would suggest a logical progression, one that came to fruition in what might be called closure, because from the earliest days, from the fourth century, the sixth century, the missionaries of Christianity had said in effect to the Jews: "You may not live among us as Jews." The secular rulers who followed them from the late Middle Ages then decided: "You may not live among us," and the Nazis finally decreed: "You may not live." [S, p. 60]

This passage hints that temporality involves displacement in the sense of repetition with change—at times disjunctive or traumatic change. But Hilberg's stress tends to be on incrementalism and anonymous, structural bureaucratic processes—a stress that may not do full justice to the distinctiveness of the Nazi genocide and the complex role of biologistic racism, scapegoating, and distorted, displaced sacrificialism in it.[21] In Lanzmann, in contrast to Hilberg, the stress tends to be on absolute uniqueness and radical disjunction. There also tends to be an insistence on naked violence and death. "It is from naked violence that one must take one's beginning and not, as one always does, from campfires, songs, blond heads of the Hitlerjügend. Not even from the fanaticized German masses, the 'Heil Hitler!' and the millions of lifted arms" (HH, p. 315). Or again:

> For there to be tragedy, the end must be already known; it must be present from the very origin of the account *[récit]*; it must scan its every episode; it must be the unique-measure of the words, of the silences, of the actions, or the refusals of action, of the blindnesses that make it possible. A chronological account . . . is essentially anti-tragic, and death, when it comes, is always on time, that is to say, it comes as nonviolence and nonscandal. [HH, pp. 315–316]

The "tragic" preoccupation with death as originally known yet violent and scandalous has implications for the making of *Shoah*. "In my film, the Final

Solution must not be the point of arrival of the account, but its point of departure" (HH, p. 315). Lanzmann also observes,

> I have always been haunted by the last moments, the last instants that precede death. Well, for me "the first time" is the same thing. I always ask myself the question of the first time. I ask it to the Pole: does he remember the first convoy of Jews he saw arriving from Warsaw on 22 July 1942? The first shock of Jews arriving. The first three hours in Treblinka. The first shock of the Nazis themselves: one day they too must arrive there. . . .
>
> The first time is the unthinkable! It is acting-out *[le passage à l'acte]:* how does one kill? [NM, pp. 288–289]

These reflections provide Lanzmann with another opportunity to excoriate historians who try to understand:

> These historians, I tell myself at times that they are going mad in wanting to understand. There are times when understanding is madness itself. All these presuppositions, all these conditions that they enumerate are true; but there is an abyss: to act out *[passer à l'acte]*, to kill. Every idea of engendering death is an absurd dream of the nonviolent. [NM, p. 289]

It would seem that the first time is, paradoxically, repeated in the last moments before death and in the reliving of a traumatic past. And the first, last, and their compulsive repetition escape all understanding. Whether or not one agrees with this extreme position, one may observe that there is an important sense in which the traumatized victim has not lived the initial experience that comes to be compulsively relived. The initial "experience" was a gap in existence typically producing a state of numbness and disorientation. The victim will come to relive or act out what was not lived, in the best of circumstances in order to work through the experience in some viable form that allows a reengagement with life in the present. While Lanzmann has little to say about working-through and seems to absolutize acting-out, it is nonetheless the case that he wants to put himself in exactly the same position as the traumatized victim who relives what has not been lived. A questioner seizes on this point and presses Lanzmann when he refers to returning to the scene of the crime or of reliving what had occurred. "As if you had already lived, as if you had already been there" (NM, p. 290). "Yes," says Lanzmann, "surely it is true . . . One only knows *[connaît]* what one recognizes *[reconnaît]*" (NM, p. 290). Then he adds,

> At the same time I never lived that! I needed to pass through a certain mental experience, which has nothing to do with what has been lived, and yet . . . I needed to suffer in making this film with a suffering that

is not that of filming in twenty-five degrees below zero at Auschwitz. A suffering . . . I had the feeling that in suffering myself, a compassion would pass into the film, permitting perhaps the spectators as well to pass through a sort of suffering. [NM, pp. 290–291]

After Lanzmann affirms that he needed to suffer in making the film and to have the viewer go through a sort of suffering as well, the questioner astutely notes, "Something that had not been lived must nonetheless be relived" (NM, p. 291).

An important consequence ensues for the very choice of "characters." Lanzmann prefers figures who are closest to death, who have an eschatological significance in that they bring together two ultimate singularities: the absolute beginning and the final end. Hence his avowed predilection among victims for members of the *Sonderkommando*, the special detail charged with the burning and elimination of bodies in the crematoria. Even more specifically, he wants people who relive the traumas of the past in front of the camera—people with whom he can identify in an unproblematically positive or negative way. He thinks, for example, that Bomba, the barber who cut women's hair before their entry into the gas chamber at Treblinka, was at first evasive, neutral, and flat. (From another perspective he might seem relatively self-possessed but still shaken by his experiences.) For Lanzmann,

> It becomes interesting at the moment when, in the second part of the interview, he repeats the same thing, but differently, when I place him back in the situation by saying to him: "What did you do? Imitate the gestures that you made." He takes the hair of his client (which he would already have cut long ago if he were really cutting his hair since the scene lasts twenty minutes!). And it is starting from this moment that the truth is incarnated and he relives the scene, that suddenly knowledge becomes incarnated. In truth it is a film about incarnation. [LP, p. 298]

Here Lanzmann is satisfied only when he is able to induce the victim to become retraumatized and to relive the past. His idea of both the best acting and of truth itself amounts to acting-out, including the breakdown of the victim who cannot go on. Here one may quote the portion of the scene leading up to Bomba's "breakdown" and note the intrusive if not inquisitorial and violent nature of Lanzmann's insistent questioning.

> [Lanzmann:] But I asked you and you didn't answer: What was your impression the first time you saw these naked women arriving with children? What did you feel?
>
> [Bomba:] I tell you something. To have a feeling about that . . . it was very hard to feel anything, because working there day and night between dead people, between bodies, your feeling disappeared, you

were dead. You had no feeling at all. As a matter of fact, I want to tell you something that happened. At the gas chamber, when I was chosen to work there as a barber, some of the women that came in on a transport from my town of Czestochowa, I knew a lot of them. I knew them; I lived with them in my town. I lived with them in my street, and some of them were my close friends. And when they saw me, they started asking me, Abe this and Abe that—"What's going to happen to us?" What could you tell them? What could you tell?

A friend of mine worked as a barber—he was a good barber in my home town—when his wife and his sister came into the gas chamber. . . . I can't. It's too horrible. Please.

[Lanzmann:] We have to do it. You know it.

[Bomba:] I won't be able to do it.

[Lanzmann:] You have to do it. I know it's very hard. I know and I apologize.

[Bomba:] Don't make me go on please.

[Lanzmann:] Please. We must go on. [S, pp. 107–108]

It is impossible to render the long pause in Bomba's speech as he literally seems to relive the past. I think it would be wrong to see this scene in terms of Lanzmann's somewhat sadistic insistence on going on. More important in Lanzmann's subject-position as filmmaker is a desire to find people with whom he may identify and whose suffering he may take up as vicarious victim. Still, it is difficult to interpret the fact that the camera is nowhere visible in the barber shop even though one is surrounded entirely by mirrors. Is this a sign of the absence of critical self-reflection in Lanzman's subject-position in the film or of an alienation effect that prompts thought and questioning in the viewer?

In the film, Poles tend to be objects of strongly negative identification except in two cases: Jan Karski and the train conductor, Henrik Gawkowski. Karski, a university professor in the United States at the time of his interview, was the courier of the Polish government in exile who told of his experiences in visiting the Warsaw Ghetto and tried to impress upon the Allies the importance of what was happening to the Jews of Europe. He breaks down right at the beginning of his testimony. His initial words are: "Now . . . now I go back thirty-five years. No, I don't go back . . . [Precipitately, he leaves the room.] I come back. I am ready" (S, p. 154). In the course of his statement, however, Karski makes a few dubious comments. Even in him there may be, mixed with undoubtedly genuine sympathy for the plight of the Jews, a refined form of the anti-Semitic prejudice that bursts forth in such populist abandon in the Polish peasants. He tells us that of the two Jewish leaders he encountered, he "took, so to say, to the Bund leader, probably because of his behavior—he looked like a Polish nobleman, a gentleman, with straight, beautiful gestures, dignified" (S, p. 158). In the Warsaw

Ghetto, however, "the Bund leader, the Polish nobleman . . . is broken down, like a Jew from the ghetto, as if he had lived there all the time. Apparently, this was his nature. This was his world" (S, pp. 158–159). Moreover, concerning the Jews in the ghetto, Karski exclaims without sufficient qualification or explanation, "It was not a world. There was not humanity" (S, p. 159).

Gawkowski is, at least for Lanzmann, an exceptionally positive figure among the Polish peasants interviewed. He is the first in the film to make the famous throat-cutting gesture to Jews as they arrive at Treblinka—a gesture that other peasants try to rationalize as a sign of warning but that Lanzmann accurately sees as a threateningly sadistic form of *Schadenfreude*. Gawkowski's gesture was not rehearsed or anticipated, and it came as something of a shock to Lanzmann. Of Gawkowski, Lanzmann states,

> I really liked him. He was different from the others. I have sympathy
> for him because he carries a truly open wound that does not heal.
> Among all the Polish peasants of Treblinka, he is the only one who has
> human behavior. He is a man who drinks, since 1942. [NM, p. 282]

One may of course wonder whether Lanzmann's liking for Gawkowski blinded him to more equivocal aspects of his character that one might detect in the film. For example, the expression on Gawkowski's face when he makes the throat-cutting gesture seems to be somewhat diabolical, and his sigh of sorrow for dead Jews seems feigned and histrionic, although it is difficult to account for one's subjective impression or the results of staging and rehearsal. Yet it is clear that Lanzmann's affective response to Gawkowski is colored by the train conductor's harrowing possession by the past. Here Lanzmann's reason for excluding from the film another testimony from a Pole is significant. As Neal Ascherson writes,

> He [Lanzmann] wanted people he questioned to relive the past in-
> stead of simply describing it. He wanted them to be "characters" [per-
> sonnages]. Asked about why he did not keep the testimony of Wladis-
> law Bartoszewski, for example, who was quite ready to give him a
> firsthand account of the manner in which the Zegota group had hero-
> ically succeeded in saving Jews under the Occupation, he answered
> that he had met Bartoszewski, whose discourse he found altogether
> boring. Bartoszewski was satisfied in simply recounting and was inca-
> pable of reliving the past.

Ascherson concludes,

> The fact of excluding Bartoszewski leads to not telling the public that
> there were Poles who, at times at the peril of their lives, tried to save
> Jews from extermination. . . . The truth is that those who see *Shoah*
> will understand it as an account of events, as a historical documentary

of a particular type, and will get no further than an idea of the way the Poles behaved with respect to the Jews, an idea that is not substantially false but marked by omissions.[22]

In his contribution to *Au sujet de "Shoah,"* Timothy Garton Ash—while in no sense downplaying the prevalence of virulent anti-Semitism in Poland, especially among the peasantry—argues that, while Lanzmann tells the truth, it is not the whole truth about Poland; the German occupation of Poland was particularly harsh, and, in spite of severe sanctions, some Poles did help Jews.[23] I would add that Lanzmann's emphasis on Poland may be excessive, especially in contrast to the limited interviewing of ordinary Germans. Frau Michelsohn, the wife of the Nazi teacher at Chelmno, is the only German interviewed who did not participate in some official capacity during the Holocaust, although, given her views, she might just as well have.[24]

This may be the point simply to list other significant, historically dubious omissions in *Shoah* that I think are prompted by Lanzmann's desire to have only characters who relive or act out the past—and who do so in ways that provide him with relatively unproblematic objects of transferential identification in either a positive or a negative sense. Among victims, one has only Jews and no mention of Gypsies (Sinti and Roma), homosexuals, or Jehovah's Witnesses. Among Jews, one has no members of the Jewish councils. (There is only a limited use made by Hilberg of Adam Czerniakow's diary, largely as a counterpoint to the evasive testimony of the former Nazi and second in command of the Warsaw Ghetto, the supreme bureaucrat Franz Grassler.) Nor is there any sense of what Levi termed the "gray zone" created by the Nazis' attempt to generate complicity among victims.

Among perpetrators, there is scant indication of the role of fanatical commitment, elation, world-historical mission, *Führerbindung,* and a heroic cult of death, regeneration through violence, and, failing total victory, total annihilation—elements that are evident, for example, in Himmler's 1943 Posen speech to upper-level SS officers. (The one inkling comes in the glint in Franz Suchomel's eye as he sings the song celebrating Treblinka.) Here original footage or at least the testimony of a historian other than Hilberg would have been necessary. Lanzmann interviews lower-level SS (such as Suchomel) or Eichmann-like bureaucrats. Nazis after the war may have assumed an evasive, bureaucratic, I-was-only-doing-my-job-and-obeying-orders-and-besides-I-didn't-know-anything attitude. But this is hardly sufficient for understanding why they became Nazis or followed the leader in executing the Final Solution. One may also observe that there are no French witnesses in *Shoah* and that the problems treated are kept at a safe distance from France.[25] Finally, the role of women, especially among victims, is very limited; they tend to appear only in cameo roles.[26]

This list of omissions is partial, but it suffices to raise the question of their basis. I have suggested that they may be understood in terms of Lanzmann's own subject-position and his desire for objects of transferential identification.

Before trying further to substantiate this claim, I would also note that the same reason may be given for Lanzmann's refusal of the *why* question. In the case of victims, it is superfluous because the point is to identify empathetically and relive their reliving. In the case of perpetrators, understanding might mitigate condemnation. For Lanzmann the Holocaust was "an absolute crime" and its character was "incommensurable" (HH, pp. 306, 308). Therefore the responsibility of those perpetrating it must be absolute. Any attempt to understand them psychologically or historically is "obscene."[27] Thus one has a linkage between an absolute refusal to understand and a belief in absolute responsibility. On the side of the victims, Lanzmann's predilection is for absolute innocence in closest proximity to death. Lanzmann states,

> The Jews of Corfu have, in my opinion, a special function in *Shoah*. It is the reason why I say there are people who are more innocent than others. The Jews of Corfu are absolutely innocent, for me. I had a breaking point myself. I think this was the most difficult thing for me to do—to shoot and edit the sequence on the Corfu Jews. [SCL, p. 99]

Lanzmann reaches his breaking point in contact with what he sees as the embodiment of absolute innocence.

I would certainly want to insist on the importance of the contrast between perpetrators and victims. But the question is how to make distinctions and critical judgments in a world in which one does not have the bedrock security or the dogmatic dictate of simple absolutes. Even with respect to the Holocaust, an idea of absolute guilt and innocence, with only minor shading to impede the inclination to identify in unproblematically positive or negative ways, is much too simple to be one's sole guide. For one thing, it leads to too many unexplained omissions. At the very least, one would have wanted omissions thematized and justified in the film to enable a better appreciation of its limits and achievements. Such a procedure would have required a more critically self-reflective role for Lanzmann in the film itself. In touching on the question of his own subject-position as filmmaker, Lanzmann is at times unguarded in affirming his participatory desire to identify, relive, and trigger the imaginary and indeed in his reliance on obsession, phantasm, and related affects. He refers to "this sort of urgency I had to relive" (NM, p. 282). Of this interviewees, he states,

> Not characters of a reconstitution, because the film is not that but, in a certain fashion, it was necessary to transform these people into actors. It is their own history that they recount. But to recount is not sufficient. They must play it, that is to say, derealize. This is what defines the imaginary: to derealize. . . . Staging *[mise-en-scène]* is that through which they [interviewees] become characters *[personnages]*. [LP, p. 301]

The next passage is particularly interesting, for in it there is a slippage from characters to Lanzmann himself—a slippage testifying to the unchecked role of obsessions and transferential identifications as the *metteur en scène* becomes part of the mise-en-scène.

> The film is not made with memories; I knew that immediately. Memory *[le souvenir]* horrifies me. Memory is weak. The film is the abolition of all distance between the past and the present; I relived this history in the present *[j'ai revécu cette histoire au présent]*. [LP, p. 301]

The paramount role of details in *Shoah* is overdetermined, but it has a special relation to Lanzmann's unchecked transferential subject-position. They testify to his affinity with Hilberg, whose *The Destruction of the European Jews* was Lanzmann's avowed "Bible."[28] In certain statements Lanzmann echoes Hilberg's memorable words in *Shoah:*

> In all of my work I have never begun by asking the big questions, because I was always afraid that I would come up with small answers; and I have preferred to address these things which are minutiae or details in order that I might then be able to put together in a gestalt a picture which, if not an explanation, is at least a description, a more full description, of what transpired. And in that sense I look also at the bureaucratic destruction process—for this is what it was—as a series of minute steps taken in logical order and relying above all as much as possible on experience. . . . And this goes not only, incidentally, for the administrative steps that were taken, but also the psychological arguments, even the propaganda. Amazingly little was newly invented till of course the moment came when one had to go beyond that which had already been established by precedent, that one had to gas these people or in some sense annihilate them on a large scale. . . . But like all inventors of institutions, they did not copyright or patent their achievements, and they prefer obscurity. [S, p. 59]

This passage is especially noteworthy because it enacts the manner in which what is presented as mere description actually tends covertly to include theory, interpretation, and even explanation. There is clearly a theory of logical incrementalism until one reaches a certain threshold at which invention becomes necessary. Moreover, there is the significance of impersonal, obscure processes that lend themselves to structural explanations. In Hilberg's famous book, the role of technological rationality and the bureaucratic machinery of destruction emerges as the interpretive center of the argument. He also downplays the importance of Jewish resistance and gives little sense of the impossible situation that often confronted members of Jewish councils.

Hilberg has a unique status in *Shoah* as "the" historian—the only nonparticipant or secondary witness.[29] And his views have the weight of authority for the viewer. Lanzmann never questions him critically. He is in the privileged position of the Lacanian "subject-supposed-to-know," providing knowledge that seems incontestably objective. In fact Hilberg is not *the* but *a* historian—a very important one, but one whose views are at times open to question. (He was trained as a political scientist, but his work measures up to the strictest standards of a certain type of history.) It is interesting that some of Lanzmann's extrafilmic comments do not conform to Hilberg's emphases, but there is little indication of this in the film itself. For example, Lanzmann responds to one questioner,

> I have the impression that you would like to take me toward the bureaucratic thesis. I am not entirely in agreement. One may always think that one has been caught in a chain! I am resolutely against the thesis of Hannah Arendt concerning the banality of evil. Each of these men, each of these consciences, knew what it was doing and in what it participated. The guard at Treblinka [Suchomel], the bureaucrat at the Railway System [Walter Stier], the administrator of the Warsaw Ghetto [Grassler] knew. [NM, pp. 291–292]

Lanzmann thus dissociates himself from the bureaucratic thesis, which is typically linked with the banality of evil, notably through the paradigmatic figure of Adolf Eichmann. In good part because of Hilberg's commentary, the image of the Nazi regime with which *Shoah* leaves the viewer is nevertheless that of a machine made up entirely of cogs with no motor. The names of prime movers such as Hitler, Himmler, Heydrich, Göring, and Goebbels are not even mentioned. Of course these figures do not bear sole responsibility or exonerate all other Germans, but the regime, its policies, practices, and ideological motivation cannot be understood without them.

In an even more thought-provoking remark, Lanzmann asserts,

> this story of the banality of evil—peace to Hannah Arendt, she wrote some things that were better, no?—I think that all these people knew perfectly that what they were doing was not banal at all. Maybe they were banal, but they knew that what they were achieving was really not banal, surely not.[30]

Here one is reminded of Himmler's Posen speech, with its reference to the annihilation of Jews as an "unwritten and never-to-be-written page of glory" in German history.[31] But, once again there is little indication of this side of the story in *Shoah*. By contrast, Lanzmann's offscreen rejection of the "banality of evil" thesis is categorical and is clearly related to his rejection of the *why* question and his desire for absolute responsibility in all perpetrators. But it has possibilities that are not exhausted by these traits, especially in the insight that banal people can do far from banal things.

Another basis for Lanzmann's insistence on details is philosophical. For him philosophy is descriptive phenomenology of experience in the sense of the early Sartre and a certain Husserl. Quite close to Hilberg's historiographical method is Husserl's famous phenomenological version (or inversion) of the dictum that God is to be found in details: "The small change, gentlemen, the small change!" Lanzmann of course began his intellectual career as a close friend, disciple, and collaborator with Sartre on *Les Temps Modernes*, which Lanzmann has himself edited for a number of years. Lanzmann's insistence on details, however, comes with a resistance to theory (if not an anti-intellectualism) that differs from Sartre's own thought and is bound up with the *Warumverbot* and the desire to relive the past.

> So why all these details? What more do they bring? In fact I believe that they are capital. It is what reactivates things, what gives them to be seen, to be experienced, and the entire film, for me, is precisely the passage from the abstract to the concrete. This, for me, is the entire philosophical process. [NM, p. 282]

The obsession with details even at times seems to lead Lanzmann to repeat, in his own voice as interviewer, aspects of the bureaucratic mentality he is investigating. It leads as well to an expression by Hilberg of a kind of archival fetishism that attests to the extraordinary fascination of documents in establishing contact or continuity between past and present:

> [Lanzmann:] But why is this document so fascinating, as a matter of fact? Because I was in Treblinka, and to have the two things together. . . .
> [Hilberg:] Well, you see, when I hold a document in my hand, particularly if it's an original document, then I hold something which is actually something that the original bureaucrat held in his hand. It's an artifact. It's a leftover. It's the only leftover there is. The dead are not around. [S, p. 131]

Yet the consuming interest in details also bears on the importance of sites and machines as incarnations of the lived and of concrete materiality. Sites and machines are among the principal characters of *Shoah*, and, at least in the film, machines do not break down. One of the indelible images in the film is created by mournfully elegiac yet melancholy shots of endlessly rolling trains. The presence of the past also persists in its ruins and material embodiments.

> These disfigured places are what I call nonplaces of memory [*non-lieux de la mémoire*]. At the same time it is nonetheless necessary that traces remain. I must hallucinate and think that nothing has changed. I was conscious of change but, at the same time, I had to think that time had not accomplished its work. [NM, p. 290]

Fully empathetic identification with people and places enabled Lanzmann to feel that he was reliving—indeed suffering through—a past he had never in fact lived. He would even be phantasmatically able to die others' deaths with them.

> The idea that always has been the most painful for me is that all these people died alone. . . .
>
> A meaning for me that is simultaneously the most profound and the most incomprehensible in the film is in a certain way . . . to resuscitate these people, to kill them a second time, with me; by accompanying them. [NM, p. 291]

I have intimated that Lanzmann seems to have been more interested in victims, especially dead or shattered victims, than in survivors—or in survivors to the extent that they remained close to their experience as victims. His identification with victims was so complete that it could justify, for him, filming from their perspective—phantasmatically seeing things through their eyes:

> It was the middle of winter, and I said, "We'll get into the train car and film the sign, Treblinka." The distance between past and present was abolished; all became real for me. The real is opaque; it is the true configuration of the impossible. What did filming the real mean? To make images starting from the real is to make holes in reality. To enframe a scene is to excavate. [LP, p. 298]

Thus one has a crucial constellation that links positive, fully empathetic, transferential identification with the victim; absolute, noncomprehending distance from the perpetrator; a general refusal of the *why* question; obsessive, imaginary acting-out or reliving of the traumatic past; the equation of the "real" with holes in reality; and a hallucinatory reincarnation of the past in details of the present without appeal to archives. One consequence is what Lanzmann himself willingly calls a lack of human respect for others. With particular reference to his interchange with Suchomel, Lanzmann states, "to lack human respect is to promise a Nazi that one will not disclose his name while it has already been given. And I did that with an absolute arrogance" (NM, p. 287). More dubious, as I have intimated, is that Lanzmann's identification with victims allows him at times to be rather blindly intrusive in the manner in which he interrogates them. He asserts that there are no real encounters or dialogic relations between people in the film even when they are in the same place. "No one encounters anyone in the film" (LP, p. 305). A major sign of this nondialogic situation is the fact that, in the film, victims for the most part do not speak in their mother tongue. The characters who speak in their own language are primarily perpetrators and more or less complicitous and collaborating bystanders. This relation or nonrelation to others and even to the self is conspicuous in the juxtaposition of Srebnik and the Polish peasants or, as Lanzmann adds, in Srebnik's alienated relation to himself.[32]

But a major question is the extent to which it may also apply to Lanzmann's own role as interviewer. His exchanges often play out his own obsessions, affects, and phantasms and do not embody the tense interaction between proximity and distance required for critical dialogic exchange. Still, through inquisitorial rigor or specular projection, they do lead others to divulge what is in them—at times, however, in ways whose desirability one might question.

Lanzmann's personal, imaginary, or phantasmatic apprehension of the nature of art itself emerges quite forcefully in a kind of death or destruction wish through which he envisions the annihilation of the 350 hours of footage not used in *Shoah*: "You want to know my deep wish? My wish would be to destroy it. I have not done it. I will probably not do it. But if I followed my inclination, I would destroy it. This, at least, would prove that *Shoah* is not a documentary" (SCL, p. 96). Art and destruction are here in the closest proximity. Still, what may be the most crucial dimension of Lanzmann's desire to be a vicarious victim is a displaced religious longing that is encrypted in his vision of art—a longing for which the term *masochism* may be too facile a designation.

One of the most disturbing scenes in *Shoah* is the almost Beckettian sequence in which Bomba breaks down and cannot go on but Lanzmann insists that he go on nonetheless. I would like to return briefly to this scene and pose again the problem of trauma with respect to the survivor-victim, the secondary witness as filmmaker or historian, and the reader or viewer. One difficulty in discussing *Shoah* as a "fiction of the real" is that in it survivors both *play* and *are* themselves. Any boundary between art and life collapses at the point trauma is relived, for when a survivor-victim breaks down, the frame distinguishing art from life also breaks down and reality erupts on stage or film. The occurrence of trauma cannot be controlled, but one may to some extent control the settings that could facilitate or check its incidence. A survivor may willingly agree to tell his or her story and find that, in the course of recounting it or answering questions, the past is relived and the self is shatteringly (re)traumatized. This at times occurs in survivor testimonies. The particular problem in *Shoah* is the motivation and insistence of Lanzmann in trying to bring this reliving about so that he may share or relive it himself. One may well believe that there is something awe inspiring about Lanzmann's willingness to subject himself to traumatization or shattering of the self and to relive the extreme suffering of others. And at times Lanzmann realizes that his wish is impossible to fulfill and that he too can only go through a sort of suffering related, however indirectly, to the trauma of victimized survivors. But the sticking point is when he, as in his exchange with Bomba, insists on going on in the face of the extreme disorientation or suffering of the other so that he may participate in it.[33]

With respect to the filmmaker or historian as secondary witness, I earlier stated that the goal should not be full empathy in the sense of an attempt to relive the trauma of the other but rather the registering of muted trauma and the transmission of it to the reader or viewer. Of course one cannot prescribe that the secondary witness limit empathy at a certain degree or dosage, nor is it plausible to construe the situation in a voluntaristic manner that occludes the role of unconscious forces. At most one may argue that the setting or staging of an interview or the formulation of problems be such that the triggering of trauma is counteracted, for example, by the manner in which questions are posed or pursued. This argument is most compelling with respect to the survivor-victim, who should not be put in impossible situations or set up to relive the past, whatever the effects may be for the film, the filmmaker, or the viewer. Needless to say, this past may be relived even if all precautions are taken not to facilitate its recurrence.

If one objected to the notion of a muted trauma and maintained that the very term *trauma* should be reserved for limit-cases that pass a certain threshold, it would be more cogent to argue that the secondary witness should reactivate and transmit not trauma but an unsettlement—or what Lanzmann terms "a sort of suffering"—that manifests empathy (but not full identification) with the victim and is at most an index of trauma. One may also argue that this attempt, insofar as possible and without avoiding or denying the insistence of acting-out, be related to the furtherance of working through problems, especially in terms of achieving a sense of agency that resists reenactment of, or helpless possession by, the past and makes ethical considerations involving responsibility and obligation not only relevant (which they always are) but also cogently applicable. They were often not applicable to the situation of victims in concentration or death camps, and they may not be for those—including secondary witnesses—who relive the traumas or bear the open wounds of the past. Of course, working-through would require different things of different people, depending on their subject-positions, and it is intimately related to the recurrent movement from the status of victim to that of survivor and agent. But in all cases—notably those born later who will soon be the only ones left—it would necessitate not only remembering what happened in the past but actively recognizing the fundamental injustice done to victims as a premise of legitimate action in the present and future.

In the preceding analysis, I have treated Lanzmann both as a principal interlocutor or character in his film (a position that is often ignored when he is seen simply as a cipher or transparent secondary witness) and as an important viewer or interpreter of it—one whose self-understanding has either influenced or coincided with the views of notable commentators. I would like to conclude with a series of open questions concerning my argument. (1) Is *Shoah* (perhaps disengaged from, or "read" against the grain of, Lanzmann's self-understanding) even closer to mourning and working-through—or at least more effective in relating acting-out and working-through—than my argument allows? Can one provide a cogent "reading" of the film that answers this question in the affirmative? (2) Would this answer be provided by an avowedly liturgical or ritual "reading" or reception of the film—one that has in fact been active, implicitly or explicitly, in many readings or reception?[34] (3) On the other hand, should any film have a liturgical function? Is this a valid role for a commercially distributed film? (4) Should *this* film have such a function to the extent that my argument is convincing and Lanzmann's self-understanding is also active in liturgical receptions? (5) What are the social, political, and personal functions of a liturgical reception, for example, in constructing a certain kind of Jewish identity, and how valid are these functions? (6) Does a liturgical reception attest to a protected core of the personality that is not questioned and that may indeed be the basis on which seemingly radical or experimental views may be deployed elsewhere? Is this a reason why criticisms of *Shoah* may provoke visceral and vitriolic responses in otherwise open-minded people? (7) Is constitutively limited understanding, along with affective response, one desirable basis of working through the past, and is historical validity, even in a film—including a film subject to liturgical reception—a component of such understanding?

Although the foregoing series of questions could be extended further, they are meant to create a movement of self-criticism in my argument as well as in certain critical responses to it. In posing these questions, I would nonetheless insist that nothing in my discussion should be taken to lessen the importance of *Shoah* as a film or its role in resisting the trivialization or dubious relativization of the Holocaust. Rather my argument should be seen as indicating and exploring the tensions among historical, aesthetic, and liturgical perspectives on the film. Indeed, while the film seems to present itself in terms of the historical, and while Lanzmann's commentaries stress the aesthetic, the printed version of the text of the film seems to point primarily in a liturgical direction. The prose of the film is set as if it were blank verse, but this typographical positioning of the words creates the effect less of a collection of poems than of a series of prayers based on the principle of call and response. Perhaps the basic point of my argument is that, at least in a secular context, liturgy is not easy to come by and that any secular work, even when taken as liturgical, must be open to certain forms of questioning. Such questioning is related to the attempt to work through the past. Working-through, of which mourning is one prominent form, should not be conflated with utopian optimism or total liberation from the past and its melancholic burdens; instead, it should be seen as a supplement and counterforce to melancholia and acting-out. It should also be disengaged from discourses of pathology or medicalization and understood in an explicitly normative manner as a desirable process, however limited it may be in terms of actual success, especially in the face of trauma and limit-events.

Notes

Unless otherwise noted, all translations are my own.

1. Simone de Beauvoir, "La Mémoire de l'horreur," preface to Claude Lanzmann, *Shoah* (Paris: Fayard, 1985), p. 10. The revised English edition, from which I shall

quote, is Lanzmann, *"Shoah": The Complete Text of the Acclaimed Holocaust Film*, trans. A. Whitelaw and W. Byron (New York: Pantheon, 1995); hereafter abbreviated *S*. According to the copyright page, this edition has been "extensively corrected and revised by Claude Lanzmann in order to conform more closely to the original film" (*S*, p. ii). (Lanzmann disavowed the 1985 Pantheon Books edition.)

2. Lanzmann, "Les Non-lieux de la mémoire," in *Au sujet de "Shoah": Le Film de Claude Lanzmann*, ed. Michel Deguy (Paris: Belin, 1990), p. 282; hereafter abbreviated NM. This book contains a series of articles on *Shoah* as well as interviews and contributions by Lanzmann himself.

3. Lanzmann, "Seminar with Claude Lanzmann, 11 April 1990," *Yale French Studies*, no. 79 (1991): 96, 97; hereafter abbreviated SCL. This was a special issue, edited by Claire Nouvet, entitled "Literature and the Ethical Question."

4. Lanzmann, "Le Lieu et la parole," in *Au sujet de "Shoah,"* p. 301; hereafter abbreviated "LP."

5. See Shoshana Felman, "The Return of the Voice: Claude Lanzmann's *Shoah*," in Felman and Dori Laub, *Testimony: Crises of Witnessing in Literature, Psychoanalysis, and History* (New York: Routledge, 1992), pp. 204–283; hereafter abbreviated RV; trans. Lanzmann and Judith Ertel, under the title "À l'âge du témoignage: *Shoah* de Claude Lanzmann," in *Au sujet de "Shoah,"* pp. 55–145. For an idea of the currency of views similar to Lanzmann's, see their role in Ron Rosenbaum, "Explaining Hitler," *The New Yorker*, May 1 1995, pp. 50–70. Gertrud Koch, "Transformations esthétiques dans la représentation de l'inimaginable," trans. Catherine Weinzorn, in *Au sujet de "Shoah,"* pp. 157–66, offers a strongly aesthetic interpretation of the film that in certain respects coincides with Lanzmann's self-interpretation. Referring to what she terms Lawrence L. Langer's "option for an aesthetic of modern times," she appeals to "the (irresolvable) aporias of autonomous art" (pp. 160, 161). Autonomous art, for her,

> draws its force from the theorem of the imagination, from the affirmation that art is not representation, but presentation, not reproduction, but expression. One accords to the imagination a proper autonomy; it is capable of conceiving, capable of annihilating being-in-society, of transcending it toward the radically other, capable of making arise in the mute body the natural substratum, however hidden, however dispossessed of expression, it may be. [p. 161]

After quoting Samuel Beckett, whom Theodor Adorno also relied on for his conception of autonomous art, Koch asserts, "modern art has stopped talking and transformed itself into an enigma: the proof of its reflection on this [Beckettian] limit" (p. 161). *Shoah* for her brings about "an aesthetic transformation of the experience of extermination" (p. 166). In what almost amounts to a begrudging concession, she notes in passing, "That the film brings, in addition, enough material and contributes to necessary historical and political debates cannot be denied." But she stresses that "the fascination it exerts, its somber beauty, is assuredly an aesthetic quality" (p. 166). My own approach to *Shoah* insists on consistently relating aesthetic qualities and historical-political issues and conceives differently the priorities Koch postulates between them. Moreover, I would be wary of aestheticized renderings of the Shoah, including the unqualified inclination to validate certain tendencies (notably the desire to have the past relived or acted out) by viewing them in exclusively aesthetic terms.

6. Lanzmann himself uses the phrase "writing of disaster" in his introduction to the text of *Shoah* (*S*, p. viii). The phrase is taken from the title of a book by Maurice Blanchot, *L'Écriture du désastre* (Paris: Gallimard, 1980), trans. Ann Smock, under the title *The Writing of Disaster* (Lincoln: University of Nebraska Press, 1986).

7. Pierre Vidal-Naquet, "The Holocaust's Challenge to History," trans. Roger Butler-Borruat, in *Auschwitz and After: Race, Culture, and "the Jewish Question" in France*, ed. Lawrence D. Kritzman (New York: Routledge, 1995), p. 31; hereafter abbreviated HC. The French version, "L'Épreuve de l'historien: Réflexions d'un généraliste," is in *Au sujet de "Shoah,"* pp. 198–208. This comment is made not only to confer genuine praise on Lanzmann but to criticize French historiography, notably the *Annales* school for its tendency to avoid recent history and emphasize *la longue durée*. One consequence has been that, in France, basic work on the Holocaust and, to some extent, on related issues, such as the Vichy regime, has until the relatively recent past often been done by figures who are not professionally trained historians.

8. Lanzmann, "Hier ist kein Warum," in *Au sujet de "Shoah,"* p. 279, hereafter abbreviated HKW.

9. Primo Levi, *Survival in Auschwitz,* in *"Survival in Auschwitz" and "The Reawakening": Two Memoirs*, trans. Stuart Woolf (1958; New York: Summit Books, 1986), pp. 28, 29.

10. Lanzmann, "De l'holocauste à *Holocauste,* ou comment s'en débarrasser," in *Au sujet de "Shoah,"* p. 316; hereafter abbreviated HH.

11. A recent object of what might almost be called Lanzmann's spleen is Steven Spielberg's 1993 film *Schindler's List*, which Lanzmann sees as the epitome of kitsch. Although Lanzmann's response is extreme, this film is, to a significant extent, sentimentally harmonizing, particularly in its upbeat ending, which depicts the Schindler figure as a saint and martyr and presents a ritual—in living color—that seems to provide consolation too facile for the wounds of the past.

12. Saul Friedlander, *Memory, History, and the Extermination of the Jews of Europe* (Bloomington: Indiana University Press, 1993), p. 132. Friedlander also writes:

> The major difficulty of historians of the Shoah, when confronted with the echoes of the traumatic past, is to keep some measure of balance between the emotion recurrently breaking through the "protective shield" and numbness that protects this very shield. In fact, the numbing or distancing effect of intellectual work on the Shoah is unavoidable and necessary; the recurrence of strong emotional impact is also often unforeseeable and necessary.
>
> "Working through" means, first, being aware of both tendencies, allowing for a measure of balance between the two whenever possible. But neither the protective numbing nor the disruptive emotion is entirely accessible to consciousness. [p. 130]

13. Cathy Caruth, "Introduction," *American Imago* 48 (Winter 1991): 417.

14. See especially Sigmund Freud, "Remembering, Repeating, and Working-Through" (1914) and "Mourning and Melancholia" (1917), *The Standard Edition of the*

Complete Psychological Works of Sigmund Freud, trans. and ed. James Strachey, 24 vols. (London: Hogarth Press, 1953–1974), 12:145–156 and 14:237–260.

15. See my discussion of this issue in *Representing the Holocaust: History, Theory, Trauma* (Ithaca, N.Y.: Cornell University Press, 1994), pp. 116–125.

16. Self-dramatization is most blatant in Felman, "Education and Crisis, or the Vicissitudes of Teaching," chap. 1 of Felman and Laub, *Testimony,* pp. 1–56, in which Felman discusses her own and a class's reaction to viewing Holocaust testimonies. In one lengthy section of her discussion of Lanzmann (see RV, pp. 242–257), Felman even interprets *Shoah* in terms of Lanzmann's personal *"journey"* or saga, thereby threatening to subordinate the film to biographical or even narcissistic concerns (RV, p. 242).

17. When her class threatens to get out of control in the aftermath of viewing Holocaust testimonies, however, Felman assumes the authoritative role of the Lacanian "subject-supposed-to-know" and presumably returns the class to the Symbolic order: "After we discussed the turn of events, we concluded that what was called for was for me to reassume authority as the teacher of the class, and bring the students back into significance" (Felman, "Education and Crisis, or the Vicissitudes of Teaching," p. 48). (In Lacan the notion of the "subject-supposed-to-know" is of course meant to ironize the position of the analyst who claims such an untenable status.) Perhaps too rapidly, Felman reaches the conclusion that "the crisis, in effect, had been worked through and overcome and . . . a resolution had been reached, both on an intellectual and on a vital level" (p. 52). The question is whether one can construe as working-through the turn to an authoritative figure in order to bring closure to disorientation and acting-out.

18. As Felman remarks in a footnote, "Cf. Lacan's conception of 'the Real' as 'a missed encounter' and as 'what returns to the same place' " (RV, p. 268 n. 44). One may argue that historical reality is a compromise formation that involves—or is repeatedly disrupted by—the Lacanian Real (trauma?) but cannot simply be reduced to or conflated with it. One may also guardedly speculate (in line with the views of Nicolas Abraham and Maria Torok) that Lanzmann's own desire to identify with the victim is based on an encrypted or hidden wound caused by the fact that he was not in reality a victim of the Shoah sharing the fate of his objects of study. Indeed his specific "trauma" may itself be this missed encounter or disturbing absence, which he converts into a lack or loss in his experience. Lanzmann never explicitly acknowledges the wound or gap caused by his not participating in the unspeakable event—an acknowledgment that may be necessary for attempting to work through his relation to victims rather than endlessly and obsessively acting it out (or intrusively "incorporating" the other). See Nicolas Abraham and Maria Torok, *The Shell and the Kernel: Renewals of Psychoanalysis,* trans. and ed. Nicolas T. Rand (Chicago: University of Chicago Press, 1994), esp. pt. 4.

19. It is noteworthy that Lanzmann has little to say about Vrba in his commentaries and interviews. Vrba was not a member of the *Sonderkommando* and does not "relive" the past. If anything, his reliance on irony is sustained and perhaps overdone. It is also interesting that Vrba is mentioned only briefly in passing in Felman's essay, and his name does not appear in the index of her book. Richard Glazar does appear in her index, but his self-possessed testimony receives relatively little attention in her comments

or in Lanzmann's. Indeed a sustained analysis of Vrba's and Glazar's testimonies, along with their extrafilmic statements, might provide one basis for a reading of *Shoah* that diverges in significant ways from Lanzmann's seemingly dominant self-understanding.

20. See Philippe Lacoue-Labarthe, *Heidegger, Art, and Politics: The Fiction of the Political,* trans. Chris Turner (Cambridge, Mass.: Basil Blackwell, 1990).

21. For the latter view, see the discussion in my *Representing the Holocaust.* I would note that there is a crucial difference between arguing that displaced religious elements—notably a distorted sacrificialism involving victimization and scapegoating—are operative in aspects of the Holocaust (especially in the outlook and behavior of certain elite perpetrators) and affirming those elements in one's own voice. Indeed detecting their possible role may be a basis for a critique of them as well as vigilance with respect to their possible recurrence. By contrast, Elisabeth Huppert, "Voir *(Shoah),*" in *Au sujet de "Shoah,"* pp. 150–156, relies on negative theology to offer a rather indiscriminate religious interpretation of the Holocaust and transfers religious qualities to Lanzmann's film and even to Lanzmann himself. Thus she writes, "It is possible that something important happened in the concentration camps—the most important thing in the history of the world. It is possible that God showed himself there" (p. 150). In the film, "the unnamable is not represented," but "we contemplate those who have gone to the brink of the abyss." Moreover, "the emptiness that we carry in ourselves is perhaps that through which we participate in the divine principle. In *Shoah* it is on the exterior of the film, but *it exists.*" Hence the film is prophetic. "To attach the term *prophet* to Claude Lanzmann is embarrassing but not to do so is a lie" (p. 151). Sami Naïr, "*Shoah,* une leçon d'humanité," in *Au sujet de "Shoah,"* pp. 167–174, offers an existential humanist interpretation with religious overtones. He sees Abraham Bomba, when he breaks down, as finally being unable "to repress his martyrized humanity" and he characterizes the ensuing dialogue between Bomba and Lanzmann, which I later quote, as "worthy of the greatest tragic works" (p. 172). "Precisely because he pursues, in spite of his tears, his relieved martyrology," Bomba "gains entry to physical ascesis. He covers himself in bruises *[il se meurtrit]* as body and consciousness in order to be liberated as word. For there is no other way than this: *to relieve in one's flesh the tragedy of tortured victims.*" Moreover, this "acceptance of ascesis. . . . imposes itself not only on witnesses but also on Lanzmann himself " (p. 173). Naïr also sees Lanzmann as "rehabilitating and transfiguring" surviving Jewish members of the *Sonderkommando* "by showing their profound *sanctity*" (p. 174). Naïr thus unguardedly affirms and validates in his own voice the possible role of quasi-sacrificial processes in the film.

22. Neal Ascherson, "La Controverse autour de *Shoah,*" trans. Jean-Pierre Bardos, in *Au sujet de "Shoah,"* p. 231.

23. See Timothy Garton Ash, "La Vie de la mort," trans. Nathalie Notari, in *Au sujet de "Shoah,"* pp. 236–255.

24. In response to Lanzmann's question concerning how many Jews were "exterminated" at Chelmno, Frau Michelsohn gives one of her more memorable answers: "Four something. Four hundred thousand, forty thousand." Lanzmann: "Four hundred thousand." Michelsohn: "Four hundred thousand. Yes, I knew it had a four in it. Sad, sad, sad!" (*S,* p. 83). Whatever one's view of the general adequacy of Lanzmann's

portrayal of the role of Poles in the Holocaust itself, it is arguable that, in the contemporary context, his emphases were instrumental in generating a controversy concerning, and a reexamination of, the nature of anti-Semitism in Poland. Indeed one might even speculate that a more qualified approach might have been less effective in helping to bring about such a reexamination, one that was also furthered by groups in Poland itself, notably in the younger generation prominent in the Solidarity movement. It is important to emphasize the point that anti-Semitism was pronounced and prevalent in Poland and remained so after the war. Moreover, before the appearance of *Shoah*, relatively little had been done in Poland to come to terms with the problem of anti-Semitism or the broader issue of the relation between Poles and Jews in the nation's history and contemporary life. On these issues, see Jean-Charles Szurek's important essay, "Shoah: De la question juive à la question polonaise," in *Au sujet de "Shoah,"* pp. 258–275.

25. On this question, see Nelly Furman, "The Languages of Pain in *Shoah*," in *Auschwitz and After*, pp. 299–312.

26. In *Tsahal* the role of women is even more limited in spite of the fact that the Israeli army is known for their participation. By and large, women are either seen and not heard or (as translators) heard but not seen. In *Shoah*, aside from supporting cameo parts for victims, the primary role of women is as translators and technical assistants. And the problem of translation as well as the role of the translator is not thematized in the film despite its major importance. Unfortunately, the one truly memorable woman is Frau Michelsohn. For an excellent discussion of the problematic role of gender in *Shoah*, see Marianne Hirsch and Leo Spitzer, "Gendered Translations: Claude Lanzmann's *Shoah*," in *Gendering War Talk*, ed. Miriam Cooke and Angela Woollacott (Princeton, N.J.: Princeton University Press, 1993), pp. 3–19.

27. At Yale in 1990 Lanzmann created a sensation when he refused even to discuss a film he was invited to discuss because he believed it provided a tendentious, apologetic psychological account of a Nazi doctor. In good academic fashion, the event turned into a discussion of Lanzmann's decision not to discuss the film. See Lanzmann, "The Obscenity of Understanding: An Evening with Claude Lanzmann," *American Imago* 48 (Winter 1991): 473–495.

28. See Raul Hilberg, *The Destruction of the European Jews*, rev. ed., 3 vols. (New York: Holmes & Meier, 1985).

29. Felman somewhat misleadingly writes, "*Shoah* is a film made exclusively of testimonies: firsthand testimonies of participants in the historical experience of the Holocaust" (RV, p. 205). She nonetheless goes on to discuss Hilberg as *the* historian yet tries to construe his role as that of "yet another witness" (RV, p. 213). She thus tends to obscure his unique position in the film.

30. Lanzmann, "The Obscenity of Understanding," p. 489.

31. Quoted in *A Holocaust Reader*, ed. Lucy S. Dawidowicz (West Orange, N.J.: Behrman House, 1976), p. 133.

32. Of Srebnik surrounded by Poles, Lanzmann observes, "at the church, he is there, silent; he understands everything, and he is terrorized by them just as he was as a child. And then he is alone in the clearing; he is double: he does not encounter himself " (LP, p. 305). The problem is whether the revictimization and internal splitting of Srebnik

can be detached from the manner in which Lanzmann has actively arranged and staged his encounter with the Poles.

33. Here one may note the exchange between Lanzmann and Bomba that precedes the latter's "breakdown." Lanzmann asks Bomba, "Can you describe [the gas chamber] precisely?" Bomba answers, "Describe precisely. . . . We were waiting there until the transport came in. Women with children pushed in to that place. We the barbers started to cut their hair, and some of them—I would say all of them—some of them knew already what was going to happen to them. We tried to do the best we could—" Lanzmann: "No, no, no. . . ." Bomba: "—the most human we could." Lanzmann: "Excuse me. How did it happen when the women came in to the gas chamber? Were you yourself already in the gas chamber, or did you come afterwards?" (*S*, pp. 103–104). What is happening at this point in the exchange between Lanzmann and Bomba? I would suggest that Bomba is going in directions Lanzmann rejects and with which he cannot identify. Lanzmann therefore becomes intrusive and insists on bringing the witness back in line with his own preoccupations and desires. This response to Bomba is in marked contrast with Lanzmann's attentive listening to Müller, for example, with whom he can identify in an almost specular manner.

34. See, for example, Michael S. Roth, "*Shoah* as Shivah," in *The Ironist's Cage: Memory, Trauma, and the Construction of History* (New York: Columbia University Press, 1995), pp. 214–227, and, especially, Robert Brinkley and Steven Youra, "Tracing *Shoah*," *PMLA* 111 (January 1996): 108–127. Particularly in film studies, *Shoah* often has the special status of an icon, or at least a largely unquestioned standard with which one measures the accomplishments of other films on related topics. For an attempt to rehabilitate *Schindler's List* that simultaneously presupposes and tries to counter this tendency, see Miriam Bratu Hansen, "*Schindler's List* Is Not *Shoah:* The Second Commandment, Popular Modernism, and Public Memory," *Critical Inquiry* 22 (Winter 1996): 292–312. See also Geoffrey H. Hartman, *The Longest Shadow: In the Aftermath of the Holocaust* (Bloomington: Indiana University Press, 1996), for a discussion of *Schindler's List* (chap. 5) and for at times critical comments on *Shoah* (esp. pp. 129–130). After completing this study, I read Tzvetan Todorov's *Facing the Extreme: Moral Life in the Concentration Camps*, trans. Arthur Denner and Abigail Pollak (New York: Metropolitan Books, 1996), which contains certain analyses and criticisms of *Shoah* similar to those I offer; see pp. 271–278. Todorov's interpretive framework is, however, in important ways different from my own. For example, he does not employ psychoanalytic concepts or emphasize the importance of Lanzmann's desire to identify with and relive the experience of the victim. Rather he relies on the concept of totalitarianism both to approximate Stalin's gulags and Nazi concentration camps and to explain the Holocaust as an effect of totalitarianism's positioning of the enemy other. He also attributes the excesses of the Nazi genocide to "the fragmentation of the world we live in and the depersonalization of our relations with others" (pp. 289–290). In Heideggerian fashion, he argues that "our industrial and technological civilization [is] responsible for the camps . . . because a technological mentality invaded the human world as well" (p. 290). I would rather stress the conjunction of a technological framework and all that is associated with it in the Nazi context (including racial "science," eugenics, and medicalization based on purity of blood) with the

return of a repressed—seemingly out of place or *unheimlich*—sacrificialism in the attempt to cleanse (or purify) the *Volksgemeinschaft* and fulfill the leader's will by getting rid of Jews as polluting, dangerous, phobic (or ritually impure) objects. Perhaps only this disconcerting conjunction helps to explain the incredible excesses of brutality, cruelty, and at times carnivalesque or "sublime" elation in Nazi behavior toward Jews.

Suggestions for Further Reading:
A Select Bibliography

Angress, Ruth K. "Lanzmann's *Shoah* and Its Audience." *Simon Wiesenthal Center Annual* 3 (1986): 249–260.

Ascherson, Neal. "The Controversy Around *Shoah*." *Soviet Jewish Affairs* 16, no. 1 (1986): 53–61.

Asseo, H. "On the Extermination of the Jews in World War II and the Film *Shoah* by Claude Lanzmann." *Les Temps Modernes*, no. 471 (1985): 530–538.

Biró, Yvette. "The Unbearable Weight of Non-Being." *Cross Currents* 6 (1987): 75–82.

Brumberg, Abraham. "What Poland Forgot." *The New Republic* (December 16, 1985): 46–48.

Colombat, André. "Claude Lanzmann's *Shoah*." In *The Holocaust in French Film*. Metuchen, N.J.: Scarecrow Press, 1993, pp. 299–344.

Deguy, Michel, ed. *Au sujet de "Shoah."* Paris: Belin, 1990.

Derrida, Jacques, Antoine De Baecque, and Thierry Jousse. "Le cinéma et ses fantômes." *Cahiers du Cinéma* (April 2001): 74–85.

Desplechin, Arnaud. "Les Films de Claude Lanzmann." *Infini* (Winter 2002): 54–64.

Dickstein, Morris. "*Shoah* and the Machinery of Death." *Partisan Review* 53, no. 1 (1986): 36–42.

Didier, E., A. M. Houdebine, and J.-J. Moscovitz, eds. *"Shoah" le film. Des psychanalystes écrivent*. Paris: Jacques Grancher, 1990.

Farr, Raye. "Some Reflections on Claude Lanzmann's Approach to the Examination of the Holocaust." In Toby Haggith and Joanna Newman, eds., *Holocaust and the Moving*

Image: Representations in Film and Television since 1933. London: Wallflower Press, 2005, pp. 161–167.

Felman, Shoshana. "In an Era of Testimony: Claude Lanzmann's *Shoah*." *Yale French Studies*, no. 79 (1991): 39–81.

———. "The Return of the Voice: Claude Lanzmann's *Shoah*." In Shoshana Felman and Dori Laub, *Testimony: Crises of Witnessing in Literature, Psychoanalysis, and History*. New York: Routledge, 1992, pp. 204–283.

Forges, Jean-François. "*Shoah" de Claude Lanzmann*. Paris: L'Eden Cinéma, 2002.

Frodon, Jean-Michel. " 'Le fameux débat' Lanzmann-Godard: Le parti des mots contre le parti des images." *Le Monde*—Supplément Télévision (June 28, 1999): 5.

Gelley, Ora. "A Response to Dominick LaCapra's 'Lanzmann's *Shoah*.' " *Critical Inquiry* 24 (Spring 1998): 830–832.

Hansen, Miriam. "*Schindler's List* Is Not *Shoah*: The Second Commandment, Popular Modernism, and Public Memory." *Critical Inquiry* 22 (Winter 1996): 292–312.

Hoberman, J. "Shoah Business." *The Village Voice* (January 28, 1986): 62–64.

———. " '*Shoah*': Witness to Annihilation." *The Village Voice* (October 29, 1985).

Howland, Jacob. "Reflections on Claude Lanzmann's *Shoah*." *Proteus* 2 (Fall 1995): 42–46.

Judt, Tony. "Moving Pictures." *Radical History Review*, no. 41 (1988): 129–144.

Kael, Pauline. [Review of] "*Shoah*." *The New Yorker* (December 30, 1985): 70–72.

Koch, Gertrud. "The Angel of Forgetfulness and the Black Box of Facticity: Trauma and Memory in Claude Lanzmann's Film *Shoah*." *History and Memory* 3 (Spring 1991): 119–134.

Kuryluk, Ewa. "Memory and Responsibility: Claude Lanzmann's *Shoah*." *The New Criterion* 4 (November 1985): 14–20.

LaCapra, Dominick. "Equivocations of Autonomous Art." *Critical Inquiry* 24 (Spring 1998): 833–836.

Lanzmann, Claude. "Ce mot de 'Shoah.' " *Le Monde* (February 26, 2005): 14.

———. "Un cinéaste au-dessous de tout soupçon?" *Le Nouvel Observateur* (January 17–23, 1991): 70–73.

———. "Filip Müller, fossoyeur et martyr." *Le Nouvel Observateur* (April 28, 1980): 135–137, 145, 154–155.

———. "J'ai enquêté en Pologne." [1978] In Michel Deguy, ed., *Au sujet de "Shoah."* Paris: Belin, 1990, pp. 211–217.

———. "Les non-Lieux de la mémoire." *Nouvelle Revue de Psychanalyse*–"L'amour de la haine" 33 (Spring 1986). Reprinted in Michel Deguy, ed., *Au sujet de "Shoah."* Paris: Belin, 1990, pp. 280–292.

———. "The Obscenity of Understanding: An Evening with Claude Lanzmann." *American Imago* 48 (1991): 473–495.

———. "Parler pour les morts." *Le Monde des Débats* (May 2000): 14–16.

———. "La question n'est pas celle du document, mais celle de la vérité." *Le Monde* (January 19, 2001).

———. "Réponse à Marcel Ophüls." *Les Cahiers du Cinéma* (April 2002): 54–55.

———. "Sartre's 'J'accuse.' Ein Gespräch mit Claude Lanzmann." *Babylon*, no. 2 (1987): 72–79.

———. "Seminar with Claude Lanzmann, April 11, 1990." *Yale French Studies*, no. 79 (1991): 82–99.

———. "*Shoah*." Préface de Simone de Beauvoir. Paris: Gallimard, 1997.

———. "*Shoah*": *An Oral History of the Holocaust*. New York: Pantheon, 1985. [Note: This volume should be used only by those who cannot read French. Lanzmann has disowned this edition.–Ed.]

———. "Why Spielberg Has Distorted the Truth." *The Guardian Weekly* (April 3, 1994): 14.

Leszczyńska, Dorota, and Reinhold Vetter, eds. "In letzter Konsequenz antipolnisch . . . Warschauer Kommentare zu dem französischen Film 'Shoah' über das jüdisch-polnische Verhältnis." *Osteuropa* 36 (November 1986): 568–578.

Liebman, Stuart. "Claude Lanzmann's *Shoah*." *Cineaste* 30 (Winter 2005): 52–54.

Meschonnic, Henri. "Pour en finir avec le mot 'shoah.'" *Le Monde* (February 21, 2005): 10.

Olin, Margaret. "Lanzmann's *Shoah* and the Topography of the Holocaust Film." *Representations* (Winter 1997): 1–23.

Rabinbach, Anson. "*Shoah*." *The Nation* (March 15, 1986): 313–317.

Rosenbaum, Ron. "Claude Lanzmann and the War against the Question Why." In *Explaining Hitler*. New York: Random House, 1998, pp. 251–266.

Saxton, Libby. "Anamnesis and Bearing Witness: Godard/Lanzmann." In Michael Temple, James S. Williams, and Michael Witt, eds., *Forever Godard*. London: Black Dog, 2004, pp. 364–379.

Todorov, Tzvetan. "*Shoah.*" In *Facing the Extreme*, trans. Arthur Denner and Abigail Pollak. New York: Henry Holt, 1996, pp. 271–278.

Turowicz, Jerzy. "*Shoah* w polskich oczach." *Tygodnik Powszechny* (November 10, 1985).

Vidal-Naquet, Pierre. "The Shoah's Challenge to History." In *The Jews*, trans. David Ames Curtis. New York: Columbia University Press, 1996, pp. 142–150.

Wajcman, Gérard. *L'objet du siècle*. Lagrasse: Verdier, 1998.

———. "'Saint Paul' Godard contre 'Moïse' Lanzmann, le match." *L'Infini*, no. 65 (1999): 26–30.

Notes on Contributors

TIMOTHY GARTON ASH is Professor of History at Oxford University. His many
books include the classic account of the overthrow of communist regimes in
Eastern Europe, *The Magic Lantern* (New York: Vintage, 1993); *In Europe's
Name: Germany and the Divided Continent* (New York: Random House, 1993);
and most recently, *Free World: America, Europe, and the Surprising Future of the
West* (New York: Random House, 2004).

FRED CAMPER is a writer and lecturer on film and art who lives in Chicago. He has
taught at several colleges and universities and since 1986 has regularly
contributed essays and reviews to *The Chicago Reader* and many other
publications. He has had a lifelong involvement with experimental/avant-garde
film and recently worked on the Criterion Collection DVD selection of Stan
Brakhage's work *by Brakhage*. His website is www.fredcamper.com.

MARC CHEVRIE is a French film critic, screenwriter, and director. His essays and
reviews have appeared in many French journals and magazines. His short film,
L'Ourse bleue, was released in 1990.

SIMONE DE BEAUVOIR, whose many books and novels include the classic feminist
treatise *The Second Sex*, was a co-founder with Jean-Paul Sartre of the journal
Les Temps Modernes.

DAVID DENBY is the film critic of the *New Yorker* magazine and the author of *Great Books* (New York: Simon & Schuster, 1997), an account of his retaking the "Great Books" course at Columbia University, and of *American Sucker* (New York: Little Brown, 2004), a memoir of his misadventures in the 1990s stock market.

GEORGES DIDI-HUBERMAN is Professor of Art History at the École des Hautes Études in Paris. His many books include *Images Malgré Tout* (Paris: Les Éditions de Minuit, 2003); *Invention of Hysteria: Charcot and the Iconography of the Salpetrière* (Cambridge, Mass.: MIT Press, 2004); and *Confronting Images: Questioning the Ends of a Certain History of Art* (State Park: Pennsylvania State University Press, 2005).

MARIANNE HIRSCH is Professor of French Literature at Columbia University. Professor Hirsch has written *Family Frames: Photography, Narrative, and Postmemory* (Cambridge, Mass.: Harvard University Press, 1997), and most recently she edited, with Irene Kacandes, *Teaching the Representation of the Holocaust* (Washington, D.C.: Modern Language Association, 2005).

JAN KARSKI, who appears memorably in *Shoah*, was a member of the Polish underground and served as a courier for Jewish leaders in the Warsaw Ghetto to Western governments during World War II. His classic account of his efforts, *Story of a Secret State*, was published in 1944 by Houghton Mifflin. At his death in July 2000, he was Emeritus Professor of International Relations at Georgetown University.

GERTRUD KOCH is Professor of Film Studies at the Freie Universität, Berlin. Her many books include *Die Einstellung ist die Einstellung* (Frankfurt: Suhrkamp, 1992), and *Siegfried Kracauer* (Princeton, N.J.: Princeton University Press, 2000).

DOMINICK LACAPRA was Bryce and Edith Bowmar Professor in the Humanities at Cornell University and is the author of many books, including *History and Memory After Auschwitz* (Ithaca, N.Y.: Cornell University Press, 1998) and *Writing History, Writing Trauma* (Baltimore: Johns Hopkins University Press, 2000).

CLAUDE LANZMANN, the editor of *Les Temps Modernes*, has directed six films, including *Pourquoi Israel* (1973), *Tsahal* (1994), *Un Vivant qui passe* (1997), and *Sobibor 14 Octobre, 16 heures* (2001), as well as *Shoah* (1985).

HERVÉ LE ROUX is a French film director and screenwriter. He has directed *Grand bonheur* (1993) and *On appelle ça . . . le printemps* (2001), for which he also wrote the scripts, as well as *Reprise* (1996), the brilliant portrait of the French labor movement after 1968.

STUART LIEBMAN is a Professor of Film Studies at Queens College and the CUNY Graduate Center in New York City. He has edited volumes on the work of German director and film theorist Alexander Kluge (1988), on Helke Sander's *Liberators Take Liberties* (1995), and on Jean Renoir's politics and cinema in the 1930s (1996). In 2006 he was selected as an "Academy Film Scholar" by the Academy of Motion Picture Arts and Sciences.

MARCEL OPHÜLS has directed many major documentaries about French and European history, including the celebrated *Le chagrin et la pitié* (1969), *The Memory of Justice* (1976), *Hôtel Terminus* (1988), and *Novembertage* (1991).

LEO SPITZER, Professor of History at Columbia University, is the author of *Hotel Bolivia: The Culture of Memory in a Refuge from Nazism* (New York: Hill & Wang, 1999), and co-editor (with Mieke Bal and Jonathan Crewe) of *Acts of Memory: Cultural Recall in the Present* (Hanover, N.H.: Dartmouth College, 1998).

ANNE-LISE STERN, who was born in Germany, emigrated to France after the Nazi takeover. A deportee to Auschwitz, she is a psychoanalyst and a member of the École freudienne de Paris, founded by Jacques Lacan. She is the author of *Le Savoir-Deporté. Camps, Histoire, Psychanalyse* (Paris: Éditions du Seuil, 2004).

JEAN-CHARLES SZUREK teaches at the Université de Paris, X. A specialist in the sociology of communism and postcommunism in Eastern Europe, he has edited *A l'Est, la mémoire retrouvée* (Paris: La Découverte, 1990); with G. Mink, he edited *La Grande Conversion: Le destin des communistes en Europe de l'Est* (Paris: Éditions du Seuil, 1999) and *Écriture de l'Histoire et identité Juive: l'Europe aschkénaze, XIXème-XXème siècle* (Paris: Les Belles Lettres, 2003).

DANIEL TALBOT is the president of New Yorker Films, a leading distributor of foreign films in the United States. His firm distributes *Shoah* and two other films by Claude Lanzmann.

ELIE WIESEL, who survived Auschwitz and other camps as a child, is the author of the classic account of the Holocaust, *Night*, and many other books. He is University Professor and Andrew W. Mellon Professor in the Humanities at Boston University. He won the Nobel Peace Prize in 1984.

LEON WIESELTIER is the Literary Editor of *The New Republic* and the author of *Kaddish* (New York: Vintage, 2000) and *Against Identity* (New York: Small Press Distribution, 1996).

Film Credits

Director: Claude Lanzmann

Cast (in credits order): Simon Srebnik, Michael Podchlebnik, Motke Zaidl, Hanna Zaidl, Jan Piwonski, Itzhak Dugin, Richard Glazar, Paula Biren, Pana Pietyra, Pan Filipowicz, Pan Falborski, Abraham Bomba, Czeslaw Borowi, Henrik Gawkowski, Rudolf Vrba, Inge Deutschkron, Franz Suchomel, Filip Müller, Joseph Oberhauser, Anton Spiess, Raul Hilberg, Franz Schalling, Martha Michelsohn, Claude Lanzmann, Moshe Mordo, Armando Aaron, Walter Stier, Ruth Elias, Jan Karski, Franz Grassler, Gertude Schneider, Itzhak Zuckermann, and Simha Rottem

Cinematography: Dominique Chapuis, Jimmy Glasberg, and William Lubtchansky; Caroline Champetier de Ribes (assistant camera), Jean-Yves Escoffier (assistant camera), Slavek Olczyk (assistant camera), Andrés Silvart (assistant camera)

Editing: Ziva Postec and Anna Ruiz; assistant editors: Bénédicte Mallet, Yael Perlov, Christine Simonot, Geneviève de Gouvion Saint-Cyr

Second Unit Director and Assistant Director: Corinna Coulmas and Iréne Steinfeldt-Levi

Sound: Bernard Aubouy (engineer), Michel Vionnet (engineer), Danielle Fillios (editor)

Other Crew: gaffer: Daniel Bernard; Hebrew interpreter: Francine Kaufmann; Polish interpreter: Barbra Janica; Yiddish interpreter: Mrs. Apflebaum; production accountant: Brigitte Faure

Production: Les Films Aleph, 1985

Claude Lanzmann: Filmography

Sobibor, 14 octobre 1943, 16 heures (2001) [English title: *Sobibor, October 14, 1943, 4 p.m.*]; B/W and color, 95 minutes. DVD edition, European zone: *Deux Films de Claude Lanzmann* (Cahiers du Cinéma/CNC).

Un vivant qui passe (1997) [English title: *A Visitor from the Living*]; color, 65 minutes. DVD edition, European zone: *Deux Films de Claude Lanzmann* (Cahiers du Cinéma/CNC).

Tsahal (1994); color, 316 minutes.

Shoah (1985); color, 566 minutes. DVD edition, American zone: New Yorker Video, #51003.

Pourquoi Israel (1972) [English title: *Israel, Why*]; color, 180 minutes.

Index

Nazi teacher at, 214, 226n24 (*see also* Michelsohn, Frau)

peasant's voice at, 118

Srebnik as familiar figure at, 117

survivors of, 12, 47–48, 54, 73, 80, 82, 116, 205 (*see also* Podchlebnik, Mordechai; Srebnik, Simon)

transport to, 141

woods at, 91

Chomsky, Marvin, 7, 49n4

Chronique d'un Été (Edgar Morin), 107

Cinema Studio, 56, 60, 67

concentration camp, 78, 83, 126, 226

discredit victims of, 127

grotesque aspect of, 196

guards at, 85

likened to Stalin's Gulag, 228

as model for "new order," 196

secrets of, 173

surviving in, 129

testimony about, 86

women in, 178

work details in, 177

Corfu, 43

innocence of Jews of, 215

Jewish community in, 177, 215

counter-myth, 35, 122, 198

Cukierman, Icchak, 164. *See also* Antek; Zuckerman, Itzhak

Czerniakow, Adam

Diary of, 150, 183, 214

Hilberg's identification with, 184

suicide of, 65, 183–184

Częstochowa, 9, 212

Darstellung, 128–129

Davies, Norman, 158

death camps, 71, 75, 114, 135, 143

experience recalled in detail, 136

literary treatments of, 127

Polish villages and farms near, 141

situations of victims in, 221

wartime anti-Semitism and, 144

de Beauvoir, Simone, 4, 152, 191

preface to script of *Shoah*, 85

relationship with Lanzmann, 18n4, 53

Deleuze, Gilles, 193

de Man, Paul, 203–204

Denby, David, 4

Derrida, Jacques, 21n28, 23n48, 193, 197

Destruction of the European Jews, The (Raul Hilberg), 216

as inspiration for Lanzmann's project, 190

Deutschkron, Inge, 178–179, 187

dialectical image, 121–122

Diary of Anne Frank, The (George Stevens), 20n10

Dickstein, Morris, 56

Didi-Huberman, Georges, 15, 23

Distant Journey, The (Alfred Radok), 22n40

Dobroszycki, Lucjan, 56, 150

Double Indemnity (Billy Wilder), 48, 49n9

Dreyfus Affair, 85

École freudienne de Paris, the, 100n7. *See also* Jacques Lacan

Edelman, Marek, 158, 172

Eden, Anthony, 174

Eichmann, Adolf, 82, 214, 217

Einsatzgruppen, 11, 21n29, 137, 193

Eisenstein (Sergei), 109

Elias, Ruth, 179, 187

engaged literature, 127

Engel, David, 160

Engelking, Barbara, 164

Evian conference, 31, 34

Express, L', 135

extermination camps, 14, 49n8, 63, 136, 138, 140–141, 154, 176

Fackenheim, Emil, 33, 109

Fahrplanordnung 587, 186

discussion with Hilberg, 186

Farben, I. G., 29

Fassbinder, R.W., 33, 56, 59, 84

Fateless (Imre Kertesz), 23n48

Faure, Edgar, 86

Felman, Shoshana, 22n36, 185, 192, 203–206, 225n16, 225n19

assumes role of "subject supposed to know," 225n17

on Lacan's conception of "the Real," 225n18

obscures role of Hilberg, 227n29

"Final Solution," the, 16, 34, 86, 90, 92, 176, 183, 185, 214

connection to offensive in East, 35n1

criminals' participation in, 84

documentary film about, 67

invention of, 209

secrecy as key to efficiency of, 180

as series of minute steps, 137

witnesses to, 85, 174

Ford, Aleksander, 22n40

Ford, John, 110

Fortunoff Archive, 5

pleasure of collaborative relationship
  with Lanzmann, 186
his position in film obscured by
  Felman, 227n29
on role of technological rationality in
  destruction, 216–217
on suicide of Czerniakow, 65
unique status in, 216–217
Himmelfahrtsweg, 48. *See also* "funnel,"
  the; *Schlauch*
Himmler, Heinrich, 40, 217
  Posen speech, 214, 217
Hitchcock, Alfred, 22n40
Hitler, Adolf, 34, 74, 176, 193, 209
  absence from *Shoah*, 136
  Churchhill's remarks about, 140
  condemnation of Jews, 31
  as evil father to Jews, 33
  as German people's "fall guy," 85
  Joachim Fest's film of, 32
  his "Night and Fog" decree, 59
  Poles' reaction to, 144, 156
  "positive aspects" of, 32
  as prime mover of Holocaust, 217
  his psychopathology, 8
  as seducer of German nation, 33
  Sultan as forerunner of, 29
  his "war against the Jews," 35n1
Hitler Jugend, 34, 209
Hlond, Cardinal, 158
Holocaust, 3–6, 8, 12, 53, 59, 74, 174. *See
  also* Shoah
  aberration theory of, 32
  accusations against Poles, 81, 144, 156,
    163, 165, 227n24
  and art, 22n39
  banalization of, 29
  bearing witness to, 206
  as bureaucratic destruction process, 28,
    92, 137, 209, 214, 216–218
  Children of the, 164–165
  conditions for, 31, 33, 137, 142, 144
  as core of Nazism, 32
  as curse on mankind, 174
  de Man's silence about, 203
  denial of, 32, 69
  disjunctive character of, 208
  distinctive horror of, 11
  education, 6
  exploitation of, 6
  and gender differences, 175–177, 182–183
  Hilberg's history of, 21n34, 76
  as historical event, 28–29, 31, 91, 208
  historiography of Holocaust cinema,
    5, 90

ignorance of, 55
immediacy of, 9
kitsch, 84, 199, 224n11 (*see also*
  Schindler's List; Segal, George)
Lanzmann's approach to, 83–84, 90, 92
as legend, 35
as limit event, 193
literature, 90
Michelsohn as German witness to, 214
as modification of Jewish universe, 33
as motif in *Tsahal*, 207
Museum, 9, 14
myth of, 7
name of, 20n19
oral history of, 192
Polish Center for Research, 164
as presence, 91, 122, 198
principles of films about, 9, 13, 16, 35,
  198–199
relativization of, 222
representation in cinema, 33, 35, 135, 174
as result of anti-Jewish hatred, 27–28, 30
sacralization of, 194
Shoah as film about, 11, 47, 67, 75, 78,
  197–198, 204–205
singularity of, 29–30, 172, 194, 208
to speak from inside, 185
specific character of, 28–29, 32, 215
studies of, 8
survivors of as basis for film, 55, 58, 64,
  171, 202
tombstone fragments as symbol of,
  23n51
as tragic story, 16
as trauma, 201–202
victimization and scapegoating in,
  226n21
as work of madmen, 31
Holocaust (Marvin Chomsky), 6–7, 20n15,
  29–30, 39, 44, 49n4, 84, 199
Home Army (Polish), 140, 159
Howe, Irving, 56
hurban, 7
Hurwitz, Leo, 22n40
Husserl, Edmund, 217–218

Insdorf, Annette, 20n11
International Psychoanalytic
  Association, 99
Isaiah 56:5, 107, 123n13
Israel, 4–5, 7, 10, 18n2, 32–33, 41, 45,
  54–55, 57
  Antek's move to, 68
  as Deutschkron's home, 178
  as land of rebirth, 207

Israel (*continued*)
  locating Srebnik in, 80
  narrator's voice from, 130
  scholars from, 150
  as site of filming *Shoah*, 171, 182, 207
  Wiesel's visits to, 68

Jakob der Lügner (Frank Beyer), 23n48
Jakob the Liar (Peter Kassovitz), 23n48
Jakubowska, Wanda, 22n41
Janion, Maria, 165
Jaruzelski, General, 144, 154, 157
Jasiewicz, Krzysztof, 164
Jedwabne pogrom, 163–165
Jehovah's Witnesses, 214
Jewish Councils, 182, 214, 216. *See also*
    Judenrat
Jewish Fighting (Combat) Organization,
    164, 207
"Jewish question," the, 32, 149, 155–158,
    160–161
John Paul II, Pope, 138
Judenrat, 150. *See also* Jewish Councils

Kael, Pauline, 19n5, 56
Kantorowski, Monsieur, 205–206
Kapo (Gillo Pontecorvo), 85, 121
Kapos, role of, 181
Karski, Jan, 16, 54, 65, 70–71, 74, 120, 176, 212
  meetings with Western leaders,
      70–71, 143
  report on ghetto conditions in Poland,
      49n8, 213
  report on wartime Polish–Jewish
      relations, 160–161
Kazin, Alfred, 56
Kielce pogrom, 162–163
Koch, Gertrud, 223n5
Koło, town of, 34
Kolwakowski, Leszek, 144
Konin, District of, 34
K.O.R. (Committee for Defense of
    Workers), 155–156. *See also*
    Solidarnosc
Korbonski, Stefan, 172
K.O.S. (Committee for Social
    Resistance), 156
Kranzbuehler, Dr., 86
Kristallnacht, 34, 40
Kwasniewski, Aleksander, 163
Krupp, 29, 86, 119
Kuron, Jacek, 155–156

Lacan, Jacques, 99–100, 193, 203, 216. *See
    also* École freudienne de Paris, the

Felman assumes role of, 225n17
  his conception of the "Real," 225n18
Lacoue-Labarthe, Philippe, 209
Lamentations of Jeremiah, 104
landscapes, 17, 39, 45, 54, 59, 64, 69,
    104–105, 110, 201
Langer, Lawrence L., 127–128
Langfus, Leib, 71
Lanzmann, Claude, 3–6, 53–56, 63–65,
    73–75, 79, 174
  Adorno's impact on, 13
  art of, 63, 127, 135–136, 187, 192–193,
      223n5
  attendance at screenings, 5, 56, 58
  attitude to history, 92
  brilliance of, 91, 93
  comparisons with Ophüls, 74, 86
  on composition and mise-en-scène
      techniques, 16, 42
  conversation with Hilberg, 65, 69, 186
  on debates with Godard, 23n46
  decision for *Shoah* as film title, 7–8, 78
  descriptive phenomenology as
      method, 217
  as editor, 18, 46–47, 105
  as follower of Sartre, 130, 218
  financial assistance for, 58–59
  on function of Jews of Corfu as
      innocence, 215
  on gender differences, 177–178, 180, 182
  on the Holocaust as impossible story, 3
  how his historiography follows
      Hilberg's, 137, 190n30, 216–217
  on identification and tranference,
      215–216, 218–221, 225n18
  interview techniques of, 17, 83, 92,
      107–108, 130–131, 136, 152–153, 162,
      177, 180, 212
  on *Introduction to Shoah*, 80
  on landscapes as "non-sites of
      memory," 115, 218
  locating of survivors and witnesses,
      9–11, 81–83, 114, 177, 181, 185
  on mimesis, 14, 105
  on miniseries *Holocaust*, 84, 199
  misunderstanding of his aims, 8, 11, 48
  mythic vision of, 187
  on need to break with chronology of,
      65, 92, 194, 198–199
  on need to create counter-myth of, 35,
      122, 198
  on need to return to sites, 118
  parallels to literary strategies, 131–132
  on Poland, 137–138, 141–145, 150, 153–154,
      156–157, 162, 173, 214

Więz, 150
Wilder, Billy, 49n9
Williams, Robin, 20n13
Wirth, Christian, 13
Wise, Rabbi Stephen, 70
Witnesses (Marcel Łozinski), 162
witnessing, 165, 185, 194
  absence of French witnesses, 214
  on breakdown of, 203–204 (see also
    Felman, Shoshana)
  community of, 22n36
  paradox of, 185
  secondary, 196, 203
  trauma of, 165
women. See also gender difference
  associated with danger, 180, 183–184
  as death without regeneration, 184
  erasure of, 177–178, 187
  Holocaust's effects on, 177

roles of, 177–178, 180, 186, 214
  their loss of generativity, 186
"writing of disaster" (Maurice
  Blanchot), 193
Wysziński, Cardinal, 160

Yad Vashem, 5, 9, 142, 161
Yerushalmi, Haim Yosef, 20n15
Young, James E., 23n51

Zaidel, Hannah, 178
Zaidel, Motke, 178
Zbikowski, Andrzej, 164
Zeit, Die, 154
Znak, 150
Znolnierz Wolnosci, 139
Zuckerman, Itzhak (Antek), 54, 207. See
  also Cukierman, Icchak
Zygelbaum, Shmuel, 70